PROSPECTS FOR PEOPLE WITH LEARNING DIFFICULTIES

EDITED BY
STANLEY S. SEGAL AND VED P. VARMA

David Fulton Publishers
London

David Fulton Publishers Ltd
2 Barbon Close, Great Ormond Street, London WC1N 3JX

First published in Great Britain by
David Fulton Publishers, 1991

British Library Cataloguing in Publication Data

Prospects for people with learning difficulties.
  I. Segal, Stanley S. (Stanley Solomon), *1919–*
  II. Varma, Ved P. (Ved Prakash), *1931–*
  371.9

  ISBN 1-85346-155-5

Typeset by Chapterhouse, Formby L37 3PX
Printed in Great Britain by Biddles Ltd. Guildford.

PROSPECTS FOR PEOPLE WITH LEARNING DIFFICULTIES

Contents

Contributors

Sally Cheseldine	Principal Clinical Psychologist Royal Scottish National Hospital
Alan D. B. Clarke	Emeritus Professor Hull University
Ann Clarke	Emeritus Professor Hull University
Judith Coupe-O'Kane	Headmistress Melland School Manchester
Margaret Flynn	Associate Consultant National Development Team Hester Adrian Research Centre University of Manchester
Bill Fraser	Professor Department of Psychological Medicine Ely Hospital
James Hogg	Hester Adrian Research Centre University of Manchester
Chris Kiernan	Professor and Director Hester Adrian Research Centre University of Manchester
Loretto Lambe	MENCAP Profound Retardation and Multiple Handicap Project Piper Hill School Manchester
Helen McConachie	Lecturer in Psychology The Wolfson Centre

Roy McConkey	Director Training and Research Brothers of Charity Services Scotland
Norma V. Raynes	Formerly of the University of Manchester
Colin Robson	Professor Huddersfield Polytechnic
Philippa Russell	Principal Officer Voluntary Council for Handicapped Children
Judy Sebba	Cambridge Institute of Education
Stanley S. Segal	Chairman International Information Centre on Special Needs in Education
Ved P. Varma	Retired Educational Psychologist
Linda Ward	Research Fellow Norah Fry Research Centre University of Bristol
Klaus Wedell	Professor Department of Special Educational Needs London University Institute of Education

Preface

This authoritative and interesting book has a double purpose. First, it is a tribute to Prof. Peter Mittler from his friends and colleagues; it marks their deep appreciation of the man and his work. It also so happens that it celebrates his sixtieth birthday. Second, and equally importantly, this collection of original and practical papers presents an up-to-date picture of research and thinking in the fields of mental handicap past, present and future. Both positive and negative aspects are discussed. Constructive suggestions are made for ways in which progress can be maintained and prospects improved. What have we learned from working in the fields of mental handicap in the past thirty years that could be applied in the future? What can we learn from the lessons of the past in education, psychology, medicine and social work, in which Prof. Mittler has played a leading and often innovatory role. This is why there are chapters from caring professionals in these disciplines. The breadth and depth of each of the contributors reflects not only the range of Prof. Mittler's interests but also his international outlook and involvement.

All too often, individuals like Prof. Mittler remain known only through their lectures and publications. But this book helps to provide some insights into the creative energy that goes on behind the scenes, that develops our understanding of a field such as special education. Joseph Lancaster remarked at the end of his life that teachers of youth need much more cheering on their way than they usually receive. It is in this spirit that the contributors to this volume offer their exceptional insights into some of the pressing concerns of special education today.

The editors would like to thank the contributors, all of them extremely busy people, for the willingness and promptness with which they responded to our request and accepted our suggestions as to the topic on which they should write.

Stanley S. Segal
Ved P. Varma

INTRODUCTION
Peter Mittler

Stanley S. Segal

When Dr Ved Varma invited me to co-edit a book for Prof. Peter Mittler there could be only one response, yes. I had known Peter Mittler for some twenty-five years, and knew of his work for even longer. In particular I had seen a combination of his many strengths during the fertile period that I was part of the National Development Group on Mental Handicap (NDG), which he chaired in the second half of the 1970s. This was a decade during which there was a tide in favour of 'better services for the mentally handicapped'. Advances were reflected and given fresh impetus in legislation within the education, health and social services. The Rt. Hon. Mrs Barbara Castle had gone further than her predecessors by setting up an inter-professional source of advice in which the three trends were represented. Their collective task was to advise her on policy and on a strategy for its implementation. There could have been no more suitable person than Peter Mittler to chair such a group, to innovate at such a level, or to produce such informed and lucid guidance to the field. Through his drive and skills, a succession of pamphlets appeared in rapid succession, all in the name of the NDG. It was Prof. Peter Mittler too, who somehow ensured that these pamphlets were given wide and free distribution.

Amongst the seven members of the Group, apart from Prof. Mittler and myself, were Mrs Peggy Jay JP, who was also engaged in chairing the Inquiry into Mental Handicap Nursing and Care, and Prof. G. B. Simon (then Dr Simon), Director of the British Institute of Mental Handicap, who was also appointed Director of the Development Team which was intended to be 'the eyes and ears' of the NDG.

Had Prof. Peter Mittler retired in 1980 when the new administration disbanded the NDG as a quango, he would already have earned a notable place in the history of mental handicap provision within the UK. The award of the CBE (which he received in 1981) would have been a fitting end to the chapter. However, he not only continues to contribute – an innovative scholar, lucid

1

speaker and prolific writer, and a much sought-after participant in the international field as in the national – but has much more to contribute if only
during the decade he must still work before reaching my age! He plainly has
no intention of retiring early, although he is currently considering his first
sabbatical.

In this book contributions are made by distinguished colleagues who range
from 'the Clarkes' who were amongst those who shaped the circumstances in
which someone of Peter Mittler's calibre could emerge to further improve
the prospects of people with disabilities, to a group for whose potential and
contributions in this field Peter Mittler has helped to create a further
launching pad.

Peter Mittler's development and the range and strength of his contributions are to be glimpsed in the bibliography. This introduction may help to
illuminate some of the factors which affected his ever-expanding
contribution.

It was once a sick joke in central Europe, that if you wanted to change
your nationality you had merely to remain where you were. It was not
surprising that tormented central Europe produced many outstanding
'citizens of the world'.

Born in Vienna in April 1930, Peter Mittler was still in his eighth year, a
well-groomed, well-conducted child, perhaps compelled to be self-reliant,
when he boarded one of the succession of 'Children's Transports', for the
UK, where he was to live with 'guarantors'. His parents had acted in time.
Several of their relatives had been in concentration camps. For a Jewish child
Nazi Europe was no place to live and grow up in.

Peter Mittler's father was on business, out of the country at this time, and
being a known anti-Nazi, dared not return to it. His mother remained to
pack a few family possessions (later burned in the bombing of London)
before she escaped into domestic service in England – grateful to be in a
supportive family. To obtain employment in domestic service was the most
promising outlet for a would-be refugee.

That these early experiences played some part in determining the quality of
Peter Mittler's later contributions in the fields of deprivation and disability
seems evident. But life is of course far too complex to suggest a neat cause-
and-consequence biography. In the mid-1960s in the USA, in a penetrating
study of Edouard Seguin, who fathered an educational approach to 'the
treatment of mentally defective children', Prof. Mabel E. Talbot actually
drew attention to the 'curious interweaving of special education and the
liberal ideology' (Seguin, 1964). It was perhaps more than a curious coincidence that Peter Mittler was working on his Fabian Society publication at
this time, the *Mental Health Services* (1966).

That the socio-political climate is particularly relevant to the prospects of
people with 'mental defects' is self evident. Along the same parameter, it was
the climate of certain long-stay hospitals which finally drove a relevant minister
to declare that they were no place for a child to live and grow up in. But we would
of course diminish human compassion and creativity as well as special
education itself, if we confined it to a relationship with a liberal ideology.

Whereas Seguin for example, in the previous century, left France for political reasons to breathe the air of political freedom in the USA; one of his great predecessors, Jakob Pereire had fled to France to escape religious persecution, to be free to be a Jew. Similarly, in creating the Camphill Trust in the UK, the Christian refugees who drew strength from Rudolf Steiner's educational teachings, could claim that they had not solely rescued some of their disabled fellows from certain death in Nazi Europe, but were providing effective prototypes of 'alternative societies' for them. When we consider the disproportionate number of refugees to be found in the leadership of the movement on behalf of people with severe learning difficulties, we could refer with equal justification to the 'curious interweaving of special education' with the Judaic/Christian teachings. Other strands soon suggest themselves.

Peter Mittler recalled a great deal of display in the Austria from which he escaped; all the razzamataz; flags waving and planes flying whilst people who were Jewish were being openly humiliated and made to scrub pavements. He had learned to travel around by himself and this degree of self-reliance no doubt helped him when in January 1939 he arrived at Liverpool Street station, totally bewildered and confused but knowing that he had 'guarantors'.

Just as on a macro scale 'the world' responded unevenly to refugees, some with open arms and compassion and others with resistance and fears for their own cultures and prospects, so on a micro scale the population of the UK responded unevenly to both refugees and, shortly after, evacuees. Central government financial assistance to those receiving evacuees however, eased the latter process. But refugee children were totally dependent upon the tide of compassion which flowed out to them and which was accompanied by individual guarantees of homes and support. Peter Mittler was to be placed with such supportive guarantors, who were to see him through a public school education until his own scholarship came to the fore at the age of sixteen when he earned a place for the next stage in his education.

His primary schooling however, was far from being smooth, logical or happy, and there were experiences and lessons to be drawn from it which were to influence his outlook as an educationist even if they did not point him in that direction as a goal.

On arrival in London, he was immediately placed in a prosperous north London school. It was a culture shock for which he had not been prepared. His mother tongue, German, was increasingly hated and ostracised. The motivation to speak English was such that he caught it in a few weeks, rather than being taught it. When the war started he found himself in a boarding school in Broadstairs, Kent to which he had been sent initially, he thought, for a summer holiday. Although both his parents were now in the UK, his mother was working for a supportive family in Northamptonshire, whilst his father had been interned as an enemy alien! Peter again had to do a great deal of independent travelling.

The boarding school, now deprived by war of most of its professional staff, was a punishing experience. Its atmosphere was oppressive. He was vividly to recall how startled he was to find that a private letter that he had written, in which he expressed his views on the school was intercepted and opened by the headmaster who issued an imperious summons to his study. The headmaster underlined to nine-year-old Peter Mittler how ungrateful a pupil he was (for not recognising how lucky he was to be accepted there and for not appreciating that he was better off in the UK than under the Nazis).

If, years later, Peter Mittler was to discover that not all long-stay hospitals were patient-centred or resident-centred, he learned very early that not all schools were pupil-centred. The cry 'people not patients' seems to have its roots here; as did his awareness of how easy it is to marginalise a child.

In 1941, when Peter was eleven, another contributing strand wove its way into his biography. His parents were able for the first time in the UK to set up home together, in Yule, Surrey. Peter's father was now employed as a research chemist, and was able to accompany Peter for an interview at Sutton High School for boys, a C of E Grammar School. His former schooling at Broadstairs had been as unhelpful as was its socio-emotional climate. Now Peter was subjected to some tests of educational attainment by the headmaster of the Grammar School who in Peter's presence told his father that the school would accept Peter as a pupil but that he was unlikely to learn anything! This did more than occasion resentment; it was also an experience of such serious teacher under-estimation, as to influence his insights in the field of special education. It was certainly to be a caution to Peter Mittler of how easily special needs could be attributed to the failings of the student rather than to the inadequacies of the system or the curriculum.

Despite the prognosis by his headmaster, Peter Mittler learned more than was on offer at the school. Two years later, when his parents moved to Liverpool, he was accepted as a fee-paying pupil at a good day public school, the Merchant Taylors school, Crosby.

In contrast with his earliest schooling, this was for him a very happy and active period. Good teaching in a good climate assisted his all-round development. His interests expanded. But there was nothing to intimate his future role in the field of special needs except perhaps that he had vague thoughts at one time of entering the medical profession. Influenced in part by the fact that one teacher had inspired in him a passion for history, he took an arts direction and for his Higher Certificate was to take History, French and German.

Reminiscent of his pre-war experiences in Austria, British Fascists with their anti-semitic solutions to the world's problems, were again extremely active at this time and pro- and anti-fascist demonstrations, some violent, were to become familiar to Peter Mittler during his later adolescence and National Service. It was far from surprising that he began to show an interest in politics and was to become a *cause célèbre* in the school in 1945 for seeking the election of a Labour government at a time when the school as a whole was in support of a Conservative administration.

At the age of eighteen, on finishing school, he was called up for his National Service, where he was brought into contact with people from all walks of life. He found that his life had been curiously sheltered and that he had never before met working-class people. His army experience brought him new experiences of people, and contributed to his understanding of them. On doing his service in West Germany, where his knowledge of German was put to some pedestrian use, he went feeling initially as if a new world was well on its way. But although he never began discussions on politics in the army, he was soon dismayed by the frequency with which he was given unsolicited and unexpected assurances from Germans that they had known nothing about the concentration camps.

His final culture shock before entering the working world was experienced after completing his National Service, when he obtained an Exhibition to Cambridge. Throughout those three years the music, the friendships, the complete liberation of the mind and the spirit in Cambridge were the major contributions to his personal development. For the first two years there he studied history. In the final year he had an opportunity to study psychology, and it may be relevant but is certainly interesting that of the other five under-graduates who took the same psychology course at Cambridge, it was another ex-refugee, Klaus Wedell, who was ultimately to occupy the Chair in Special Education at the University of London.

It was at Cambridge too, that Peter Mittler met Helle, who was to become his wife. Indicative of their recreations and interests at this time, both were taking part in the play by T. S. Elliot, *Murder in the Cathedral* when they met.

They shared much in common. Her parents, like his, were Austrian, although she herself was born in Russia where her parents were working at the time. An anti-Jewish pogrom in 1934 led them to leave Russia and they eventually reached the welcoming shores of England after periods in Greece and Sicily. Over a period of some forty years, Helle was to enrich Peter's personal and professional life. She shared and influenced the development of his thinking and practice and contributed in her own right to several joint publications on partnership with parents, such that 'the Mittlers' seem set to join the company of other well-known and much appreciated partnerships.

When Peter Mittler graduated from Cambridge, there was no career guidance for him, and no work. He was living in Stoke Newington in London, where an army friend found him a route to employment as a trainee exports-manager in a sector where the product was uninspiring. Having benefitted from a galaxy of talented professionals during his psychology course, Peter Mittler began desperately to look for an opening where he could use his psychology degree. On seeing an advertisement for a clinical psychologist it was not surprising that he applied, although until that moment it had not occurred to him that there was such a profession. His professor however, had been Oliver Zangwill, internationally known as a brilliant neuro-psychologist, and from the regular clinical sessions attended at Fullbrook Hospital, Cambridge, conducted by Dr Russell Davies, who taught psychopathology, Peter Mittler had learned something of mental handicap and mental illness.

Understandably he did not get the job, but on his return journey (with the successful candidate who was at the Maudslay Hospital) he was receptive to her suggestion that he met Dr Monty Shapiro and get enrolled on a course in clinical psychology there. He now found that although he was accepted for the course there was no route to a grant to enable him to attend it. Encouraged by Helle he wrote to innumerable hospitals to enquire about the possibility of a traineeship, and one of his letters finally proved successful. In September 1954 he was accepted as a probationer clinical psychologist in the Warneford Hospital, Oxford and qualified as a clinical psychologist in 1957.

By this time a confluence of forces in the UK was influencing both the climate in which this work was taking place, and advances in what might be described as the pre-history of special education in the UK for people with mental disabilities. This preparatory period might be seen as reaching a foothill in 1959–62 with the new Mental Health Act and the Scott Committee's report.

By 1955 the parents' movement which had been sparked off by a mother in 1946 (Judy Fryd) had become the powerful National Society for Mentally Handicapped Children. That organisation in turn owed something to the three organisations which had merged in 1946 to form the National Association for Mental Health (now MIND). A succession of other parent-influenced movements, not least the Spastics Society, followed. A scatter of scandals, brilliant professionals and forward-looking organisations created or transformed resources and outlooks. By 1954 for example, the seminal work by Jack Tizard and Neil O'Connor on 'The Social Problem of Mental Deficiency' was out, and the Medical Research Council was giving consider-able encouragement to relevant research. On the educational front Dr W. D. Wall, already known internationally as an educationist had become the Director of the National Foundation for Educational Research and was ensuring visibility and encouragement to class-room based research. In the field of Child Care a range of forces was *en route* to creating what is now known as the National Children's Bureau and under the leadership of Dr Mia Kellmer Pringle became a powerful social educator. A Voluntary Council for Handicapped Children was to come into its own under the leadership of Philippa Russell, its principal officer.

Dr Herbert Gunzburg and the Clarkes were amongst the early influences upon Peter Mittler who was to refer to them all with warmth and respect. Dr Herbert Gunzburg was to be described as one of the most modest but influential people in our world, a pioneer in rehabilitation and training. His PAC (Progress Assessment Charts) produced a clear bridge between assessment and training and brought out the importance of social competence and social skills.

Educational organisations were also influencing professional attitudes by this time. The UK's first post-qualification Diploma Course in the Education of Handicapped (ESN) Pupils at the University of London, sparked off a Guild of Teachers of Backward Children which by 1955 was organising a multiprofessional National Conference on the Education of the Backward Child and by 1956 was publishing the journal *Forward Trends in the Treatment of the Backward Child*. By 1960 – reflecting the impact of depart-mentalisation and professional training – educationists found themselves organising an International Conference on the Education of the Backward Child at the very time that the National Association Mental Health (NAMH) had sparked off an international London Conference on Mental Deficiency (which was to herald the International Association for the Scientific Study of Mental Deficiency). Similarly the powerful National Union of Teachers was central to a movement chaired by Dr W. D. Wall which brought together a substantial representation of organisations in special education in a proposed National Council for Special Education – at the very time that, unknown to them, forces in the social services and care world were moving towards the creation of the National Bureau for Cooperation in Child Care (now the NCB). These are sufficiently representative of the way that developments were going.

By the mid-1960s the UK was seeing the possibility of, as well as the justification for, nurturing education even at this extremity of the 'normal curve'. Appropriate scholarship and leadership was now required in this area to take advantage of the growing potential for human advance.

It was shortly after starting work in Oxford that Peter and Helle married and in 1955 the first of their three children, Paul, was born two months prematurely. In those days a birthweight of three and a half pounds was really quite serious. There were worries about Paul's development, but no clear indication from the hospital as to what the problem might be; and it was only when their son was eighteen months old that Peter and Helle learned that Paul had cerebral palsy (a left hemipaegia). A fresh and powerful motivation for Peter Mittler's interest in the causes and treatment of disabilities now contributed to his development.

At the Churchill hospital, where Paul was taken regularly, Peter Mittler met a model Occupational Therapist (a Miss Shaw) whose work was not only of a high quality but who related with parents and saw them as partners in a joint effort to assist Paul. She explained what she was doing and why; proposed exercises and made suggestions for activities which could be carried out at home. They were also impressed by the work of the physiotherapists who showed parents a respect and consideration which left its mark.

Peter Mittler began to play a part in a local Spastics Society which had the support of a leading neurologist Dr Richy Russell in seeking to create a day centre in the grounds of Churchill Hospital. Still in training as a clinical psychologist, Peter Mittler was getting a wider and wider range of experience; 'sitting at the feet of Oliver Zangwill and Elizabeth Warrington (who now has a Chair there); and learning about the assessment of people with neurological damage' (Mittler, personal communication). This he found fascinating, although as yet it offered little to help anyone afflicted. 'The excitement came from the skill of diagnosing precisely what was the matter. The neurologists had their techniques, the psychologists had theirs' (Mittler, personal communication), whilst Prof. Oliver Zangwill seemed to Peter Mittler to have a special gift of correctly anticipating diagnoses that were subsequently confirmed by autopsy.

In 1954, Peter Mittler saw Warneford Hospital as something like an

Oxford College. A stimulating environment, with staff who formed a kind of academic community. Some patients were undergraduates or members of the university, and many of the staff acted as tutors. In charge of clinical psychology was a remarkable woman, May Davidson, who played a senior role in the British Psychological Society, and whose main interest was psychotherapy with undergraduates. She had raised the status of psychology and psychologists not only in Warneford hospital but nationally. Dr May Davidson threw Peter in at the deep end. There he got a wide range of experience, was 'pitchforked into research' and played 'a small but instructive' part in a National Child Development Study, a local longitudinal study of normal children who had first been subjected to a range of assessments at seven. This taught him something about child development and gave him an opportunity to study it at first hand. He also learnt about research methods and data analysis. Park hospital – associated with the Warneford – was transformed at this time into an acute childrens' psychiatric unit run by Dr Christopher Ounstead, and it was from the latter together with May Davidson that Peter Mittler felt he learned most at the time.

The training – which had brought Peter Mittler into the intellectually stimulating world of London teaching hospitals – was by this time coming to an end and he was to spend a period at the Warneford Hospital as a qualified clinical psychologist. It was on a one-day visit to Manor Hospital in Epsom that he met Alan and Ann Clarke who talked about their work and left him considerably impressed by what psychologists could do. The Clarkes were in charge of rehabilitation work, played a leading part in planning the discharge of residents from the hospital, were engaged in research and follow-up, and pinpointed social and psychological factors associated with successful and less successful rehabilitation. By contrast, psychologists working with the mentally ill did not seem to Peter Mittler to be engaged in much rehabilitation in the field of adult psychiatry. Their work was seen to involve a great deal of more humdrum, routine assessment. It was the Clarkes, working on their book *Mental Deficiency: The Changing Outlook* (1958), who finally fuelled his commitment to mental handicap. The Warneford Hospital had however made its contribution to his readiness for his emerging role and it is to this period at Warneford that Peter Mittler traces his interest in mental handicap.

In July 1958 Peter Mittler followed Michael Humphrey – his predecessor at the Warneford – to become Senior Psychologist (later Principal Psychologist) for a group of hospitals in Berkshire. Whilst his base was at Fairmile Hospital in Wallingford, a group of hospitals was associated with it, notably the Smith Hospital, a small unit for psychotic and autistic children. There was also a Child Psychiatric Clinic in Reading.

With the freedom and variety that came with his responsibilities in Berkshire, Peter Mittler's contribution, competencies and qualities became more widely known. The obvious commitment of staff and their person-centred approach – not least in Borocourt – endeared themselves to him, and it was for him a matter of great sadness many years later that Borocourt of all hospitals was subject to adverse publicity.

By this time Peter Mittler knew the strengths and weaknesses of both the detached clinical approach and the more interactive or person-centred one; the contrast between a distant approach where the cognitive competencies of the professional can over-awe, and a less remote approach, which might more readily create or release unsuspected resources.

Through his involvement with Dr Kevin Murphy, at the Nuffield Audiology Research Unit, he became familiar with speech therapists and with the world of speech and language disorders. Another important influence on Peter Mittler at this time was the Smith Hospital and its Medical Director, Dr Gerry O'Gorman, a highly original person, with unique theories on autism. Just as the Warneford was like a part of a university, Smith Hospital pulsated with debate, discussion, case conferences; and ideas came thick and fast. But Peter Mittler also saw in the Smith Hospital an adverse side. He was far from enamoured of the day to day regime, and tried to reduce the glaring contrast between the high-powered discussion of the professionals and the poor quality of the basic care for the children.

At the Child Psychiatric Clinic there was another rich and profitable range of experiences, and in Dr Gerry Simon, who became registrar of Borocourt and Smith hospitals, Peter Mittler was to find not only a colleague, but a friend and advocate. Their association was highly productive. Dr Simon who came to medicine late was described by Peter Mittler as 'first and foremost a good doctor'. Beginning with a thorough study of the children Dr Simon found many of them growth-retarded. The level of blood lead was found to be abnormally high in a number of cases. A range of biochemical disorders began to be uncovered at a time when the study of genetics was also going into a new dimension. Dr Simon organised careful cytogenetic studies in association with laboratories in Oxford. This was also a time when the electroencephalogram was being rapidly developed and when computerised methods of recording EEGs were being developed at Bristol by Dr Walter Grey. By the later 1950s and early 1960s Peter Mittler was taking two or three of the children at a time to have detailed EEGs with computer analysis.

During World Mental Health Year (1960) the ground was being prepared for the later extension of the educational umbrella to excluded children. The appointment of the Scott Committee which investigated the supply and training of staff for mentally handicapped people, was arousing interest amongst teachers. Whilst it was possible for me to express confidence at the 1960 International Conference that 'the Special Training Centre will ultimately be seen as part of the educational provision in this country and not as a sector apart', it was to take some years before the issue was really 'in the air'.

The period 1959–62 not only rounded off the first post-war stage in the history of 'mental deficiency', it enriched its international connections and potential. It was around about this time that Peter Mittler's interest in the planning of services began to mature.

In the UK, the response by activists in the field of mental handicap to the 1959 Mental Health Act was their insistence upon the publication and implementation of the Scott Committee's Report (1962) which followed it.

In a period of remarkable growth, health authorities began to build a mini-education system of their own for people with mental handicaps. This comprised Junior Training Centres, Adult Training Centres and a Training Council chaired by Prof. Alan Clarke which had an oversight of staff training for both kinds of training centre.

On the international front the election of President Kennedy, in 1961, who had a sister with a mental handicap, prompted a Presidential initiative on a breath-taking scale. The times were ripe for this. The London Conference on the Scientific Study of Mental Deficiency and the International Conference on the Education of the Backward Child had taken place barely a year earlier. The form and content of provision; definitions, theory, attitudes, research, were all under the microscope.

The Royal College of Psychiatrists and others had argued that the main criteria in mental handicap should be social competence, with intellectual disability being seen as relevant but not essential, whereas the British Psychological Society (BPS) approach differed significantly. The Royal Commission however, whose report led to the 1959 Mental Health Act – accepted the definition of mental subnormality recommended by the BPS and supported by the National Council for Civil Liberties (NCCL). They insisted that if people were to be called mentally subnormal, some subnormality of intelligence had to be shown; and the BPS was at least able to define what it understood by subnormality of intelligence. It was when the question arose of how the recommendations of the 1959 Mental Health Act were being implemented, that Peter Mittler's growing stature was seen in his chairmanship of a working party set up by the BPS, composed of several distinguished contributors to the field. In this, his first piece of public research in the field, a survey was designed to reach all the mental handicap hospitals in the country where there was access to clinical psychologists. The survey (in two parts, one on children and one on adults) established that a large number of people coming into mental handicap hospitals still had IQs that were way above 70. The recommendations of the BPS were that the term 'mental subnormality' should not be used for anyone with an IQ above 70, and that where IQs were below 55, the term 'severe subnormality' should be used.

It followed that the pattern of hospital admissions in 1961 reflected neither the spirit of the Royal Commission's recommendations nor that of the Mental Health Act itself. Peter Mittler's interest in service planning and delivery was now further nourished. It took him to meetings across the country where he learnt of what was going on in other long-stay hospitals and about the early days in the development of community services. It also provided his first contacts with government departments.

In 1963, although he thought of continuing in clinical psychology, fresh changes were taking place around him. The assassination of President John F. Kennedy – was later to lead to the creation of the Hester Adrian Research Centre which Peter Mittler was to head from 1968 for fourteen years.

It was during the 1960s that I was to meet Peter Mittler with increasing frequency and in a variety of situations. As I was also to play some part in the events leading up to the creation of the Hester Adrian Research Centre, it is relevant to include here a little known fact which gives the flavour of the times.

The assassination of President Kennedy led to a considerable desire nationally for a suitable memorial. Such had been the impact of President Kennedy on this field that the Guild of Teachers of Backward Children obtained considerable support in its campaign for a living memorial in the form of a President Kennedy Institute of Special Education. In my discussions with a junior minister at the time there was unsolicited reference by him to the possibility of a four million pound Institute. Both the health and the education departments showed this kind of interest and enthusiasm. A committee chaired by Lord Franks was ultimately set up by the Prime Minister to consider the various proposals, and to widespread disappointment finally decided upon a memorial at Runnymede. There was still sufficient steam in the campaign for a President Kennedy Institute however, for it to continue on a reduced scale. Fortunately it had a powerful protagonist in the NAMH whose general secretary was Mary Appleby. A committee was reconvened under the chairmanship of Lady Hester Adrian. Almost immediately, a grant of £100,000 from the Sembal Trust enabled a beginning to be made with serious approaches to universities. This was of course a time of university expansion (The Robbins Report). Professor Jack Tizard and I were asked to visit these universities, a request which I felt unable to undertake as a practising headmaster, and which Professor Tizard readily agreed to do. A number of universities had responded positively to the query as to whether they would be prepared to house this project if the money was forthcoming. Manchester was chosen. The entire process took years rather than weeks or months. It was during the process however, that Lady Hester Adrian who had spearheaded the effort, died. Appropriately, the Hester Adrian Research Centre was born in 1968.

Up to 1963 Peter Mittler had seen his career continuing in clinical psychology. He not only found it stimulating but enjoyed the company of his colleagues. That they enjoyed his company was not surprising. When my wife and I first met Peter Mittler we saw a charming, beautifully spoken scholar, friendly and a little diffident. Our paths crossed and coincided on many occasions. He was to visit the special school in Kings Cross (for educationally subnormal pupils) when I was its headmaster early in the 1960s and he was to visit the special school in Swiss Cottage (for physically handicapped pupils) when I was its headmaster in the second half of the 1960s. Similarly we were to meet frequently during the 1970s when I became resident Principal of a Village 'for the lifelong education and care of the mentally handicapped'.

By the early 1960s however, he had developed specific and absorbing interests, and saw himself as a practitioner rather than a scholar or researcher; an applied psychologist to whom it did not occur that he might end up in an academic career. The times had their impact however, and with his appointment to a lectureship in developmental psychology at Birkbeck he saw an opportunity to redress what he felt to be his lack of grounding in mainstream child development.

It was a considerable shift. It immediately brought Peter Mittler into closer contact with experienced teachers who formed two-thirds of the psychology students at Birkbeck. He plunged into the study of child psychology, which he found fascinating. His research at Birkbeck where he worked from 1963-8, was largely on language development and language disorders and in seeking a topic for his Ph.D. - which he began to work on almost immediately - the language development and language disorders of twins readily suggested itself. In 1959, the year that Luria's book on the psychological development of twins was published, Peter Mittler had seen a set of twins in Berkshire - who were found to be hyperkinetic and had no language. Peter Mittler read Luria's book with great interest and was attracted to the approach of Russians to the study of language. Adapting methods used by Luria, everything was done by Peter Mittler to persuade the parents to express the individuality of the children, by using their individual names instead of calling them 'the twins', dressing them differently, and so on. The twins did remarkably well. Their IQs and their attainments rose. Other twins with autism and language disorders were already known to Berkshire. Peter Mittler went straight back to the audiology unit in Reading, where he had valuable collaboration from Dr Kevin Murphy and his staff. As many as possible of all the twins born in Berkshire in 1961 and 1962 were traced. In all, 100 sets of twins and 100 singletons, were seen within two weeks of their fourth birthday, and Peter Mittler could soon claim to be an expert on children who were aged 48 months precisely - no younger and no older!

Peter Mittler's Ph.D. (1969) and his widely read penguin book on *The Study of Twins* (1971) followed. Although his work at Birkbeck was largely in the field of child development and psychological assessment, it was accepted that some of his research and interests would be in the field of mental handicap. In fact 'mental handicap' was a very visible part of Peter Mittler's ongoing interest. It was during his period at Birkbeck that he edited and contributed to *Psychological Assessment of Mental and Physical Handicaps* (1970) which remained a standard work for many years.

In work on neo-natal and early child development, for example, he was intrigued by the fact that a newborn baby had at its disposal skills and competences which it would not really need for months if not years; and he saw here implications for children who are mentally handicapped. Another research interest of his at this time was concerned with psychotic and autistic children. There was so little work going on in this area at the time that he felt that any research here was valuable. One such study followed up leavers from Smith Hospital; another was concerned with the siblings of autistic children. He was also given responsibility for editing the book on *Aspects of Autism* (1968) which was a report on a BPS conference at the time. In fact, Peter Mittler continued with his follow up study of autistic children during the mid- to late-1960s, travelling to different parts of the south of England. This study however was a depressing one, for with few exceptions he found that they were not doing well at all.

In Birkbeck, he was still interested in Service Delivery issues, when Shirley Williams who was then Secretary of the Fabian Society asked him to write two Fabian pamphlets, one on Mental Health Services in the community, which drew the attention of many people to his interest in these matters. The pamphlets were extremely well received.

Again, at Birkbeck Peter Mittler played a notable role in the campaign to transfer the responsibility for Junior Training Centres from the Health to the Education authorities. He chaired committees set up by both MENCAP (where I was again to meet him) and the BPS where he spoke and wrote on the issue. It was during this period that Grace Rawlings first mentioned to Peter Mittler the proposal for a Kennedy Institute of Special Education. At that time it had not yet been agreed where it should be.

Against this background Peter Mittler's concern for the future of his son Paul must also be recognised. Its relevance to Peter Mittler's insights into strengths and weaknesses of the schooling process is apparent. In 1960 Paul was five and attended a special school for physically handicapped pupils in Reading, which subsequently began to include pupils with other disabilities. He was happy there, but the headmaster thought that Paul had more potential than the school was able to realise. A more academic special school was proposed. This was to stretch Paul intellectually but at some cost. There was frustration and tears. Paul was later assessed at the Spastics Society and given a place at a good residential special school. The dilemma posed to any caring parent was highlighted in the experience of Paul's parents. Whereas at the first special school it had been the headteacher who thought that Paul could be stretched (as he obviously could), at the new school the educational psychologist was concerned that Paul's parents were too demanding of Paul! Another concern for Paul's parents (and particularly for Peter Mittler in view of his own early school experiences) must have been the decision to send Paul to a boarding school. Certainly they feared that the price could have been too high. Peter Mittler worried that they may have deprived Paul of both a home life and of the opportunity for integration. Paul however, not only succeeded in his GCE exams but progressed to come within close sight of an Open University degree.

When the advertisement duly appeared for a Director of the Hester Adrian Research Centre (HARC), Peter Mittler was encouraged by various people to apply. During this period I recall some of his fears about the funding in particular; a fear which at the beginning of the 1990s must raise fresh spectres in our minds – not least of what is already being denied to other potential pioneers. It was to give me immense satisfaction to learn recently that he had found the Hester Adrian period the most exciting and productive period of his life. He took up this post in autumn 1968, at a time when 'oysters were opening everywhere'.

In the process of being selected for the post he had to write a document on what his aims would be as Director. Whilst there was not sufficient funding for all these things to happen, a great many did. It is notable that Peter Mittler not merely attracted able staff but that HARC retained so many for so long. In the early days, largely funded by the then SSRC (Social Sciences Research Council) there were a group of projects on language and communication. Dr James Hogg, who worked as Deputy-Director until 1990 and who now has a Chair in Profound Mental Handicap at Dundee University, directed two SSRC projects on attention and discrimination learning which again had practical implications for 'personality factors' in learning. Another of the HARC founder members, Peter Herriot worked on aspects of memory and how memory training could be developed in adults with mental handicap. Cliff Cunningham (who later held the Chair in the Psychology of Mental Handicap in Nottingham) joined HARC during this phase and worked on Programme Learning and the early teaching machines. He also personally directed three substantial research projects on language development and teaching, two funded by the SSRC and the third, a school-based project, by the Schools Council.

Amongst the greatest achievements of HARC was its research and development programme relating to different approaches to parents and professionals working together. It was hardly surprising from Peter Mittler's background that he could later look back on this work with particular satisfaction. There was no royal road to parental involvement. There were many different approaches; and there were a number of people who developed this work, held it together and took it into new directions. The main contributors were Cliff Cunningham and Dorothy Jeffree, working both together in the early parent workshops (1971-2) and later individually. Indeed, HARC was to cover all age groups. At a time when it was rare to work with babies, Dr Cliff Cunningham and his team worked with 'Downs syndrome' infants as young as a few weeks, going into the homes, supporting and counselling parents and helping them to devise their own strategies. Then Dorothy Jeffree and Roy McConkey carried out a series of studies with pre-school children which led to assessment tools, ideas on play and early intervention. Together with Sally Cheseldine, Dorothy Jeffree also carried out a survey of all school leavers from the SSN (Severely Subnormal) schools (with both Peter Mittler and his wife Helle participating as interviewers in this project). Additionally a series of studies on adults and people in Adult Training Centres (by Ed Whelan and Barbara Speake) resulted in the very influential books in the Souvenir Press series, *Learning to Cope* (1978) and *Getting to Work* (1981).

Peter Mittler was particularly delighted by the success of the Anson House, pre-school project funded mainly by Barnados, which offered an integrated pre-school facility for handicapped and normally developing children and their families and which aimed to apply the findings of research in the classroom and in working in partnership with parents. This project was directed at various phases of its nine-year life by James Hogg, Cliff Cunningham and Sally Beveridge.

A key feature of HARC policy was integration of theory and practice coupled with systematic dissemination of research. HARC set out to ensure as policy and practice that information about research reached practitioners (including parents) and that their ideas about what research should be done influenced the HARC research teams. Of the stream of publications which flowed out, the down-to-earth Souvenir Press series was probably the best known. All reflected the same approach, that of research workers distilling the essence of what they had learnt into language that was accessible to readers at various levels.

Peter Mittler saw very early on the vast gap between what was already known and what was being done; and that between the required number of suitably trained staff and the numbers actually available. A particularly effective HARC initiative was the EDY project (the education of the developmentally young), developed by Tom Foxen and Judith McBrien, a 'cascade' project which took the form of a series of one-week workshops for five educational psychologists. These were held in a school and were directly concerned with the training of the staff of the school in behavioural methods which in the mid-1970s were very fashionable. The idea of the workshops was that they would not only train the psychologists in behavioural methods but would train them to train others. The original hundred psychologists trained have since 'cascaded' into five thousand people, and a second edition of EDY has now been developed by Peter Ferrell, one of Peter Mittler's present colleagues.

The range of Peter Mittler's influence and of HARC's activities was considerable. It came as no surprise to me to receive from HARC, in the early 1970s, a submission for the Ravenswood Adventure Playground Design competition; nor that the judges recommended the HARC contribution for an award. The network of friends built up by HARC was enormous.

In 1975 Peter Mittler was rung by Dr Rodney Wilkins from the DHSS to say that the government was thinking of setting up a special advisory group on mental handicap, and Peter Mittler was asked to consider being Chairman of that group. Reference has already been made to this highly productive development. For Peter Mittler it was particularly interesting to be so close to government, with ready access to ministers and senior civil servants, feeling close to policy development and presentation. In those days the Local Authority Associations had an agreement that no circulars would be produced by ministers without resource allocation; a practice from which we might all have benefitted had subsequent governments followed suit. There was as a result a virtual embargo on the government giving advice, whereas the NDG (National Development Group for the mentally handicapped) was not shackled by the constraints of the circular; and the DHSS was not committed to the advice offered. It was accordingly a most valuable innovation in which Peter Mittler's approach to theory and practice and to its dissemination outwards was very visible. His book *People not Patients* (1979) was a product of this period, seeking to summarise progress and problems in planning, policy-making and service delivery, at that time.

Unfortunately, the fact that the Jay Committee was sitting prevented us looking at the question of staff training, as Peter Mittler would undoubtedly have wished to do. With hindsight I feel that the entire field would have benefitted had there been an opportunity to look even more comprehensively at the issue of staff training than could the Jay Committee – across all relevant departments and professions. It could also be argued, that a great deal of unnecessary anguish and confusion would have been avoided had the

1970 Education (Handicapped Children) Act been extended vertically to the Adult Training Centres. Life, however, as W. D. Wall frequently reminded us, is untidy.

In 1977, as one of the three professors in the Department of Education, administrative and teaching duties were added to Peter Mittler's post. The publication of the substantial Warnock Report (DES, 1978) which squarely confronted the fact that 20 per cent – not just 2 per cent – of the school population had special needs posed new demands upon the comparatively small but expanding group of pioneers in special education. In due course a special needs element had to be introduced into all initial teacher training and new training and retraining opportunities needed to be made available to teachers and other professionals.

Prof. Mittler was also to seize upon mainstream developments which could be developed to the benefit of children with learning difficulties, such as the Trans-vocational Educational Initiative (TVEI) programmes and Records of Achievement. Above all he saw in the new GCSE which was intended as a process of teaching and assessment and examination for all, a means of ending the divisiveness between the GCE and CSE.

In the M.Ed. in Special Education programme which his department introduced Prof. Mittler began from a mainstream base, looking at special needs in terms of school effectiveness, curriculum reform and curriculum access. The weaknesses of an anaemic academic–cognitive curriculum in the mainstream were simultaneously leading to a greater awareness of the need for a blood-transfusion (of the kind normal in good special schools) which ensured a respect for human dignity; and where the curriculum recognised the part which the emotions and the creative arts had to play in the creation of citizens. Prof. Mittler was himself to be inspired by the main movement to curriculum reform associated with David Hargreaves (*Challenge for the Comprehensive School*), which inserted humanity into the cognitive–academic approach, rather than 'diluted' it.

Nationally as internationally, the 1980s which had opened with great promise, came up against growing obstacles. International Year of Disabled People, 1981, encouraged legislation and innovation across the globe. In the UK, the legislation which stemmed from the Warnock Report was at last introduced. Resources however trailed far behind the need. In those circumstances, the impressive but cot-sized blanket of special provision which could not yet cover even the 2 per cent adequately could certainly not be spread over the 20 per cent. It was however tugged at by many hands – and was in danger of being ripped to pieces in a mounting confusion. However much Peter Mittler welcomed worthwhile 'integrative' approaches he was not to lose sight of the dangers; nor was he insensitive to the relevance and merits of special schools. But fresh initiatives and new resources were required everywhere and not least in staff recruitment and training. The EDY project at one extreme and the creation of the M.Ed in Special Education at the other are indications of how the new situation was tackled at Manchester. A master's degree in Special Education, organised jointly by Manchester University and Manchester Polytechnic, will survive after the end of the current joint diploma course in special needs.

Even when with great heart-searching, Peter Mittler resigned from HARC in 1982 and took on full-time responsibilities in the Department of Education, his new offices were only a floor below HARC!

The sudden ministerial decision to promote a 'Great Education Reform' bill which showed no awareness of special needs alarmed Peter Mittler considerably. He saw in it a threat to marginalise an even greater section of the school population; and his acceptance of an invitation to join SEAC (on which he sat for two years) was a measure of his determination to ensure there a watchdog for special needs. One result owing much to him as well as to the 'SEN-friendly' attitude of his fellow members of Schools Examination and Assessment Council (SEAC) was that the GCSE in 1994 will be graded on a ten level system as opposed to the present A to G. Whilst he feels that the whole National Curriculum will have to be slimmed down he sees a general commitment to the principle that the National Curriculum is for everybody, and that it is a landmark – although its implications have still to be worked out.

Recently he has worked with a group of teachers seconded by Manchester to develop and publish examples of ways in which pupils with special educational needs, particularly those with severe learning difficulties, can gain full access to the National Curriculum.

Today the centre for Educational Guidance in Special Needs at Manchester has ten staff plus visiting professionals and is international, with staff and students from some twenty countries, many from Asia and Africa. Its brief extends to educational psychology, guidance and counselling, in essence an extension of special needs interests into the mainstream. As Deputy Director of the School of Education, the largest outside London, Peter Mittler has responsibility for a hundred teaching staff and an overview of teaching and research over the whole field of education. This provides a challenging perspective from which to view special needs issues.

Given his experience of marginalisation, his fertile mind, training and concern for his eldest son, it was not surprising that his work stretched from the detailed and immediate to the broad and universal. Today Paul lives independently in semi-sheltered accommodation. A second son Stephen, is a Health Service Manager in Bromley whilst the third is a sound engineer, innovating in pop music. Helle Mittler who shared her husband's interests from the beginning was able to resume her career once her family had grown up.

On many of their visits abroad, Peter and Helle manage to combine business with pleasure, resulting in, for example, two Himalayan and one Andes trekking expedition and more recently, a trip to Tibet. As often as they can, they go for less ambitious walks in the Peak and Lake Districts. In search of further recreation and enrichment, Peter started to learn the piano and discovered for himself what it is to experience specific learning difficulties in sight reading and motivation and in finding excuses for not practising.

It is appropriate at this point to return to Vienna, Peter Mittler's starting place sixty years ago, which, poignantly, today houses the UN Centre for Social Development and Humanitarian Affairs. He attends a meeting there annually and is also able to take part in all inter-agency meetings of UN organisations dealing with disability. He was commissioned by the UN to prepare a discussion paper on the future of the Decade of Disabled People (1982–92), what should happen during its last two years, and beyond; and after consultation that paper went forward to the UN General Assembly in October of 1990. Notwithstanding economic constraints everywhere, some of its recommendations were agreed.

The international dimensions of Peter Mittler's interests are most clearly reflected in his voluntary work with the International League of Societies for Persons with Mental Handicap, a world-wide federation of voluntary organisations, now numbering 130 in 75 countries. He was an active innovative President in the period 1982–6 and continues to represent the League within the UN system. He also worked for some years with the League's sister organisation, the International Association for the Scientific Study of Mental Deficiency, editing the proceedings of their international conferences in Washington and Jerusalem. These international contacts and activities help to bring a wider perspective in the context of deteriorating public services for disabled people in the UK.

It is relevant that Helle Mittler has not only produced some joint publications but engaged in joint assignments abroad, as a social worker and later Staff Development Officer for a Social Services Department. This international dimension began to expand in the 1980s, perhaps to counter in some measure the downward pressures of economy and climate in the UK. By 1990 Prof. Mittler had visited some sixty countries. Much of his effort abroad was in the form of lecture tours, India, Japan, Australia, New Zealand and so on, but more importantly he organised some practical work along workshop lines. One example of this took place as early as 1981 (IYDP, in Hong Kong) when the International League of Societies for the Mentally Handicapped organised an intensive 'family training' workshop along Peter's 'Noah's Ark Principle'. In this case, a parent, a teacher and a community worker from each country were brought together for a course which concluded with each trio producing an action plan for their own countries. After the intensive workshop on early intervention and teaching techniques, each trio returned to their countries to implement these in their very different contexts. Similar initiatives took place in Nairobi where policy implementation in twelve African countries was considered, and in 1986 a workshop was conducted with money from the EEC and the ILO which concerned itself with mentally handicapped adults.

Two 'citizens of the world', the Mittlers have a great deal of achievement to look back and forward to. They have now been to China five times where they have been involved in workshops, together with Peter Farrell a psychologist and teacher–trainer.

Enormous tasks face all the specialist, voluntary and parents' movements which seek a more compassionate and creative world community. In contributing to this book, the contributors salute Peter Mittler in a way he will best appreciate by further disseminating and contributing to our growing knowledge.

References

Clarke, A. M. and Clarke, A. D. B. (1958) (eds) *Mental Deficiency: The Changing Outlook*. London, Methuen.

Department of Education and Science (1978) Special Educational Needs. Report of the Committee of Enquiry in the Education of Children and Young People. (The Warnock Report) London, HMSO.

Hargreaves, D. (1982) *Challenge for the Comprehensive School*. London, Routledge & Kegan Paul.

Luria, A. R. and Yudsvitch, F. I. (1959) *Speech and the Development of Mental Processes in the Child*, J. Simon (ed.). London, Staples Press.

Mittler, P. (1968) (ed.) *Aspects of Autism*. London, BPS.

Mittler, P. (1970) (ed.) *Psychological Assessment of Mental and Physical Handicaps*. London, Methuen.

Mittler, P. (1971) *The Study of Twins*. London, Penguin.

Mittler, P. (1979) *People not Patients: Problems and Policies in Mental Handicap*. London, Methuen.

Seguin, E. (1964) Teachers College Series in Special Education. University of Columbia, Bureau of publications.

Speake, B. (1981) *Getting to Work*. London, Souvenir Press.

Whelan, E. (1978) *Learning to Cope*. London, Souvenir Press.

CHAPTER 1

Research on Mental Handicap: Past, Present and Future

Alan D. B. Clarke and Ann M. Clarke

This chapter will chiefly consider the period 1950–90, but will attempt to place research into its preceding and contemporary historical context. We will use 'mental retardation' as the international global term for the many conditions which have been variously designated as mental deficiency, mental subnormality, mental handicap, mental impairment, learning disability and doubtless others still to come.

Developments in the nineteenth century stemmed from the watershed in human thought provided by Darwin (*The Origin of Species*, 1859) who showed that in evolution the fittest became ascendant in the struggle for survival, passing on their characteristics to their progeny. The unfit had a smaller chance of so doing, and this biological theory was extended simplistically to cover social matters. The 'threat of the unfit' became the major factor in the move to sterilise or to incarcerate the mentally retarded in institutions. Galton, a cousin of Charles Darwin, stated that

> the wisest policy is that which results in retarding the average age of marriage among the weak, and in hastening it among the vigorous classes, whereas unhappily for us, the influence of various social agencies has been strongly and banefully exerted in precisely the opposite direction.... Its effect would be such as to cause the race of the prudent to fall, after a few centuries, into an almost incredible inferiority of numbers to that of the imprudent... [it would] bring utter ruin upon the breed of any country. It may seem monstrous that the weak should be crowded out by the strong, but it is still more monstrous that the races best fitted to play their part on the stage of life, should be crowded by the incompetent, the ailing and the desponding. (Galton, 1869: 352–6)

These views gained increasing credence at the beginning of this century. By this time compulsory education had revealed wide differences in scholastic ability. Concurrently, an oversimple view of the manner in which genetic influences operated was popularised, leading in this country to Galton's Eugenics Society and to widespread alarm that the higher breeding rates of the 'least fit' would lead to national degeneracy. A number of extraordinarily naïve investigations fanned the flame of this alarm. Thus the study of the Kallikak family by Goddard (1912) purported to show that intelligence and social fitness were inherited along simple lines. A Martin Kallikak took up with a purportedly feeble-minded tavern woman while a soldier during the American Revolution. She bore him a son, Martin Kallikak junior, from whom were descended vast numbers of social parasites. Martin senior, on returning to civilian life, thoughtfully provided an apparent control group by marrying a girl of good stock, from whom virtuous citizens were descended. Much of the evidence was incomplete, anecdotal or fragmentary, and, of course, heredity and environment in both streams of descendants were hopelessly confounded.

The simplistic view of heredity propounded by Goddard (1914) among others, led to the widespread practice of segregation and/or sterilisation. Earlier nineteenth century views on aetiology had been even more primitive. Correlates were often mistaken for causes and thus tuberculosis and alcoholism were considered to be major aetiological agents in mental retardation. Moreover, Langdon Down (1866) who first identified 'mongolism', had proposed a theory of racial 'atavistic regression' to explain the origin of various clinical conditions. By contrast, a number of educational and medical pioneers undertook work which gave a promise that mental retardation might be ameliorated. Finally, the beginnings of 'mental measurement' are to be found towards the end of the century. A decade later, Binet in France combined a deep humanism with a scientific objectivity in pioneering the assessment of backwardness and mental retardation.

For very different reasons two social trends in the early part of this century combined to influence the collection of information on the nature and extent of the problems posed by mental retardation. On the one hand, liberal concerns about the disadvantaged in society began to emerge; on the other, the eugenics movement (see Barker, 1983, 1989) as noted, reflected alarm about the future population. Institutions were seen as a solution, and some became research centres (e.g. the Vineland Training School, USA, Stoke Park Hospital, UK). As laws governing societies' methods for dealing with this field came into operation, it became a relatively straight-forward process to collect information relating to prevalence, causation and treatment. Epidemiological studies in the 1920s, 1930s and 1940s proved to be informative and influential. In 1938, for example, the late L. S. Penrose published the famous Colchester Survey; among other far-sighted observations, this documented clear distinctions between the two sub-populations (severe versus mild impairment) in the field of mental retardation, and also indicated that prevalence had strong age associations, with a marked decline after the school years.

In the immediate post-war period, several influences combined to accelerate scientific advances. First, the spirit of optimism and humanism, characteristic of those times, caused many to become more aware of the disadvantaged, to be attracted to these fields and to seek preventive or remedial measures. Second, the belief that scientific methodology had much to offer became more widespread, and its successes more obvious. Third, the parents of the severely handicapped began to initiate pressure groups and to influence the laws and practices which catered for the mentally retarded.

In 1949, Penrose's *The Biology of Mental Defect* proved to be a landmark in recording the already considerable advances in the biomedical field. A less impressive book, though a landmark in the sense of recording for the first time what was known in the psychosocial field, was S. B. Sarason's *Psychological Problems in Mental Deficiency* (1949). Of its ten chapters, however, only one was devoted to treatment, the remainder being largely descriptive. Within a few years the situation had altered radically. An edited text by Hilliard and Kirman (1957) included non-medical contributions, and Clarke and Clarke's (1958) *Mental Deficiency: The Changing Outlook* was almost entirely written by psychologists. Here seven chapters out of eighteen were explicitly concerned with training and others forms of treatment. By now a surge of scientific work was taking place in all disciplines.

The major thrust of this chapter will be concerned with description, prevention and amelioration. The distinction between the latter two sub-headings is not as firm as perhaps it may sound, for secondary prevention (that is preventing the continuation of an existing handicapping condition) could equally be termed amelioration. An example is the successful use of dietary treatment in Phenylketonuria (PKU) (Woolf *et al.*, 1955).

A further important distinction must be made between conditions resulting in severe or milder impairment. These differ considerably in aetiology, developmental level and prognosis for independence, as noted by E. O. Lewis (1933).

The more severe forms of mental handicap arise from pathological disturbance of the Central Nervous System (CNS) having their roots in rare genetic or environmental accidents such as infections, toxic conditions or traumas. Milder cases may, in some 20 to 30 per cent of the administratively identified, be due to the aforementioned factors affecting development to a milder degree. A larger number in industrialised Western communities occur as a combination of polygenic influences (Scarr, 1981; Plomin, 1989), often interacting with adverse social conditions including malnutrition (Wilton and Irvine, 1983; Clarke and Clarke, 1986; Dowdney *et al.*, 1987; Pollitt, 1988; Baumeister, 1990).

Description of the mentally retarded

Accurate description may be possible at many different levels, chromosomal, biochemical, skeletal and behavioural to name but a few. It may serve a number of different functions ranging from research to clinical or educational practice.

Overall description of a mentally retarded person will normally include a record of family and personal history, an assessment of present level of functioning (intellectual, social and emotional), a note of any special features of the diagnostic process and so forth. In turn these may provide broad hints about the prospects for treatment, with provisional indications of prognosis. Appropriate assessments may offer base-lines against which effective or ineffective interventions may be evaluated (e.g. Gunzburg, 1974).

Here we will consider briefly the two aspects of mental retardation which together are associated with administrative action, namely sub-average intellectual functioning together with problems of adaptive behaviour (Grossman, 1983).

During the period 1960–80 the IQ, as a descriptive and prognostic indicator, fell into disrepute in many quarters. Court cases in the USA concerned the labelling of poor (often black) children as mentally retarded and in need of special education. Books and articles poured forth from the pens of protagonists who argued for or against the use of IQ tests as the sole or even part-description of persons with learning disabilities. Apart from unfortunate eugenic overtones already mentioned, IQ tests were regarded as too far removed from the presenting difficulties exhibited by retarded persons. These seemed, especially to the many unsophisticated critics, to demand descriptions in terms of educational failure and social competence. Berger and Yule (1985, 1987) provide a spirited and careful defence of the IQ in mental retardation practice; in the former chapter, for example, they offer nine cogent points for its clinical utility. In our own view the IQ provides the single most valid criterion of retarded functioning. For a strong argument in favour of this view, see Zigler and Hodapp (1986). Furthermore, researchers are becoming increasingly interested in the components of intellectual abilities/disabilities, and progress in delineating the basic processes of intelligence is likely to occur (see Detterman, 1987).

For many decades social incompetence, a somewhat vague concept, was used as one of the criteria for the diagnosis of mental retardation, and indeed has been a main route for official administrative action. Much more recently, deficits in adaptive behaviour have been included, with attempts to objectify these criteria (see Balthazar and English, 1969; Nihira et al., 1974). The development of such scales (and there are now over a hundred) was encouraged as an alternative to the maligned IQ. The best known is the Adaptive Behaviour Scale (ABS) of Nihira et al. (1974) subsequently revised. Bortner (1978) offers an excellent early review of the 1974 revision. The ABS represents an important attempt to objectify the concept of social competence, covering between twenty-one and twenty-four areas of functioning, ranging from ratings of self-direction, responsibility and socialisation to withdrawal, inappropriate interpersonal manners, hyperactive activities and sexually aberrant behaviours. It is appropriate for ages between three years and adulthood. Part I relates to personal independence and part II measures maladaptive behaviour. Percentile norms were based on 4000 institutionalised retarded persons, but a public school version offers norms on 2600 children in grades 2 to 6. Inter-rater reliabilities for part I range from 0.71 to 0.93, with a median 0.86 for the ten domains of the scale. Reliabilities for the fourteen domains of part II range from 0.37 to 0.77 with a median of 0.57, the latter value being unimpressive.

Bortner points out that various studies suggest the existence of meaningful factors or aspects of adjustment, and the ability of different parts of the scale to discriminate successfully between variously labelled groups. However, since adaptive behaviour can only be defined in terms of a particular setting, and since there is a variety of settings to which individuals may differentially adapt, it will be important to evaluate the diagnostic validity of the scale in terms of the variety of criteria that are applicable to such settings. It is possible that the correlations between behaviour of institutionalised persons and their adaptation in the wider context of the community after proper training may not be very high. It is important, too, to recognise that scores may represent current levels of functioning without possessing a necessary predictive validity for individuals, especially in the upper ranges of intelligence.

In accord with the earlier work it seems clear that part II of the ABS is less reliable than part I. This is unfortunate, to say the least, because it is maladaptive behaviour that produces problems for the retarded (see Bean and Roszkowski, 1982, who indicate that part I ratings appear to be influenced by general cognitive ability, and that item analysis of part II indicated that 39 per cent possess undesirable psychometric characteristics).

The burgeoning research on adaptive behaviour underscores a conclusion reached by Grossman (1983) that adaptive behaviour scores yield information that is sometimes closely correlated with IQ. A recent example is given by Brems et al. (1990) who attempted to establish reliability and validity of the Developmental Record which employs five sub-scales of adaptive behaviour, using 1,069 records of institutionalised persons. They established very high reliability and correlations of 0.84 with Stanford-Binet scores and of 0.72 with the Vineland Adaptive Behaviour composite scores. For this large institutionalised population, the IQ predicted the adaptive behaviour well.

An important review of the use of adaptive behaviour measures in reported research has been provided by Hawkins and Cooper (1990). They trace the increasing combined use in articles of intellectual and adaptive behaviour measures. They conclude about the latter that prediction will be much more accurate if the initial level of functioning is very low, and is associated with low IQ, and repeat our warning that perfect adaptation within an institution may have no bearing upon adaptation in a wider community.

Refined descriptive procedures, of course, are useful not only in connection with individual people and plans for their future, but also for determining prevalence both as a scientific and an administrative question of importance.

By the beginning of our period, the work of O'Connor and Tizard on the IQ distribution in adolescent and adult males classified as 'feeble-minded' in twelve institutions was well known. It implied that mental deficiency hospitals were being used as dumping grounds for social problem cases, for the mean IQ was about 70 points; a similarly disturbing picture was later provided by Mittler (1963, 1966). At the same time, the employment and employability of such persons was also studied (O'Connor and Tizard, 1956). Another interesting survey by Goodman and Tizard (1962) contrasted the prevalance of severe subnormality in Middlesex with figures from a 1920s survey by E.O Lewis. While the number of surviving Down's syndrome persons had greatly increased, other forms of severe mental handicap decreased, but these were in balance and overall prevalance was unaffected. McLaren and Bryson (1987) give an excellent overview of epidemiological studies of mental retardation with an emphasis on prevalence, associated disorders and aetiology. Massively the IQ was used as the defining criterion both for mental retardation and for sub-categories. Many of the (on the whole minor) differences in reported rates are attributed to methods of definition (i.e. whether incidence is included with prevalence) and ascertainment at various stages, which is highest between ten and twenty years of age.

These authors include a consideration of European as well as American research on prevalence, but ignore the attempt by the Bishop Bekkers Foundation, Utrecht to compare prevalence rates in Third World countries (Belmont, 1981; Serpell, 1988). For those interested in the methodology of conducting surveys in remote districts of Africa and Asia these reports make fascinating reading.

Prevention

An understanding of the causes of particular conditions can lead ultimately to prevention. Sometimes correlates may suggest preventive action; high maternal age in Down's syndrome is an example. Matters are taken much further, as will be noted, when chromosomal anomalies are identified.

Many conditions result from interacting rather than single factors. Most of the administratively identified mildly retarded persons exemplify this point. A complex array of biological and pervasive environmental adversities combine to promote low levels of functioning. The precise weighting of each of these factors undoubtedly varies in individual cases. Preventive action for this group as a whole seems beyond our grasp. Indeed, with current social disruption typical of developed societies one can foresee an increase in the numbers of these unfortunate people.

Penrose's (1949) *The Biology of Mental Defect* and its later editions (1954, 1963, 1972) recorded immense changes in the understanding of aetiologies which have continued since that time. For example, although, as noted, the association with maternal age was already well known for Down's syndrome, a variety of explanations were offered. The major advance came in 1959 with Lejeune, Gautier and Turpin's discovery of the extra chromosome. This, in turn, led to the development of the pre-natal diagnosis, to accurate genetic counselling for many conditions and currently to new banding techniques allowing the detection of many different chromosomal anomalies (Berg, 1986). Alphafetoprotein assays for spina bifida and anencephaly (for example, Brock, 1976) and even more recent chorion biopsy techniques represent further advances (for example, Rodeck and Morsman, 1983) as do ultrasonography and fetoscopy.

Another break-through was the discovery by Lubs (1969) of the fragile-X chromosome and its associated phenotype which may account for at least 2 per cent of retarded males (Evans and Hamerton, 1985), although Hagberg and Hagberg (1985) quote much higher prevalence rates. Gosden *et al.* (1986) point out that it is second only to Down's syndrome in its importance as a genetic disease associated with moderate to severe mental handicap. Possibilities of treatment are thought to exist (see also Baraitser, 1984).

Stimulated by the advances in research in the 1950s and 1960s an unwise forecast was made by the President's Committee on Mental Retardation (1972) which stated that 'Using present knowledge and techniques from the biomedical and behavioural sciences, it is possible to reduce the occurrence of mental retardation by 50 per cent before the end of the century'. In 1976, one of the present authors indicated that, since three-quarters of the mentally retarded are of mild grade and since no significant impact on their prevalence had been, or was likely to be, demonstrated, the overall forecast must be largely incorrect. The Committee (1976) implicitly conceded this point in the same year, confining its prediction to the more severe forms of mental retardation.

Two further notable advances in genetics have more recently been reported. First, the gene for tuberous sclerosis has been located on the distal long arm of chromosome 9, representing the first step towards the development of prenatal and presymptomatic tests (Fryer *et al.*, 1987). Second, as St Clair (1987) indicates in a review, a genetic link has now been established between Down's syndrome and Alzheimer's disease. The gene responsible for amyloid plaques and deposits, and probably also for neurofibrillary tangles, is located on chromosome 21, confirming the view that dementia in middle-aged Down's syndrome persons is qualitatively indistinguishable from the effects of Alzheimer's disease. He indicates that the resources of molecular biology will now be aimed at learning more about the pathological segment of chromosome 21 involved in both conditions.

Wahlström (1990) has presented an impressive gene map concerning diseases, enzymes and proteins of interest in connection with mental retardation, involving 503 diseases, 69 of which were mapped to an autosome and 73 to the X-chromosome. The number of genes located on chromosomes is increasing rapidly and, as the author states, could be of value in understanding disorders connected with mental retardation.

Cytomegalovirus has come to the fore as an important aetiological agent during our period (Crome, 1961; Stern *et al.*, 1969; Dudgeon, 1984). The development of a safe vaccine will be very difficult, and several authorities, including Dudgeon (1984), believe that genetic engineering recombination techniques may provide a future prospect for prevention. Berg (1985) quotes frequencies for congenital cytomegalovirus infection ranging from 0.5 per cent to 2.5 per cent in screening studies of infants, although only a minority show evidence of the disease in infancy. Nevertheless, the problem represents an even greater potential viral hazard than rubella.

Equally important advances have occurred in understanding the biochemistry of some forms of retardation, from early work on PKU and onwards (for a review see Stern, 1985), and the stream of research initiated by Dobbing has identified particular vulnerabilities in brain growth during the last trimester of pregnancy and the first two years of post-natal growth (for example, Dobbing, 1968, 1984; Dobbing and Sands, 1973).

Amelioration

Amelioration of mental retardation can take place through different approaches. For example, surgery has been effective for some forms of hydrocephalus; dietary treatment has had some favourable results in cases of PKU. For most forms of amelioration, however, attempts to change behaviour have been pre-eminent.

At the beginning of our period (1950–90), the Mental Deficiency Act of 1913 was still operative in this country with its underlying philosophy of protecting citizens from the mentally retarded and from national degeneracy. This resulted in the forcible incarceration of large numbers of handicapped infants, children, young people and adults in institutions, predominantly located in the countryside where they would be segregated from society and, so far as the sexes were concerned, from each other. A similar situation applied across the Atlantic.

In the 1940s H.C. Gunzburg had been appointed as a training officer/psychologist at Monyhull Hospital and by 1948 Tizard and O'Connor had joined the Social Psychiatry Research Unit at the Maudsley Hospital, England. Their brief, under the direction of Aubrey Lewis, was to investigate the social problem of mental deficiency. The early work of all three marked the starting point of post-war research into rehabilitation in the UK. Other appointments to clinical posts were soon to follow and since research training formed part of the background for most of these persons, and since very little was known about the psychology of mental retardation, the field was wide open. By 1956, O'Connor and Tizard had produced a small book which recorded their findings.

Conditions in 'mental deficiency' hospitals and occupation centres were then so impoverished, and their inmates so deprived, that several psychologists rapidly moved away from the descriptive work which had characterised earlier research towards the notion of developing techniques of amelioration. Clearly the nature of, and constraints upon, retarded learning were of prime interest and a better understanding of these was seen as a key strategy in producing behavioural change.

The late Jack Tizard was the first to perceive the importance of learning studies for the severely retarded. His early work showed that these adults possessed an unsuspected capacity to learn simple tasks, to respond to incentives, to retain learning and transfer these effects to other tasks (see Clarke and Tizard, 1983). Others were to follow and to establish that

Tizard's laboratory studies possessed 'real-life' validity (e.g. Clarke and Hermelin, 1955). Simple industrial tasks were shown to be well within the capacity of such persons and became widely practised in sheltered conditions. The contrast between the passive, dependent handicapped person, and the same one fully employed was very marked. More recently, Gold in Canada replicated and extended this early work and recorded the development of skills in the same dramatic fashion (for example, Gold, 1973). During this same period, assessment methods such as the Portage Project (for reviews, see Shearer and Shearer, 1972; Shearer and Loftin, 1984) were developed to identify both the assets and deficits of individuals so that programmes of remediation could be employed. The authors developed the training of home visitors to teach parents how to employ behavioural techniques for assisting the development of their handicapped children.

As noted, in the 1950s several psychologists started to challenge the prevailing views held by the predominantly medical and nursing authorities, and meanwhile there was a change in society's outlook with a (sometimes glib) environmentalism replacing the former belief in heredity. The economy expanded, there was a period of very full employment, parents started to raise their voices on behalf of their handicapped progeny, and the mentally retarded were increasingly perceived as 'people not patients' (Mittler, 1979) for whom normalisation programmes were required (Bank-Mikkelsen, 1969; Nirje, 1969, 1970; Gunzburg, 1970; Wolfensberger, 1972) in order that they might be as fully as possible integrated into society.

The success of the early research led to the foundation at the University of Manchester of the Hester Adrian Research Centre for the study of learning processes, under its first Director, Peter Mittler. His research and that of colleagues such as Cunningham, Hogg, Whelan, Jeffree and more recently, Kiernan, have made a major impact upon practice.

Among the more powerful techniques used in encouraging socially adaptive skills and eradicating maladaptive behaviour is systematic behaviour modification. There are two somewhat different methods having their origins in animal experiments on classical conditioning (Pavlov, 1927) and instrumental or operant conditioning (Thorndike, 1911; Skinner, 1938), respectively. Application to the mentally retarded has been overwhelmingly along the lines developed by Skinner and his colleagues and elaborated for retardation by Bijou (1963, 1966) and in Britain by members of the Hester Adrian Centre. See also Yule and Carr (1980, 1987). Kiernan (1974, 1985) has presented succinct accounts of research in this field, together with extensive references. In general, he believes that his review of studies on the development of new skills and the elimination of unacceptable behaviour indicates considerable success in the use of behavioural techniques, although their application to the development of communication skills has so far yielded less satisfactory results. However, experts acknowledge the dangers of the over-enthusiastic use of behaviour modification by practitioners lacking an understanding of the complexity of some of the target behaviours and also the procedures required to bring about a lasting change. A recent useful overview of the use of behavioural techniques in the treatment of sexually deviant behaviour in mentally retarded people is provided by Foxx *et al.* (1986).

The notion of a potential upward shift in psycho-social abilities dated from the 1930s but the methodology of such research was weak. Later work, from the 1950s and onwards, however, yielded some support to the view that, within certain limits, the levels of functioning, whether intellectual, scholastic or social of previously deprived persons might be enhanced (for example, Clarke and Clarke, 1958, 1976). From varied approaches, it became obvious that some forms of familial mild retardation, particularly those associated with prolonged social adversity, show spontaneous improvement (Clarke *et al.*, 1958; Cobb, 1972; Svendsen, 1982). Such persons often benefit from and, initially at least, rely upon unofficial help from 'benefactors' in the community (Edgerton, 1967; Edgerton and Bercovici, 1976; Edgerton *et al.*, 1984). Since these processes of improvement appear to occur naturally, there are prospects of enhancing and accelerating such changes by deliberate intervention.

In the 1960s, in some quarters, it seemed to be believed that anything termed intervention, however, brief, would have effects similar to those recorded in children who had experienced prolonged ecological change. Hence short pre-school Head Start programmes were launched in the US with results which, to say the least, were disappointing. High-quality early intervention programmes have, however, resulted in modest gains in educational and social status in later life. A self-sustaining motivational process both in parents and children seems to have been initiated by pre-school experience (Lazar and Darlington, 1982; Schweinhart and Weikart, 1980, 1981). By contrast, Head Start programmes appear not to have been similarly successful (for example, Evans, 1985) but, for an evaluation of immediate and longer-term effects, see McKey *et al.* (1985) and Clarke and Clarke (1989).

The general message is that only powerful and prolonged ecological change is likely to have really significant effects. This has occurred for individuals by adoption or fostering, but programmes for groups have not in recent times been recorded, apart from a fascinating French study of children from deprived backgrounds, adopted between four and six years, with an initial mean IQ of 77. On follow-up between eleven and sixteen years, more than a quarter had IQs above 100, paralleled by scholastic achievement (Duyme and Dumaret, 1986; for an English summary, see Clarke *et al.*, 1985: 458-9).

The emphasis of much behavioural research during the last decade has shifted towards evaluations of various types of service. Sensitivity to these needs is to be welcomed, and there has been a clearer indication of the ideal requirements of community care (Mittler and Serpell, 1985).

Recently, problems of adjustment in the community have given rise to the concept of challenging behaviour, especially in those with severe retardation. McCool *et al.* (1989) indicate that these behaviours may arise in those who are resistant to the new demands placed upon them to indulge in acceptable behaviour. These persons will not respond to unstructured opportunities in ordinary settings, but require intensive structured help, following a careful analysis of the particular circumstances promoting inappropriate responses.

Prospects

For the reasons of space this review has been selective. Although there remain large areas of ignorance, the advances in research over the last forty years have been impressive in all fields. Moreover, from having been almost a medical monopoly in 1950, the development of multi-disciplinary approaches has been significant, reflected world-wide by the foundation in 1964 of the International Association for the Scientific Study of Mental Deficiency.

Advances in biomedical areas have been very considerable, and ultimately hold prospects for a reduction in the incidence of more severe forms of mental retardation. With increased survival at birth and longevity, however, overall prevalence may well be much the same as earlier. As noted, the President's Committee on Mental Retardation (1972) made a wildly optimistic forecast concerning a 50 per cent reduction in incidence of all forms of mental retardation by the end of the century. Its later limitation (1976) to the more severe conditions is likely to prove equally erroneous (see Stratford and Steele, 1985, concerning Down's syndrome).

New knowledge relating to aetiology, especially of the apparently undifferentiated group of severely retarded persons, can confidently be expected. Gene mapping and genetic engineering recombination techniques hold high promise for the future.

In the psychosocial field the potentials for amelioration have been well demonstrated, although there remains a lack of application of research findings to ordinary practice in many areas. For those with milder handicaps, the prognosis in the past, as shown in dozens of follow-up studies has, on average, been relatively good. This reasonably optimistic picture, however, may well no longer hold in the light of widespread social problems (for example Zetlin and Murtaugh, 1990) and the possibility of an intergenerational under class (see Baumeister and Kupstas, 1990).

The move towards community care, signalled by the normalisation movement, was prompted by a number of influences. Tizard's (1962) Brooklands experiment comparing the effects of community living versus institutionalisation was one influential factor arising from research. Although care in the community became official policy thirty-one years ago, its fruition in this country is, to say the least, very incomplete, as Rose-Ackerman (1982) implies for the US. The relatively recent identification of challenging behaviour has been influenced by the decanting of poorly prepared individuals from long-stay hospitals, as well as by the reluctance of many citizens to tolerate unusual behaviour. Lack of human and material resources threatens advances in community care. Further work on social skills training is urgently needed.

Policy makers are, of course, constrained by their political masters and usually by finance. Hence they tend to choose only to implement those aspects of research findings which suit their overall plans. It is up to research workers to urge the proper monitoring and evaluation of innovative ideas, and to bring to public attention their findings. In such endeavours Peter Mittler has been pre-eminent, nationally and internationally.

References

Balthazar, E. E. and English, G. E. (1969) A system for the social classification of the more severely retarded, *American Journal of Mental Deficiency*, 74, 361–8.

Bank-Mikkelsen, N. E. (1969) A metropolitan area in Denmark: Copenhagen, in R. B. Kugel and W. P. Wolfensberger (eds) *Changing Patterns of Residential Services for the Mentally Retarded*. Washington, D.C., President's Committee on Mental Retardation.

Baraitser, M. (1984) Chromosomal aspects of mental retardation, in J. Dobbing, A. D. B. Clarke, J. A., Corbett, J. Hogg and R. O. Robinson (eds). London, Macmillan and The Royal Society of Medicine.

Barker, D. (1983) How to curb the fertility of the unfit: the feeble-minded in Edwardian Britain, *Oxford Review of Education*, 9, 197–211.

Barker, D. (1989) The biology of stupidity: genetics, eugenics and mental deficiency in the inter-war years, *British Journal of the History of Science*, 22, 347–75.

Baumeister, A. A. and Kupstas, F. (1990) The new morbidity: implications for prevention and amelioration, in P. Evans and A. D. B. Clarke (eds) *Combatting Mental Handicap*. London, A.B. Academic Publishers.

Bean, A. G. and Roszkowski, M. J. (1982) Item domain relationships in the Adaptive Behaviour Scales (ABS), *Applied Research in Mental Retardation*, 3, 359–67.

Belmont, L. (1987) International studies of severe mental retardation, *International Journal of Mental Health*, 10, 3–7.

Berg, J. (1985) Physical determinants of environmental origin, in A. M. Clarke, A. D. B. Clarke and J. M. Berg (eds) *Mental Deficiency: The Changing Outlook* (4th edn). London, Methuen.

Berg, J. (1986) Etiology update and review: I. biomedical factors, in J. Wortis (ed.) *Mental Retardation and Developmental Disabilities*. New York, Elsevier.

Berger, M. and Yule, W. (1985) IQ tests and assessment, in A. M. Clarke, A. D. B. Clarke and J. M. Berg (eds) *Mental Deficiency: The Changing Outlook* (4th edn). London, Methuen.

Berger, M. and Yule, W. (1987) Psychometric approaches, in J. Hogg and N. V. Raynes (eds) *Assessment in Mental Handicap*. London, Croom Helm.

Bijou, S. W. (1963) Theory and research in mental (developmental) retardation, *Psychological Record*, 13, 95–110.

Bijou, S. W. (1966) A functional analysis of retarded development, in N. R. Ellis (ed.) *International Review of Research in Mental Retardation*. New York, Academic Press.

Bortner, M. (1978) AAMD Adaptive Behavior Scale, 1974 revision in O. K. Buros (ed.) *The Eighth Mental Measurements Yearbook*. Highland Park, N. J., The Gryphon Press.

Brems, C., Kowalski, D., Powell, J. and Tucker, D. R. (1990) The Developmental Record: reliability and validity in a clinical population, *American Journal on Mental Retardation*, 94, 649–53.

Brock, D. J. H. (1976) Prenatal diagnosis – chemical methods, *British Medical Bulletin*, 32, 16–20.

Clarke, A. D. B. (1976) From research to practice: presidential address to the International Association for the Scientific Study of Mental Deficiency, Washington, D.C., in P. Mittler (ed.) (1977) *Research to Practice in Mental Retardation*, Baltimore, Md., University Park Press.

Clarke, A. D. B. and Clarke A. M. (1986) Etiology update and review: II. psychosocial factors: correlates or causes?, in J. Wortis (ed.) *Mental Retardation and Developmental Disabilities*, 14, 36–49. New York, Elsevier.

Clarke, A. D. B., Clarke A. M. and Reiman, S. (1958) Cognitive and social changes in the feebleminded: three further studies. *British Journal of Psychology*, 49, 144–57.

Clarke, A. D. B. and Hermelin, B. F. (1955) The abilities and trainability of imbeciles, *Lancet*, ii, 337–9.

Clarke, A. D. B. and Tizard, B. (1983) *Child Development and Social Policy: The Life and Work of Jack Tizard*. Leicester, British Psychological Society.

Clarke A. M. and Clarke, A. D. B. (1958) (eds) *Mental Deficiency: The Changing Outlook*. London, Methuen.

Clarke A. M. and Clarke, A. D. B. (1976) (eds) *Early Experience: Myth and Evidence*. London, Open Books.

Clarke A. M. and Clarke, A. D. B. (1989) Editorial: the later cognitive effects of early intervention, *Intelligence*, 13, 289–97.

Clarke A. M., Clarke, A. D. B. and Berg, J. M. (1985) (eds) *Mental Deficiency: The Changing Outlook* (4th edn). London, Methuen.

Cobb, H. V. (1972) *The Forecast of Fulfilment*. New York, Teachers College Press.

Crome, L. (1961) Cytomegalic inclusion-body disease, *World Neurology*, 2, 447–58.

Darwin, C. (1859) *The Origin of Species*. London, John Murray.

Detterman, D. (1987) Theoretical notions of intelligence and mental retardation, *American Journal of Mental Deficiency*, 92, 2–11.

Dobbing, J. (1968) Vulnerable periods in developing brain, in A. N. Davidson and J. Dobbing (eds) *Applied Neurochemistry*. Oxford, Blackwell.

Dobbing, J. (1984) Pathology and vulnerability of the developing brain, in J. Dobbing, A. D. B. Clarke, J. A. Corbett, J. Hogg and R. O. Robinson (eds) *Scientific Studies in Mental Retardation*. London, Macmillan and The Royal Society of Medicine.

Dobbing, J. and Sands, J. (1973) The quantitative growth and development of the human brain, *Archives of Disease in Childhood*, 48, 757–67.

Dowdney, L., Skuse, D., Heppinstall, E., Puckering, C. and Zur-Szpir, S. (1987) Growth retardation and developmental delay amongst inner-city children, *Journal of Child Psychology and Psychiatry*, 28, 529–41.

Dudgeon, J. A. (1984) Commentary, in J. Dobbing, A. D. B. Clarke, J. A. Corbett, J. Hogg and R. O. Robinson (eds) *Scientific Studies in Mental Retardation*. London, Macmillan and The Royal Society of Medicine.

Duyme, M. and Dumaret, A. (1986) La reversibilite de la debilite legere: une therapeutique sans therapeute, CNAMS-INSERM, 144, 553–62.

Edgerton, R. B. (1967) *The Cloak of Competence: Stigma in the Lives of the Mentally Retarded*. Berkeley, Ca., University of California Press.

Edgerton, R. B. and Bercovici, S. M. (1976) The cloak of competence ten years later, *American Journal of Mental Deficiency*, 80, 485–97.

Edgerton, R. B., Bollinger, M. and Herr, B. (1984) The cloak of competence after two decades, *American Journal of Mental Deficiency*, 88, 345–51.

Evans, E. D. (1985) Longitudinal follow-up assessment of differential preschool experience for low income minority group children, *Journal of Educational Research*, 78, 197–202.

Evans, J. A. and Hamerton, J. L. (1985) Chromosomal anomalies, in A. M. Clarke, A. D. B. Clarke and J. M. Berg (eds) *Mental Deficiency: The Changing Outlook*, (4th edn). London, Methuen.

Foxx, R. M., Bittle, R. G., Bechtel, D. R. and Livesay, J. R. (1986) Behavioural treatment of the sexually deviant behaviour of mentally retarded individuals, in N. R. Ellis and N. W. Bray (eds) *International Review of Research in Mental Retardation*, 14, 291–317. London, Academic Press.

Fryer, A. E., Chalmers, A., Connor, J. M., Fraser, I., Povey, S., Yates, A. D. and Osborne, J. P. (1987) Evidence that the gene for tuberous sclerosis is on chromosome 9, *Lancet*, i, 659–61.

Galton, F. (1869) *Hereditary Genius*. London, Macmillan.

Goddard, H. H. (1912) *The Kallikak Family*. New York, Macmillan.

Goddard, H. H. (1914) *Feeble-mindedness: Its Causes and Consequences*. New York, Macmillan.

Gold, M. W. (1973) Research on the vocational habilitation of the retarded, in N. R. Ellis (ed.) *International Review of Research in Mental Retardation*. New York, Academic Press.

Goodman, N. and Tizard, J. (1962) Prevalence of imbecility and idiocy among children, *British Medical Journal*, i, 216–19.

Gosden, C., Webb, T., Rodeck, C., Nicolaides, K. and Primrose, D. (1986) in J. M. Berg (ed.) *Science and Service in Mental Retardation*. London, Methuen.

Grossman, H. J. (1983) (ed.) *Classification in Mental Retardation*. Washington, D.C., American Association of Mental Deficiency.

Gunzburg, H. (1970) The hospital as a normalizing training environment, *Journal of Mental subnormality*, 16, 71–83.

Gunzburg, H. (1974) Educational planning for the mentally handicapped, in A. M. Clarke and A. D. B. Clarke (eds) *Mental Deficiency: The Changing Outlook*, (3rd edn). London, Methuen.

Hagberg, B. and Hagberg, G. (1985) Neuropaediatric aspects of prevalence, aetiology, prevention and diagnosis, in A. M. Clarke, A. D. B. Clarke and J. M. Berg (eds) *Mental Deficiency: The Changing Outlook* (4th edn). London, Methuen.

Hawkins, G. D. and Cooper, D. H. (1990) Adaptive behaviour measures in mental retardation research: subject description in AJMD/AJMR articles (1979-1987) *American Journal on Mental Retardation*, 94, 654-60.

Hilliard, L. T. and Kirman, B. H. (1957) *Mental Deficiency*. London, J. and A. Churchill.

Hutton, W. O. and Talkington, L. W. (1974) *The Developmental Record (Manual)*. Portland, Portland State University, Division of Continuing Education Publications.

Kiernan, C. (1974) Behavior modification, in A. M. Clarke and A. D. B. Clarke (eds) *Mental Deficiency: The Changing Outlook* (3rd edn). London, Methuen.

Kiernan, C. (1985) Behaviour modification, in A. M. Clarke, A. D. B. Clarke and J. M. Berg (eds) *Mental Deficiency: The Changing Outlook* (4th edn). London, Methuen.

Langdon Down, J. (1866) Observations on an ethnic classification of idiots, *Clinical Lectures and Reports of the London Hospital*, 3, 259-62.

Lazar, I. and Darlington, R. (1982) Lasting effects of early education, *Monographs of the Society for Research in Child Development*, 47, 1-151.

Lejeune, J., Gautier, M. and Turpin, R. (1959) Etudes des chromosomes somatiques de neuf enfants mongolien, *Comptes Rendues Hebdomadaires de l'Academie des Sciences*, Paris, 248, 1721-2.

Lewis, E. O. (1933) Types of mental deficiency and their social significance, *Journal of Mental Science*, 79, 298-304.

Lubs, H. A. (1969) A marker-X chromosome, *American Journal of Human Genetics*, 21, 231-44.

McCool, C., Barrett, S., Emerson, E., Toogood, S., Hughes, H. and Cummings, R. (1989) Challenging behaviour and community services: 5, structuring staff and client activity, *Mental Handicap*, 17, June 1989, British Institute of Mental Handicap.

McKey, R. H., Condelli, L., Ganson, H., Barrett, B. J., McConkey, C. and Plantz, M. C. (1985) *The Impact of Head Start on Children, Families and Communities*. Department of Health and Human Services. Publ. No. (OHDS) 85-31193, Washington, D.C.

McLaren, J. and Bryson, S. E. (1987) Review of recent epidemiological studies of mental retardation: prevalence, associated disorders and etiology, *American Journal on Mental Retardation*, 92, 243-54.

Mittler, P. (1963) Report of the working party on subnormality, *Bulletin of the British Psychological Society*, 16, 37-50.

Mittler, P. (1966) *Children in Hospitals for the Subnormal*. London, British Psychological Society.

Mittler, P. (1979) *People not Patients: Problems and Policies in Mental Handicap*. London, Methuen.

Mittler, P. and Serpell, R. (1985) Services: an international perspective, in A. M. Clarke, A. D. B. Clarke and J. M. Berg (eds) *Mental Deficiency: The Changing Outlook* (4th edn). London, Methuen.

Nihira, K., Foster, R., Shellhaas, M. and Leland, H. (1974) *AAMD Adaptive Behavior Scale*. Washington, D.C., American Association on Mental Deficiency.

Nirje, B. (1969) The normalization principle and its human management implications, in Kugel, R. B. and Wolfensberger, W. (eds) *Changing Patterns in Residential Services for the Mentally Retarded*. Washington, D.C., President's Committee on Mental Retardation.

Nirje, B. (1970) The normalization principle – implications and comment, *Journal of Mental Subnormality*, 16, 62–70.

O'Connor, N. and Tizard, J. (1956) *The Social Problem of Mental Deficiency*. London, Pergamon.

Pavlov, I. P. (1927) *Conditioned Reflexes*. Oxford, Oxford University Press.

Penrose, L. S. (1938) A clinical and genetic study of 1280 cases of mental defect, *Special Report Series*, Medical Research Council, No. 229. London, HMSO.

Penrose, L. S. (1949) *The Biology of Mental Defect*. (2nd edn 1954, 3rd edn 1963, 4th edn 1972). London, Sidgwick & Jackson.

Plomin, R. (1989) Environment and genes: determinants of behavior, *American Psychologist*, 44, 105–11.

Pollitt, E. (1988) Developmental impact of nutrition on pregnancy, infancy and childhood: public health issues in the United States, in N. Bray (ed.) *International Review of Research in Mental Retardation*, 15, 33–80. London, Academic Press.

President's Committee on Mental Retardation (1972) *Entering the Era of Human Ecology*. Washington, D.C., Department of Health, Education and Welfare, Publ. No. (OS) 72–7.

President's Committee on Mental Retardation (1976) *Mental Retardation: Century of Decision*. Washington, D.C., Department of Health, Education and Welfare, Publ. No. (OHD) 76–21013.

Rodeck, C. H. and Morsman, J. M. (1983) First trimester chorion biopsy. *British Medical Bulletin*, 39, 338–42.

Rose-Ackerman, S. (1982) Mental retardation and society: the ethics and politics of normalization, *Ethics*, 93, 81–101.

Sarason, S. B. (1949) *Psychological Problems in Mental Deficiency*. New York, Harper.

Scarr, S. (1981) *Race, Social Class and Individual Differences in IQ*. Hillsdale, N. J., Lawrence Erlbaum.

Schweinhart, L. J. and Weikart, D. P. (1980) *Young Children Grow Up: The Effects of the Perry Preschool Program*. Ypsilanti, Mich.: High/Scope Press.

Schweinhart, L. J. and Weikart, D. P. (1981) Perry preschool effects nine years later: what do they mean?, in M. J. Begab, H. C. Haywood and H. L. Garber (eds) *Psychosocial Influences on Retarded Performance*. Baltimore, Md., University Park Press.

Serpell, R. (1988) Assessment criteria for severe intellectual disability in various cultural settings. *International Journal of Behavioral Development*, 1, 117–44.

Shearer, D. E. and Loftin, C. R. (1984) The Portage Project: teaching parents to teach their preschool children in the home, in R. F. Dangel and R. A. Polster (eds) *Parent Training*. New York, Guilford Press.

Shearer, M. and Shearer, D. E. (1972) The Portage Project: a model for early childhood education, *Exceptional Child*, 36, 210–17.

Skinner, B. F. (1938) *The Behaviour of Organisms*. New York, Appleton-Century-Crofts.

Stern, J. (1985) Biochemical aspects, in A. M. Clarke, A. D. B. Clarke and J. M. Berg (eds) *Mental Deficiency: The Changing Outlook* (4th edn). London, Methuen.

Stern, H., Elek, S. D., Booth, J. and Fleck, D. G. (1969) Microbial causes of mental retardation: the role of prenatal infections with cytomegalovirus, rubella virus and toxoplasma, *Lancet*, iii, 443–8.

St Clair, D. (1987) Chromosome 21, Down's syndrome and Alzheimer's disease, *Journal of Mental Deficiency Research*, 31, 213–14.

Stratford, B. and Steele, J. (1985) Incidence and prevalence of Down's syndrome – a discussion and report, *Journal of Mental Deficiency Research*, 29, 95–107.

Svendsen, D. (1982) Changes in IQ, environmental and individual factors: a follow-up of educable mentally retarded children, *Journal of Child Psychology and Psychiatry*, 23, 69–74.

Thorndike, E. L. (1911) *Animal Intelligence*. New York, Macmillan.

Tizard, J. (1962) The residential care of mentally handicapped children, *Proceedings of the 1960 London Conference on the Scientific Study of Mental Deficiency*, 2, 659–66. Dagenham, May & Baker.

Wahlström, J. (1990) Gene map of mental retardation, *Journal of Mental Deficiency Research*, 34, 11–27.

Wilton, K. and Irvine, J. (1983) Nutritional intakes of socio-culturally mentally retarded children vs children of low and average socio-economic status, *American Journal of Mental Deficiency*, 88, 79–85.

Wolfensberger, W. (1972) *The Principle of Normalization in Human Services*. Toronto, National Institute on Mental Retardation.

Woolf, L. I., Griffiths, R. and Moncrieff, A. (1955) Treatment of phenylketonuria with a diet low in phenylalanine, *British Medical Journal*, i, 57–64.

Yule, W. and Carr, J. (1980) *Behaviour Modification for the Mentally Handicapped*. London, Croom Helm.

Yule, W. and Carr, J. (1987) (eds) *Behaviour Modification for People with Mental Handicaps*, (2nd edn). London, Croom Helm.

Zetlin, A. and Murtaugh, M. (1990) Whatever happened to those with borderline IQs?, *American Journal on Mental Retardation*, 94, 463–9.

Zigler, E. and Hodapp, R. M. (1986) *Understanding Mental Retardation*. Cambridge, Cambridge University Press.

CHAPTER 2

Teaching and Learning: Retrospect and Prospect

Judith Coupe-O'Kane

Introduction

Over the past few years, educators of children with a mental handicap have gained respect and recognition from colleagues for their expertise, skills and competence in meeting individual needs. As the stereotyped clichés for this 'dedicated', 'patient' group of 'caring' adults gradually diminish, children with Severe Learning Difficulties (SLD) have become recognised as being educable (DES, 1973). Government reports and legislation such as Warnock (DES, 1978) and the 1981 Education Act have reinforced this and sanctioned the need to identify and meet the individual needs of children in partnership with their parents.

The mentally handicapped are now accepted as pupils who, like any other children between five and sixteen years, are entitled to attend school and receive a broad, balanced, relevant and differentiated education (DES, 1988).

The SLD school curriculum

To ensure that a qualitative education was delivered to SLD pupils, a process evolved through which teachers could identify and meet individual needs with greater precision. In the 1970s and early 1980s behaviourism 'ruled OK' and this approach brought with it the underlying principles for acquiring sensitive skills in assessing, teaching and evaluating behaviours actually observed in pupils. In service training courses, particularly the Education of Developmentally Young (EDY) (Foxen and McBrien, 1981) assisted all staff

37

in understanding and applying such basic strategies as baselining, setting behavioural objectives, establishing a criterion for success, teaching by trials, task analysing skills, prompting and shaping behaviours, rewarding, recording etc. Without doubt, this approach has influenced and enhanced the quality of educational delivery. However, whilst EDY provided good basic teaching strategies, it was apparent that the content of education remained restricted and that a wider and more imaginative, range of strategies was required.

A variety of published curricula models subsequently provided the basis for expanding curricular content and intervention. For instance, the Schools Council funded a project to consider the education of mentally handicapped children with particular reference to teaching language and communication (Leeming et al., 1979). Gardner and Murphy (1980) highlighted a Skills Analysis approach providing a framework for organising the skills identified as needing to be taught. An environmental model designed for secondary aged pupils had implications for all age groups. What does the pupil need to be able to do in the kitchen, lounge, cinema etc? (Brown et al., 1978). Ainscow and Tweddle (1979) expanded the objectives approach and, whilst this was directed at teaching pupils with moderate learning difficulties, it had great relevance to the SLD field. Also under consideration was the concept of an open and closed curriculum which balanced core areas of development, for example, cognition, language and communication, with a wide range of relevant lessons and activities such as drama, religious education and educational visits. Developmental theories, assessments and checklists were absorbed accordingly (Uzgiris and Hunt, 1975; Bluma et al., 1976) and it was gradually seen that the various models and theories need not be mutually exclusive. Hence, a more eclectic stance was taken where the strengths from all approaches could be drawn together (Coupe and Porter, 1986; Wilson, 1981).

The Curriculum Intervention Model (Coupe, 1986) advocated this eclectic approach and outlines a practical route for developing a school curriculum document which can be utilised for intervention (see Figure 2.1). Stemming from a stated philosophy, based on the aims of schooling (DES, 1985), the main core and experience curriculum areas can be identified. Each area can be considered in its own right and broken down as required in to goal areas with subsequent behavioural objectives. Through this formula, schools can, as required, utilise aspects of any model or theory.

Having developed a curriculum document the process of Assessment, Programme Planning, Recording and Evaluation will then apply to any intervention. The pupils can be assessed and monitored, priority and general areas of learning can then be defined and whilst teaching occurs, the child's response and performance can be recorded. Following on from this, regular evaluation ensures accountability for progress, appropriateness of programmes etc.

It is evident that teachers of SLD pupils have acquired the expertise to assess and teach individual pupils. However, there has tended to be a lack of opportunity for the pupils themselves to exert and initiate control over their

Figure 2.1 Curriculum intervention model

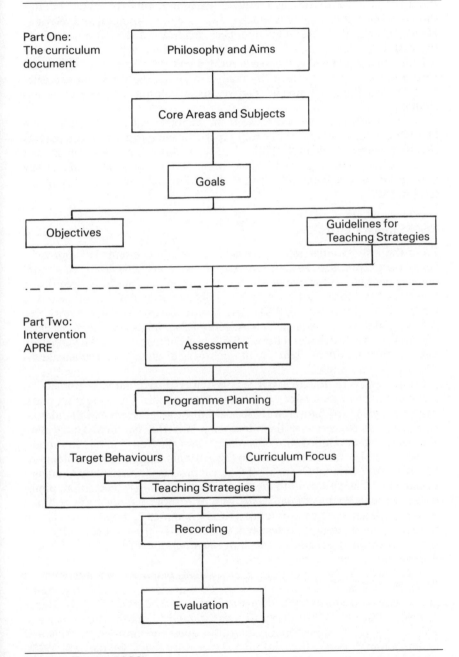

(*Source*: Coupe, 1986)

learning and experiences. Working to a clear statement of what the child should be expected to learn as a result of teaching is still to be valued, but this should be placed in a context which is functional, meaningful and relevant. Hence, a crucial development has been made towards safeguarding the successful components of intervention and complementing this with teaching being planned and carried out in a context where the pupil has the need and motivation to learn. By really examining the skills and strategies used for teaching, a more interactive, social approach to education has resulted.

By the 1980s teachers could use their school's own curriculum to plan individual educational priorities and experiences in partnership with parents (Rectory Paddock School, 1983). Through classroom management and organisation, teaching could then occur in a balanced, functionally appropriate and accountable way, with a commonly understood range of terminology.

The National Curriculum

From the now familiar terms of teaching strategies, interactive approach, behavioural approach, baselines, task analysis, target behaviours, classroom management etc. – a whole new range of 'jargon' has suddenly been thrust upon teachers of SLD pupils, for example, National Curriculum (NC), Education Reform Act (ERA), Attainment Targets (ATs), Levels, Key Stages, Standard Assessment Tasks (SATs), Programmes of Study, Schemes of Work, Cross Curricular Themes, Skills and Dimensions etc. Never before has new legislation brought about such radical change and challenge to educators of all pupils.

From Policy to Practice (DES, 1989) was disseminated nationally to introduce the new mandatory requirements to schools. The mere three and a half pages given to children with Special Educational Needs (SEN) did little to dispel the concerns of their teachers. Was this National Curriculum conceived and developed with only mainstream children in mind? In support of the principle of full entitlement to the National Curriculum for all pupils, however, the National Curriculum Council produced Curriculum Guidance Document 2, which set out to 'access the National Curriculum for all pupils who have special educational needs, with or without statements in ordinary schools, special schools and units' (NCC Guidance 2, 1989). This offered some hope and support to teachers who from 1990 have been subject to tightly controlled schedules for implementing the orders for core and foundation subjects as they are received.

In essence, the NC sets out to offer a broad, balanced and differentiated education which is relevant to the individual needs of all pupils 'providing progression and continuity from five to sixteen and beyond' (NCC Guidance 3, 1990). It has been introduced to 'raise standards, enhance relevance and give each pupil a unique opportunity to acquire the knowledge, skills and understanding' to take them into the 21st century (NCC Guidance 3, 1990). Through the NC, carefully planned programmes of study and schemes of work may complement the content of subjects and skills to be taught. Ten subjects, plus religious education, have been established, of these the three core areas are English, maths and science. The seven foundation subjects consist of technology, history, geography, art, music, physical education and from eleven years, a modern foreign language. Each NC subject incorporates a number of attainment targets (ATs). For instance, the core subject English has five ATs: speaking and listening, reading, writing, handwriting and spelling. Subsumed within each AT are objectives or Statements of Attainment for each of up to ten levels of attainment.

To augment this basic curriculum three cross curricular elements of themes, skills and dimensions are incorporated. The five identified themes are seen as essential parts of the whole curriculum – economic and industrial understanding (NCC Guidance 4, 1990), health education (NCC Guidance 5, 1990), careers and guidance (NCC Guidance 6, 1990), environmental education (NCC Guidance 7, 1990) and education for citizenship (NCC Guidance 8, 1990) and should, therefore be applied in a deliberate and complementary way.

> The themes have in common the ability to foster discussion and questions of values and belief: they add to knowledge and understanding and they rely on practical activities, decision making and inter-relationship of the individual and the community. (NCC Guidance 3, 1990)

It is also considered that a number of basic skills 'can be developed coherently throughout the curriculum' (NCC Guidance 3, 1990). Whilst the individual school will be required to identify and develop its own core skills, NCC recommends six skills which are seen to be essential and which should be fostered across the curriculum in a planned and measured way. These six skills comprise of communication, numeracy, study, problem solving, personal and social education and information technology. It is claimed that 'what is beyond dispute is that in the next century these skills, together with flexibility and adaptability will be at a premium' (NCC Guidance 3, 1990). Equal opportunities for all pupils and a recognition that 'preparation for life in a multicultural society is relevant to all pupils should permeate any aspect of the curriculum' (NCC Guidance 3, 1990) forms the basis for introducing cross curricular dimensions to the curriculum.

The whole curriculum

National Curriculum now rules, though its speedy introduction has inevitably created problems for schools throughout the country. Whilst its delivery is mandatory, professionals are, quite rightly, expressing their concerns about teaching to such a rushed, tight, imposed content, along with the restrictions and additional workload involved in assessing pupils on prescribed Standard Assessment Tasks (SATs) at the key stages of seven, eleven, fourteen and sixteen years. Indeed many professionals involved with teaching pupils with severe learning difficulties have been active in voicing those type of issues along with concerns more specifically related to the needs of their particular pupils.

Typical concerns include: are SLD pupils working towards or within level 1? Are subjects such as algebra, geography or a modern foreign language relevant to SLD pupils? Why should schools drop core areas such as cognition, language and communication, motor skills etc? Why should the results of hard work in curriculum initiatives and development be lost in order to implement the National Curriculum? Isn't national Curriculum a nonsense for some of our pupils? How can pupils with profound and multiple learning difficulties be involved in the identified subjects? Is it fair for these particular pupils to be stuck within level 1 for their school life? (Emblem and Conti-Ramsden, 1990; Fagg *et al.*, 1990; Sebba, 1991).

Perhaps in attempting to get to grips with the NC, many professionals have yet to appreciate the spirit of the Education Reform Act (DES, 1989) and its central philosophy. If we truly believe in the concept of a broad balanced relevant and differentiated curriculum for all pupils we should celebrate the constructive nature of the 'Whole School Curriculum' notion. It is recognised that National Curriculum alone will not provide the necessary breadth (NCC Guidance 3, 1990), additional subjects and extra curricular activities need to be included. Indeed 'there will be intangibles which will come from the spirit and ethos of each school, its pupils and its staff' (NCC Guidance 3, 1990). Contributions to the whole school curriculum can also be made by the 'deployment of the most effective teaching method' (NCC Guidance 3, 1990) along with efficient and imaginative management of the curriculum and the school.

Consider then the high level of expertise achieved by many SLD schools in developing and implementing their philosophy and school curriculum to meet individual needs. For them curriculum development has traditionally been perceived as an ongoing, never ending process. This should not change. It is essential for this process to continue and for SLD schools to maintain their process of reviewing, revising and developing their approaches to teaching and learning. The experience and expertise need not be lost in order to implement and deliver NC. Instead, it should be constructively and imaginatively blended and developed to produce a richer, broader, more balanced, relevant and differentiated curriculum than ever before.

The whole school curriculum model

In developing a whole school curriculum it may be that teachers of SLD pupils are at a greater advantage than many colleagues. The actual framework adopted for the NC has strong parallels with the curricular models already used and as Figure 2.2 demonstrates, it is quite possible to imaginatively blend the two to form a whole school curriculum model. Dakin *et al.* (1991) have similarly outlined a dynamic process which will assist school staff in developing this type of curriculum change.

The curriculum document for SLD schools has provided staff with a plethora of subjects and behaviours to be taught along with policy

Figure 2.2 Whole school curriculum model

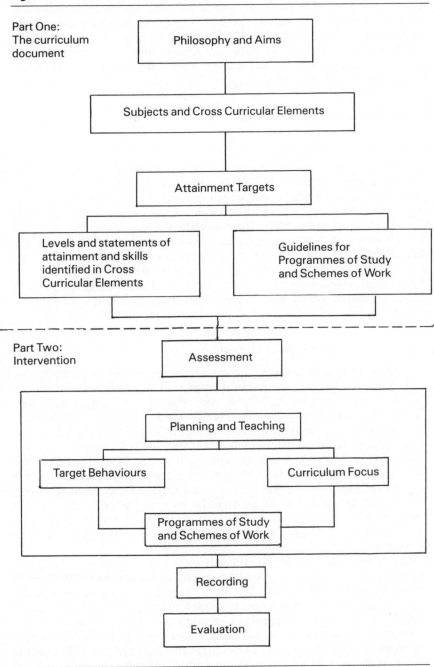

Part One:
The curriculum
document

Philosophy and Aims

Subjects and Cross Curricular Elements

Attainment Targets

Levels and statements of attainment and skills identified in Cross Curricular Elements

Guidelines for Programmes of Study and Schemes of Work

Part Two:
Intervention

Assessment

Planning and Teaching

Target Behaviours

Curriculum Focus

Programmes of Study and Schemes of Work

Recording

Evaluation

statements and guidelines for intervention so that individual needs can be identified and met. The National Curriculum document proports to provide this too. With cross curricular elements permeating the whole curriculum, subjects are identified and divided into Attainment Targets which are subsequently expanded by Statements of Attainments in up to ten age related levels of achievement. Intervention then incorporates Assessment, Programmes of Study and Schemes of Work.

Part 1: the curriculum document

Philosophy and aims

The philosophy and aims of schooling must be the same for pupils regardless of their abilities and needs. SLD schools like any other, have had to produce their individual statements as advised by their Local Authority and the Department of Education and Science in the policy documents related to Curriculum 5-16 (DES, 1985). The Education Reform Act further sanctions this, proposing that all pupils have access to a broad, balanced, relevant and differentiated curriculum which is relevant to their individual needs. Stated aims identify that each school should have a curriculum which '(a) promotes the spiritual, moral, cultural, mental and physical development of pupils at the school and of society; and (b) prepares such pupils for the opportunities, responsibilities and experiences of adult life' (DES, 1989).

Subjects and cross curricular elements

Until now, SLD schools have generally identified and taught the basic core areas of language and communication, cognition, fine and gross motor skills and life and social skills. Along with this the curriculum has been complemented with more traditional subjects such as cookery, early literacy, PE, expressive arts etc. In a similar way the National Curriculum stipulates three core and seven foundation subjects. These link quite readily with many and the SLD schools core areas and subjects. However, of most significance is the importance given to cross curricular themes, skills and dimensions. These underpin all elements of the curricular established so far in the SLD schools and should be welcomed as an essential part of the new whole school curriculum. In this way, those aspects of development and learning which are most sensitive to the varying needs of SLD pupils can continue to be considered.

Admittedly, some of the NC subjects may, at first, appear to be low in priority and, taking into account the severity of the learning difficulties of some pupils, rather irrelevant. But why? Without realising it, many of the subjects, lessons and experiences organised in the past have incorporated aspects of geography, technology, algebra etc. Educational visits and residentials, for instance, are abound with these subjects. In fact, if analysed the 'open' and 'hidden' school curriculum delivered to pupils in the past has absorbed all NC subjects along with the cross curricular elements.

A modern foreign language from eleven years: how relevant is this? Some SLD pupils are already multi-lingual and all have a right to experience and perhaps learn to appreciate that other countries and cultures exist and that alternative languages are equal in providing channels of communication. The NC may be different, it may not have been developed with SLD pupils in mind, but it should be viewed as a welcome orientation. In this way we can create a broader and more balanced range of content and overcome some of the limitations evident in past curricular. Sebba and colleagues (1990) for instance found little or no evidence of history and geography in the curricular of many SLD schools. They found too that science has been limited to multi sensory content, technology limited to computer use and maths to work on numbers.

Levels, statements of attainment and skills identified in cross curricular elements

Curricular objectives have clearly defined the pupil behaviours to be considered in any goal area. As appropriate they may have been developmental or have stemmed from an analysis of a particular skill or activity. Likewise, the NC identifies statements of attainment which are defined within the statutory orders for each subject and are related appropriately to ten levels of attainment.

It may be that teachers of SLD pupils will find those statements of attainment to be somewhat woolly forms of objectives, lacking in precision and clarity. The expertise gathered so far in developing an objective based model of curriculum should not be lost. Instead, it is quite feasible to group all appropriate objectives from past curriculum documents with a particular statement of attainment. By doing so each level and corresponding statement

Figure 2.3   Curriculum core area: mathematics

Attainment Target: 14 Handling Data

LEVEL 2

Statement of attainment:

> (1)   The pupil should recognise that there is a degree of uncertainty about the possible outcome of some events and other events are certain or impossible.

(1)   The pupil will recognise that something is certain e.g. it will get dark tonight.

(2)   The pupil will recognise that something is impossible e.g. I will be 50 tomorrow.

(3)   The pupil will recognise that something is uncertain e.g. it might rain tomorrow.

of attainment, particularly up to level 3 will be expanded, accommodating all relevant milestones and skills (see Figure 2.3).

Past curricular content can similarly be amalgamated into the cross curricular elements. Health education, one of the cross themes for instance, addresses such areas as substance use and misuse, sex education, family life education, safety, health-related exercise, food and nutrition, personal hygiene, all of which can be expanded if required.

Guidelines for programmes of study and schemes of work

Within the whole school curriculum document it is essential that guidelines for intervention are incorporated. Programmes of study are therefore concerned with 'the matters, skills and processes' (DES, 1989) which must be taught to all pupils at each key stage 'for them to meet the objectives set out in attainment targets' (DES, 1989). The schemes of work therefore complement the programmes of study. By accounting for mandatory requirements, cross curricular issues, the schools' aims, teaching and learning processes, assessment procedures and resources, these schemes of work focus on curriculum content and how the work will be achieved by class pupils over a period of time.

Part 2: intervention

Assessment

Assessment must reflect the strengths and needs of the individual pupil and provide a positive direction for future intervention. In the spirit of the ERA, assessment should not be used merely to place a pupil in the NC, and should not act as a competative device for comparing pupils against one another. The School Examinations and Assessment Council (SEAC, 1990) is currently preparing final orders for prescribed assessment tasks (SATs) which will inform teaching and assist in enhancing the development of the whole child.

Planning and teaching

From the assessment the teacher can plan the individual scheme of work for each pupil. Accounting for all subjects, individual priorities and the general focus of teaching can be stated and referenced to the attainment target level, statement of attainment and the appropriate objective. Similarly account can be taken of what is to be introduced and taught through cross curricular themes, skills and dimensions including programmes of integration, speech therapy and physiotherapy along with reference to any group or class topic. In addition, this whole stage of planning and teaching will need to include explicit details of programmes of study for the individual.

Recording

The teachers will take responsibility for selecting suitable methods of recording which can be practically used and understood by classroom staff. Recording could be as detailed as the numerical system devised by Foxen and McBrien (1981) or as simple as a tick. What is important is for the staff to record the pupil's performance in an individual or group context as immediately as possible with speed and accuracy.

Evaluation

Regular evaluation provides information about what the pupil has learned and the effectiveness of the teaching. In turn, this should aid in determining what to teach next and how. If, on evaluation, the pupil has successfully learned the skill being taught, re-assess and define a new priority or focus for teaching. If the skill has not been achieved then review factors affecting the teaching and context for learning.

Towards the future

Whilst many concerns are still voiced and the notion of SATs and teacher assessment remains an issue, the ethos of a school and the range and breadth of education offered can certainly be enhanced by carefully blending the existing curriculum with the requirements of the ERA and NC. School staff should continue to value their expertise and willingness to consider, consolidate, discuss, update and disseminate new initiations and developments.

The National Curriculum Council have actively welcomed feedback and recommendations from practitioners. Furthermore, they have demonstrated their commitment to SLD pupils by establishing a one year research project to address their particular needs in relation to NC. Local education authorities too are seconding teachers of SLD pupils to develop aspects of the whole school curriculum. It is clear that teachers need not feel isolated and that they can be actively involved in determining the direction of education for the future. All will have opportunities for access to one or more of the regional NC development groups now established throughout the UK. Indeed the North West Regional group and the West Midlands group in conjunction with the British Institute of Mental Handicap (BIMH) have initiated the first national conference along with establishing a national data base.

To conclude this chapter is no easy task as so many new initiations are in the early stages of development. However, it is clear that a positive and imaginative approach to meeting the individual needs of SLD pupils can continue through the concept of a broad, balanced, relevant and differentiated education.

48

References

Ainscow, M. and Tweddle, D. A. (1979) *Preventing Classroom Failure: An Objective Approach*. London, Wiley.

Bluma, S., Shearer, M., Frohman, A. and Hilliard, J. (1976) *The Portage Guide to Education*. Wisconsin, Co-operative Education Service.

Brown, L., Branston, M. B., Hamre-Nietupski, S., Pumpian, I., Certo, N. and Gruenwald, L. (1978) A strategy for developing chronological age appropriate and functional curricular content for severely handicapped adolescents and young adults (draft paper), University of Wisconsin.

Coupe, J. (1986) The curriculum intervention model, in J. Coupe and J. Porter (eds) *The Education of Children with Severe Learning Difficulties*. London, Croom Helm.

Coupe, J. and Porter, J. (1986) (eds) *The Education of Children with Severe Learning Difficulties*. London, Croom Helm.

Dakin, A., Dawson, H., Smith, B., Tweats, W., Turner, C. and Staveley, R. (1991) *A Rational for Blending Own Curriculum (SLD) and National Curriculum* North West National Curriculum Development Group (in press).

Department of Education and Science (1973) Education Act (Handicapped Children). London, HMSO.

Department of Education and Science (1978) Special Education Needs. Report of the Committee of Enquiry into the Education of Children and Young People. (The Warnock Report). London, HMSO.

Department of Education and Science (1981) Education Act. London, HMSO.

Department of Education and Science (1985) The Curriculum from 5–16. London, HMSO.

Department of Education and Science (1988) Education Reform Act. London, HMSO.

Department of Education and Science (1989) National Curriculum From Policy to Practice. London, HMSO.

Emblem, B. and Conti-Ramsden, G. (1990) Towards level one: reality of illusion, in *British Journal of Special Education*, 17, 3.

Fagg, S., Aherne, P., Skelton, S. and Thornber, A. (1990) *Entitlement for all in Practise*. London, David Fulton.

Foxen, T. and McBrien, J. (1981) *Training Staff in Behavioural Methods: Trainee Workbook*. Manchester, Manchester University Press.

Gardner, J. and Murphy, J. (1980) A curriculum model, in *Curriculum Planning for the ESN(S) Child* N. B. Crawford (ed.), British Institute of Mental Handicap.

Leeming, K., Swann, W., Coupe, J. and Mittler, P. (1979) *Teaching Language and Communication to the Mentally Handicapped*. Schools Council Curriculum Bulletin 8, Evans/Methuen Educational.

National Curriculum Council (1989) *Curriculum Guidance 2. A Curriculum For All*. York, NCC.

National Curriculum Council (1990) *Curriculum Guidance 3. The Whole Curriculum*. York, NCC.

National Curriculum Council (1990) *Curriculum Guidance 4. Education For Economic and Industrial Understanding*. York, NCC.

National Curriculum Council (1990) *Curriculum Guidance 5. Health Education*. York, NCC.

National Curriculum Council (1990) *Curriculum Guidance 6. Careers Education and Guidance*. York, NCC.

National Curriculum Council (1990) *Curriculum Guidance 7. Environmental Education*. York, NCC.

National Curriculum Council (1990) *Curriculum Guidance 8. Education for Citizenship*. York, NCC.

Rectory Paddock School (1983) *In Search of a Curriculum*, (2nd edn) Mere Publications.

Sebba, J. (1990) Paper presented to National Curriculum Council. Conference on Pupils with Special Needs.

Sebba, J. (1991) *Why use the term 'Within level one'?* National Curriculum Council Project. Schools Examination and Assessment Council.

SEAC School Assessment Folder. Key Stage 1. (1990)

Uzgiris, I. C. and Hunt, J.McV. (1975) *Assessment in Infancy: Ordinal Scales of Psychological Development*. Illinois, University of Illinois Press.

Wilson, M. D. (1981) *The Curriculum in Special Schools*. Schools Council Programme 4.

CHAPTER 3

Special Educational Provision in the Context of Legislative Changes

Klaus Wedell

Introduction

In this chapter I will focus on one aspect of the way in which legislation affects special educational provision. I will examine the effect of legislation on the way in which decisions are made about the provision of special education for individual children or young people.

Countries which provide education for all children within their age range of compulsory schooling, usually set up official or semi-official decision-making procedures for making special educational provision for individual pupils. Such procedures may serve a variety of purposes, and they will reflect both the prevailing conception of children's special educational needs (SENs), and also the nature of the existing educational provision. In the UK, the statutory procedure for decision-making was most recently changed in the 1981 Education Act (DES, 1981). The Act provides a good example of the relationship between legislation and provision, and in this chapter I intend to explore the way in which decision-making has been determined by developments in legislation and its interpretation.

Decisions to give a child access to special education may be made on a variety of grounds. At one extreme, the decision may reflect a positive concern to further the development of the individual, and to provide additional resources to support this either in an ordinary class, or a setting as nearly similar to this as possible. At the other end of the continuum, the decision may be aimed at ensuring that the prevailing methods and approaches to education in the classroom are not disrupted, and at removing a pupil who might be an obstacle to the teacher's management of the

50

curriculum in a class. In many instances the decision may actually r
compromise between these aims. The way the decision falls out, wil
the extent to which the general system of education is or is not reg
alterable to meet the needs of individual pupils. For example, in th
Public Law 94–142 reflected concern that children with SENs sh
educated 'in the least restricted environment'. This expressed commitment to
the rights of the individual child to an educational experience which was as
little different from 'ordinary' education as possible. By contrast in other
countries, special educational provision is seen as separate, and is even
administered by a different government department, such as the Ministry of
Social Welfare. The decision-making procedure thus moves the child to a
separate administrative system.

These contrasting outcomes of decision-making show that they are based
on evaluations both of the child's needs, and of the child's educational
setting. Frequently, it is only the child's needs or 'deficiencies' which are
made explicit, while the consideration of the relevant features of the
environment is left implicit. This point applies also to decisions about the
education of children below school age, the only difference being that in
these instances, the child is considered in the context of a future rather than a
current school setting. In this chapter, I will focus on the effect of legislation
on decision making about special educational provision in England and
Wales.

The present situation in the UK

In the 1981 Act, children are considered to fall into three groups. The first
group consists of all children of compulsory school age, and these
consequently fall within the responsibility of the Local Education Authority
(LEA). Included within this group are those pupils who have special
educational needs which can be met by the special educational provision
which is 'generally made in ordinary schools'. In terms of the
epidemiological data mentioned in the Warnock Report (DES, 1978), this
group of pupils is likely to include about 18 per cent of the school population.
The third group consists of those pupils who are regarded as having needs
which cannot be appropriately met in this way, and for whom the special
educational provision has to be individually 'determined' by the LEA. This
group is estimated to include approximately 2 per cent of the school
population. These proportions are, of course, an estimate for the general
school population, and will not necessarily reflect the proportions in any
particular school or LEA. In our research on the implementation of the 1981
Act (Goacher *et al.*, 1988), we found that rural LEAs tended to higher
percentages of pupils in the third group than urban LEAs. No doubt this
reflected the fact that it was easier to make support more generally available
to schools in more densely populated areas.

For this third group of pupils who have to be individually identified by the
LEA, a specific decision-making procedure is needed. The 1981 Act
prescribes a procedure by which a LEA 'determines the provision' to be

made for these pupils. The procedure involves a multiprofessional assessment of the child by a teacher 'with experience of the child', an educational psychologist, and a medical doctor. These three professionals form the minimum group for assessment, and the psychologist and the doctor have to be ones nominated by the LEA for this purpose. The function of the assessment is to enable the LEA to decide whether it should maintain a 'statement' of the special educational provision it determines as appropriate to meet the child's needs.

By definition, this third group of pupils are those for whom the statement procedure gives access to resources over and above those made generally in the LEA's schools. The statement legally binds the LEA to maintain the provision while the pupil needs it. The original Circular (DES, 1983) described this process as giving the child the 'security' of a statement. This is an interesting concept, since it seems to imply that the LEA acknowledges that there is a risk to the provision being maintained unless the LEA makes itself legally accountable for the decision. It is tempting to speculate what form this risk might take, considering that any change is solely within the power of the LEA in any case. On the other hand, the 'security' of the statement also reflects a recognition of accountability to the pupil and the parents.

The LEA, in maintaining a statement for a pupil, acknowledges that it is giving a particular pupil priority of access to resources over other potential pupils who might actually need them. Other pupils who have SENs are only able to receive provision 'made generally' in the LEA's schools. In other words, the determination of the provision for a particular pupil is made in relation to the limits of the resources at the disposal of an LEA, and not necessarily only in relation to the perceived SENs of the child. Consequently, there is an implicit competitive element in the LEA's agreeing to maintain a statement for a pupil. A pupil may be given the 'security' of a statement, only if that pupil's needs are sufficiently great in the perception of the LEA.

Special educational provision is clearly not made on an open-ended resource basis. The allocation of the available resources is ultimately a resource decision made by the elected members of the local authority, and the total finance available is determined by the amount granted to the local authority by central government. The 'LEA' is normally represented in the statement process by an administrator, who acts within the general policy and funding allocation established by the elected members of the LEA, and has to make a lay decision on the basis of the evidence provided.

The enactment of the 1981 Act was not accompanied, in contrast to similar legislation in many other countries, by additional resource provision to LEAs. The government expressed the hope that the reduction in pupil numbers following the declining birthrate at that time would result in LEAs being able to allocate a greater proportion of resources to pupils with SENs in both ordinary and special schools. In our research on the implementation of the 1981 Act, we found that LEAs did in fact, allocate a larger proportion of their funds to supporting pupils with SENs, particularly in ordinary schools (Goacher et al., 1988). It might be presumed that such a direction of resources would raise the level of 'generally made' provision, with the result that fewer pupils would require LEA-determined provision through the statement procedure. However, the fact is that there was previously insufficient support for the 18 per cent of pupils with SENs in ordinary schools in any case. Also, since the LEA continued to make its 'determined' provision on a competitive allocation of limited resources, as outlined above, there was no reason for the proportion to change from its previous approximate 2 per cent.

It was generally recognised that LEAs would not be able to maintain a preferential allocation of resources to pupils with SENs in perpetuity, and certainly not once central government funding of LEAs came to be more tightly controlled and limited. This came about in the later 1980s. In addition, following an education act which came into force in 1988, and which was called the Education Reform Act (DES, 1988), the government introduced the requirement that LEAs should devolve financial resources to individual schools predominantly in proportion to pupil numbers. Schools thus became responsible for their own funding at the very time when funds were in any case more limited. The 1988 Act also promoted the principle that schools should compete for pupils on the basis of their assessed performance in a newly prescribed curriculum for all pupils.

It was not surprising that reports started to appear in the press, and in anecdotal personal communications among those concerned, that the demand for statements for pupils was increasing, and even that more statements were being maintained by LEAs. The demand for statements seemed likely to be a consequence of a combination of factors. The coupling of LEAs' constrained finances with the devolving of budgets to schools, probably faced schools with a more immediate awareness of the financial implications of making provision 'generally' for pupils' SENs. The promotion of competition on the basis of achievement within the prescribed curriculum faced schools with a conflict about allocating resources to high or low attaining pupils. The obvious way out of this dilemma was to make a claim on LEA 'determined' provision for pupils with SENs.

These developments strikingly illustrate the impact of legislation, and its consequences for the provision of special educational resources.

The definition of Special Educational Needs

The developments mentioned in the previous section also show how the definition of SEN in the 1981 Act focuses assessment on the educational context as well as on the particular needs of the individual child: 'a child has special educational needs if he has a learning difficulty which calls for special educational provision to be made for him' (DES, 1981). This remarkable definition makes clear that it is just as important to know why the learning difficulty 'calls for' special educational provision, as it is to know what the need is (Wedell et al., 1987).This interactive view of SEN did not always prevail.

The 1944 Education Act referred to children's SENs in terms of 'disability of mind or body'. This focused assessment on factors within the child. Not surprisingly, the assessment of these 'disabilities' was made the duty of medical officers, although this was no doubt also because none of the other professions which might have been thought relevant were at that time sufficiently developed to take on the task. Special educational provision was organised according to ten statutory categories of handicap. Pupils were assessed by medical officers, and allocated to provision on the basis of a diagnosis in terms of one or more of these categories of handicap. The diagnosis was recorded on designated 'Handicapped Pupils' forms. Pupils could also be deemed 'ineducable', on the grounds of severe disability, and the responsibility for the pupils was then moved from the education services to the health services.

In subsequent years, it was recognised that children's SENs were primarily met through educational provision. In 1970, the responsibility for the education of all pupils was given to the LEAs in which they lived. By 1975, the concepts of SEN and of provision had developed considerably. It was recognised that the causation of SENs was complex, and that their manifestation did not necessarily occur within the boundaries defined by the ten statutory handicap categories. The focus on educational intervention led to the demand that decisions about educational provision should most appropriately be based on developmental and educational, rather than medical expertise. All the same, the relevance of medical considerations was not denied.

The government of the day issued Circular 2/75 (DES, 1975) in the context of the development of these ideas. In the Circular, the multiple causation of SENs was recognised by a recommendation that assessment should have an educational and psychological as well as a medical component. The Circular recommended that LEAs should replace the HP (Handicapped Pupils) forms with SE forms, which were designed to be filled in by teachers and psychologists as well as medical personnel. The developmental aspect of the SEN was stressed in the Circular's emphasis on early identification, and on the need for assessment to be based on an on-going evaluation of the child. The corollary that parents consequently had a significant contribution to make was also recognised.

These points were echoed in the Warnock Report (DES, 1978).The Report concluded that SEN was a relative concept. No clear line could be drawn between the handicapped and non-handicapped, or indeed between children deemed to have different types of handicaps. The Report also recognised that such a relative view of SEN required that assessment of the needs of a child should include the assessment of the resources and deficiencies of his or her setting. Such a view inevitably placed emphasis on the parents' contribution both to assessment and to intervention, and the Report went on to stress the rights of parents to participate in decision-making concerning their children's SENs and the provision proposed for them.

The process of decision-making

The Warnock Committee specified five stages of assessment in their report. The stages referred to assessment of children who were already in school. In the first stage, the headteacher would be consulted by the teacher who was concerned about a pupil. Together they would consider all the available information about the pupil, to arrive at a decision about how the pupil could be helped within the existing resources of the school. If this did not resolve the problem, a specialist advisory teacher from within or outside the school would be consulted about the nature of the pupil's needs, and about a programme for meeting them. If it was felt that further specialist advice was needed, stage three involved the expertise of specialist advisory teachers from outside the school, and of educational psychologists. At this stage it was envisaged that any action could still be taken within the resources of the school.

Further assessment beyond stage three was seen to be needed when higher levels of professional expertise or a multiprofessional assessment were required. Stages four and five were differentiated only by the call for increasing levels and breadth of expertise. It was also recognised that such levels and breadth of expertise were less available, and so could be called on less easily. It was recommended that, at stage four, the 'SE Form' procedure should be used for assessing pupils and allocating them to appropriate provision. This linking of level of expertise in assessment with the administrative process of giving access to special provision has led to great confusion.

In our research on the implementation of the 1981 Act, we drew a distinction between the *process* of decision-making about allocating special educational provision, and the *procedure* prescribed in the statutory formulation of laws, regulations and circulars. The appropriateness of procedures for decision-making clearly depends on whether they match the processes which are inevitably involved in the decision-making.

The first three stages proposed in the Warnock Report are concerned with the way a teacher monitors the achievements of a pupil in relation to the progression of the curriculum. 'Curriculum' here needs to be considered in its broad sense, as outlined, for example, in the DES document published in 1979. The two-dimensional framework provided by the range of content of such a curriculum, and by its progression over successive stages, provides the teacher with a basis both for assessing the pupil's achievement, and for choosing the next step for learning. At the same time, the teacher's knowledge of the pupil leads to the choice of effective teaching methods. Evaluation of the pupil's response to teaching leads to a continuation of this cycle of teaching and evaluation. The same model of assessment, teaching and evaluation can, of course, be applied to the progress of children before school, as their parents support and observe their development.

The first three Warnock stages cover the situations where the teacher notices that the pupil is not making expected progress, and where teachers have recourse to advice and consultation with others. It has often been assumed that the Warnock Committee's stages of assessment inevitably require the teacher to seek advice from others in a sequence of increasing expertise. This was never envisaged, and in any case, many expert professionals have now gone over to regular consultation work within schools. As a result, a teacher who is just starting to seek further advice may well meet with a 'higher' level expert in either an informal or more organised way in a school, and so cut across the sequence of stages of consultation.

Children may of course also be taken to see professionals working either on their own or in multiprofessional teams, at levels of expertise corresponding to the Warnock Committee's stages four and five, without these professionals being directly involved in making administrative decisions about the allocation of special educational resources.

The distinction between seeking and obtaining an effective assessment of a pupil, and the decision to 'call' for special educational provision to be 'determined by the LEA' has not been clearly recognised. The latter occurs, when assessment indicates that the 'generally made' provision in a school is not likely to meet a pupil's SEN. The process then switches to the administrative requirements of making a case for an individual pupil to be given priority of access to provision which is not 'generally made' by an LEA.

If the assessment of the pupil has followed the cycles of thoughtful evaluation implied by the Warnock stages, a considerable amount of information about the pupil's needs will have been collected. It may well be that the psychological and medical professionals normally concerned with making assessments on behalf of the LEA have been concerned in this process. Also, if the parents have been appropriately involved, they are likely to have come to recognise the need for additional provision for the child.

It can therefore be seen that the 'call' for special educational provision may occur at the point where a careful assessment of a pupil's SENs has already been made. Unfortunately, the *procedure* prescribed in the 1981 Act requires that at this point a multiprofessional assessment is carried out on behalf of the LEA, to decide whether the LEA should maintain a statement for the pupil. This illustrates how a procedure may not necessarily match the process it is intended to mediate. For the LEA, the main decision is about whether the particular pupil should be given access to provision which is not 'generally made'. Because this is inevitably a matter of resource allocation, the question becomes one of assessing the pupil's priority of access. Although such a decision requires a good understanding of the pupil's needs, the LEA's decision more importantly involves comparing that pupil's needs with the claims of others. Those making the assessment of the pupil are therefore concerned in making a case to be decided by the administrators of the LEA's resources. They, in their turn, are making the decision on behalf of the elected members of the LEA.

Assessment information in statements has often been criticised for not being sufficiently detailed. It seems clear that such a view may result from an erroneous view of the purpose of an assessment for a statement. In the light of the above analysis, the assessment for a statement has four main purposes:

(1) to make an appropriate case for the child to receive the necessary provision,

(2) for these grounds to be stated in a way which allows the efficacy of the provision, if made, to be evaluated,

(3) to enable all, including the parents, to understand how the provision is intended to match the need, and

(4) to justify the priority of access of the individual pupil to the provision proposed.

It is clearly important that decisions about priority of access to provision are open to scrutiny by all concerned, particularly where it is decided *not* to allocate the provision demanded. Similarly, it is important that the appropriateness of the provision can be evaluated. According to the 1981 Act procedure, this should occur at each of the child's annual reviews or more frequently.

If a pupil's parents do *not* agree that the LEA should be asked to determine the provision for their child, then there is a clear need for a separate and new assessment to be made when the LEA is approached to maintain a statement. Parents may not agree to an approach to the LEA for a number of reasons. They may not have been appropriately involved in the early stages of their child's assessment, and so may not feel that there is sufficient evidence that the school is unable to meet their child's SENs. In such an instance the need for an additional assessment for a statement may reflect inadequate professional practice on the part of those concerned. On the other hand, there may be a genuine difference of opinion even following the best practice. In such cases, there is a clear need for recourse to further opinions, and further assessment at the point of the approach to the LEA.

If the details of assessment and recommended provision are limited specifically to the information requirements for a statement, one is still left with the question about how the information and recommendations needed by those serving the pupil in a school should be communicated.

It is well-known that there is considerable dissatisfaction with the information provided in statements. This dissatisfaction is expressed by different people who are involved in different ways. Those who are expected to provide for the pupil as the result of provision decisions in the LEA's statement may be dissatisfied with the lack of detail of information offered. In the light of the above analysis, this may well reflect the fact that the statement was written specifically to meet the administrative rather than the individual assessment requirements.

The obvious way to meet the information needs of those who are about to take on responsibility for a pupil's SENs when a statement has been made, is for them to be in direct communication with those who have been concerned with the pupil's previous education on a day to day basis, and with those who have provided assessment and advice. It seems obvious that the statement would under any circumstances, be a much too limited means of communication to serve these purposes.

Recently, another source of concern about the informational content of statements has arisen. Educational psychologists have been said to be constrained by their employing LEAs in what they are permitted to write in their contributions to statements. Educational psychologists are in a particularly invidious position, since they carry out assessments for statements as employees of the LEA. As professionals they are concerned with the wellbeing of their 'client' the child, but as employees of the LEA, the latter can make 'client' claims on them.

The professionals involved in assessing a pupil's SENs are clearly concerned to establish these needs irrespective of the resource implications of the scale and nature of the provision required to meet the needs. Indeed, Circular 22/89 (the revision of Circular 1/83), specifically requires the professionals carrying out the assessment not to allow themselves to be influenced by resource implications in stating the pupil's needs (DES, 1989). However, the Circular distinguishes between formulating needs and formulating the LEA's allocation of provision to meet the pupil's needs. This distinction is one which can be made fairly clearly in theory, but not so easily in practice.

An educational psychologist may specify the pupil's needs in relation to specific developmental or educational goals. The educational psychologist may also specify the pupil's need for the forms of educational and other intervention which may be required to enable the pupil to progress towards these goals. The Circular seems to distinguish both of these senses of need from the specification of how the LEA should arrange for the needs to be met. Any specification of provision in a statement of course becomes legally binding for the LEA. In view of this rather fine distinction between different senses of need it is not surprising that conflict has arisen.

Circular 22/89 reaffirms the point made in Circular 1/83, that the assessment of need should be made independently of the availability of resources, in order to ensure that discrepancies between need and provision can be demonstrated. This is particularly important in the light of the 1981 Act's arrangements for parents to be able to appeal to a tribunal against the provision specified for their child by an LEA. The professionals' assessment has to be expressed in the senses of needs mentioned above, so that the Appeal Tribunal is provided with criteria for deciding whether the provision specified by an LEA matches the need. These grounds provide the basis on which parents can claim that the LEA is not meeting its obligations. Our research demonstrated that there was still considerable confusion on these points. It had been hoped that Circular 22/89 would clarify the misperceptions both of the procedures and of the meanings of the central concepts of 'need' in the Act (Norwich, 1990).

Conclusion

In this chapter I have traced some of the effects of changes in legislation on decision-making about provision for children with SENs. I have used the example of English legislation, although I indicated that the legislative framework has a direct effect on provision in many other countries. I have also described how legislation may be misinterpreted, with the result that its purposes are not realised.

In this country, the 1981 Act had a profound effect on the way in which children's SENs were met, not least because the Act reflected the changed concept of SENs themselves. The positive and negative effects on provision were compounded by the difficulty which was experienced in interpreting the new conceptions of 'need' in the legislation. Eight years after the Act came into force, these difficulties still persist. The consequences of the 1988 Act have further emphasised the gap between the decision process involved, and the statutory procedures intended to mediate these processes.

Changes in legislation continue to effect decision-making about provision for pupils with SENs. The changes instigated by the 1988 Education Act have now altered the way in which LEAs can carry out their obligations under the 1981 Act, particularly because the LEAs have been required to devolve financial resources increasingly to schools (Wedell, 1988). As a result, the change in context is altering the significance of the decisions made. For example, it is already evident that the changed financial allocation is having an influence on schools' attitudes to using their funds to support provision for pupils' SENs. This will have an immediate effect on the 1981 Act's requirements for the integration of pupils with SENs. As has already been mentioned in this chapter, the problem is currently emerging in schools' increased demands for statements, as a means of attracting resources. However, without additional funds to provide for any increase in the proportion of pupils with statements, LEAs will be faced with more conflicts in deciding about provision. It is not at all clear how an LEA will be able to ensure the 'security' of the provision which would be specified in a statement.

The conflicts facing educational psychologists in making decisions may also increase. It seems possible that the devolving of funds to schools will mean that LEAs will no longer employ educational psychologists centrally. In this case, schools themselves will have to employ psychologists to carry out assessments for statements. In such a situation, the psychologist will have a conflict between responsibility to the child, the 'customer' relation to the school, and the awareness of the lack of resources available to the LEA.

There seems to be no doubt that educational legislation has important direct and indirect consequences for the way in which decisions can be made – and are made – about provision for pupils with SENs. However, one is often left to conclude that the instigators of legislation lack awareness of the practical consequences which their laws have for the individual pupil.

References

Department of Education and Science (1975) The discovery of children requiring special education and the assessment of their needs (Circular 2/75). London, HMSO.

Department of Education and Science (1978) Special Educational Needs (The Warnock Report). London, HMSO.

Department of Education and Science (1981) Education Act. London, HMSO.

Department of Education and Science (1983) Assessments and statements of Special Educational Needs. (Circular 1/83). London, HMSO.

60

Department of Education and Science (1988) The Education Reform Act. London, HMSO.

Department of Education and Science (1989) Assessments and statements of Special Educational Needs: procedures within the education, health and social services. (Circular 22/89). London, HMSO.

Goacher, B., Evans, J., Welton, J. and Wedell, K. (1988) *Policy and Provision for Special Educational Needs*. London, Cassell.

Norwich, B. (1990) *Reappraising Special Needs Education*. London, Cassell.

Wedell, K. (1988) The new Act: a special need for vigilance, *British Journal of Special Education*. 15, 3, 98–101.

Wedell, K., Evans, J., Goacher, B. and Welton, J. (1987) The 1981 Education Act: policy and provision for special educational needs, *British Journal of Special Education*. 14, 2, 50–3.

CHAPTER 4

People with Profound and Multiple Disabilities: Retrospect and Prospects

James Hogg and Loretto Lambe

The arrival of Peter Mittler in Manchester as Director of the Hester Adrian Research Centre (HARC) in 1968, for his first year in splendid isolation before his staff began to join him in the autumn of 1969, coincided with significant movements in relation to children and young people with intellectual disabilities, movements that culminated in the Education Act of 1970 and the Act's implementation in April 1971. This coincidence of Peter's arrival and such legislative change was, of course, no fortuitous coincidence. He had contributed substantially to the debate on integration of children with intellectual disabilities into educational services and there can be little doubt that he was perceived at the time as someone who could direct research that would influence the consequences of the outcome of that debate. For those joining him in HARC in 1969, therefore, a special dynamic had been established which set an agenda for much of the initial research in which we, his colleagues, engaged. As significantly, however, this agenda through various transformations has continued over two decades, despite substantial changes in HARC's research programme and the changing position of the Centre in the spectrum of national and international activities in this field.

Within the range of issues emerging in the early 1970s, following the legislative changes noted above, none was more important than the inclusion of children with profound intellectual, physical and sensory disabilities within the responsibility of education departments. Such an outcome was by no means inevitable. Despite the arguments of Segal (1974) and others, exclusion of children with extensive and multiple disabilities was contemplated and may have become a reality, as indeed is still the case in some putatively more enlightened European countries. In this chapter we will take the opportunity to consider HARC's response to the educational, and indeed social, challenges this state of affairs offered. However, it would be incorrect to suggest that HARC's was the first, the only, or even the greatest contribution in this area. We will be mindful of the wider context of issues, services and research in which the Centre's work was undertaken. We will also show how interests in HARC converged with those developing in the voluntary sector and recent developments of such collaboration.

The early days of HARC coincided with a burgeoning interest in what at the time we comfortably referred to as 'behaviour modification' and which subsequently we came to call 'applied behaviour analysis' (ABA). It was not only the apparent rigour and effectiveness of the well-documented studies being reported from the US that attracted many of us to ABA, nor even the philosophical attractions of radical behaviourism. In the context of the challenge confronted by educators of pupils with severe and profound intellectual disabilities, here was an ostensibly total approach that offered close ties between theory and practice, research and classroom activities. It would be misleading to suggest that HARC was primarily a behavioural department, though there is little doubt that this was how it was perceived in some quarters; nor indeed was Peter himself ever what Jack Tizard ironically referred to as 'one of the brethren'. However, for those of us moving into this field from an essentially experimental psychological background, and indeed, even for some of us with teaching experience, ABA and the experimental methods surrounding it were highly attractive. With respect to people with profound disabilities in particular, here was a set of procedures, and indeed a philosophical framework, in which we could engage with them and begin to explore their behaviour and their understanding of the world. It may be recalled that in an earlier terminology (and one still being used and actively defended in the 1960s), people with profound intellectual disability were classified as 'idiots'. The origin of this term, the Greek *idiotes*, denoted 'a private person', perhaps one who does not share his or her thoughts readily, or is difficult to fathom. To describe some one as 'profound', therefore has similar connotations, and to plumb that profundity it was felt that behavioural exploration might well provide a sensitive and systematic approach.

It was also clear that however subtle behavioural analysis might be in providing a vehicle to explore such profundity, the wider organisation of behaviour and its changing structure were essential prerequisites to such understanding, and that developmental psychology, most notably that drawing on the work of Piaget, merited investigation. Those of us taking this first initiative in studying people with profound intellectual and multiple disabilities in HARC did not in the early 1970s, however, start in a vacuum. Behavioural investigations had begun decades before in Fuller's (1949) seminal paper exploring operant conditioning in a person regarded then as 'a vegetative organism'. A limited number of studies had followed in the 1950s and 1960s, primarily undertaken in the USA, and reviewed by Hogg and Sebba (1986: 228–44). With respect to a developmental framework, some of the most innovative work of the late 1960s and early 1970s was being undertaken by Bill and Diane Bricker in the USA, work which was to have a significant influence on many HARC enterprises (e.g. Bricker, 1970). Nearer to home, however, Mary Woodward had for many years undertaken a series of studies formally examining the applicability of methods of assessment based on Piagetian theory (e.g. Woodward, 1959, 1979; and reviewed by Hogg and Sebba, 1986: 188–93). This highly innovative and sadly undervalued series of studies may subsequently have been eclipsed as the US passion for pinning down the jelly which yielded first the Uzgiris-Hunt Scales of Ordinal Development (Uzgiris and Hunt, 1975) and the even more formalised version produced by Dunst (1980) came to prominence. (For Mary Woodward the clinical nature of Piagetian assessment would preclude any such standardisation, and Ina Uzgiris herself was heard to say at a conference in 1979, 'If I'd known how they were going to use my scales, I'd never have published them'.)

The background against which we set out to investigate profound and multiple disability in HARC with support from the Department of Education and Science (DES) in the early 1970s, therefore, was one of evolving techniques and instruments. In a series of studies a variety of learning situations were explored, as was the feasibility of characterising such people through both Gessellian and Piagetian assessment. These studies of respondent learning (Hogg et al., 1979b), instrumental learning (Hogg, 1983; Remington et al., 1977), attempt to bring the growing sophistication in experimental design that was the hallmark of the experimental analysis of behaviour to studies of profound disability. The behaviour of the same young people was in parallel explored through use of both standard developmental scales, as well as some of those from Uzgiris and Hunt (1975).

The wider educational context described above, however, was not lost in the preliminary application to undertake the learning and developmentally based work just noted. The development of staff training for those working with children with profound disabilities was proposed. The pilot course was developed in what was then Swinton Children's Hospital, Salford, and involved State Registered and State Enrolled Nurses, and physiotherapists and teaching staff. The course material was based on a modified version of Kiernan and Riddick's (1973) Programme for Training in Operant Techniques utilising video material illustrating many of the children who had been involved in experimental studies (Hogg et al., 1979a). The course was evaluated (Hogg et al., 1981) and became the basis for a further application to the DES to begin the national dissemination exercise that became known as the EDY Project (Education of the Developmentally Young Project) and which has led through a pyramid training method to several thousand staff in schools for pupils with intellectual disabilities (McBrien and Foxen, 1987). Despite the general success of this venture, two observations are in order. In disseminating the original approach, the focus was broadened to embrace more able pupils than those on whom the original work had concentrated. In addition, as ideas regarding the education of pupils with profound and multiple disabilities have evolved, so the need to broaden appreciably from the narrow behavioural focus we developed has emerged, and such training must now be regarded as very partial. We will return to this issue in our final considerations.

A further development that evolved in parallel to the dissemination undertaken in the EDY Project and which has had a significant bearing on provision for children with profound and multiple disabilities, was the setting up and running of the Anson House Preschool Project. This Project was conceived some years before its inception in 1975 by the first author and Cliff Cunningham, and was strongly influenced by the Brickers' development of the *Toddler Research and Intervention Project* at IMRIDD (Institute of Mental Retardation and Developmental Disabilities), in Nashville. The Project, which ran until 1984, was primarily supported by Barnardo's, the initial idea gaining credibility with that organisation through Peter Mittler's close association with the initial proposals. The Project was notable for providing a fully integrated pre-school for children of all levels of ability, from those with profound and multiple disabilities to some who were sufficiently above the developmental test scale averages to suggest genuinely high intelligence. All children were involved in a comprehensive assessment and curriculum framework and participated equally in the classroom setting. The feasibility of such integration and its benefits were amply demonstrated.

The Anson House service also embodied a crucial element of HARC's overall orientation in its early years, that is the opportunity for parents to participate and to learn from the on-going work. This strand of work had begun early in HARC's history with the innovative workshops of Dorothy Jeffree and Cliff Cunningham. Such approaches in Anson House again embraced all children and their parents, including those with multiple disabilities. A carefully evaluated programme of teaching was established with demonstrably positive outcomes (Beveridge, 1986; Sebba, 1978).

However, this work led to further important insights into how best parents could be supported. HARC in its early days was almost exclusively concerned with cognitive and educational aspects of support to families and their offspring. It became clear that this focus had to be broadened to embrace both social and emotional considerations. This insight was not unique to staff in HARC, there being a growing awareness in the field of factors influencing family stress and coping. The pre-school service, therefore, broadened its activities and staffing to embrace counselling and social work support as essential elements of a comprehensive service, these being nowhere more relevant than for parents with a son or daughter with profound and multiple disabilities.

With the 1980s, and particularly with Peter Mittler's departure from HARC, work in the Centre showed a progressive movement away from educational concerns and a shift in the populations studied. As with the earlier impact of the Education Act (1970) on HARC's programme of research, wider changes in society's view of intellectual disability contributed substantially to this shift. The growing emphasis on community care, the impact of normalisation philosophy, the emergence of an ageing population of people with intellectual disabilities, and particularly closure of the large hospitals, dictated a shift to specific adult groups of interest to policy makers. This is not to say that HARC had hitherto not concerned itself with adults, as is evidenced in the work undertaken by Ed Whelan since HARC's inception.

These changes did not of themselves preclude continued work on profound and multiple disability, and indeed, such people have continued to constitute significant proportions of much of the on-going research. In the educational field, *Project Impact* (in service and special educational needs) under the joint direction of Colin Robson, Judy Sebba and Peter Mittler developed several in-service teacher training packs of relevance to profound and multiple disability, dealing specifically with this group in Sebba's (1987) resource pack on this subject. The increasingly social orientation of HARC also led to a programme of work focusing exclusively on the subject of leisure provision for adults with profound and multiple disabilities. The impetus for this study came from Peter Mittler's close involvement in the International League of Societies of Persons with Mental Handicap, and resulted in the first European Commission grant to HARC, directed by the first author, by Peter himself, and by Judy Sebba. The investigation itself involved extensive case studies in European Commission countries to identify models of leisure provision. It was undertaken by Judith Cavet and resulted in an illuminating account of the diverse initiatives that have evolved in recent years in a hitherto neglected field (Cavet, 1990).

From the standpoint of an exclusive focus on profound and multiple disability, the strands of work HARC had developed up until 1984 were drawn together in a unique collaboration between HARC and the voluntary sector. The then Secretary-General of The Royal Society for Mentally Handicapped Children and Adults (MENCAP), Sir Brian Rix, was deeply concerned to increase the role of his organisation in supporting families with sons and daughters with profound and multiple disabilities, regardless of their age. Aware of the work undertaken on this subject in HARC, he drew both authors of this chapter into a working party that was established to develop, within available resources, a national support service for such parents. In 1985, the Profound Retardation and Multiple Handicap Project (PRMH Project) was established with three aims: first to undertake a national survey of the needs of parents and carers of those with profound intellectual and additional disabilities; second, in the light of this research, to establish a programme of workshops primarily for parents, but also for other carers, to be evaluated and disseminated nationally; and third, the development of a computerised information resource on this subject.

This Project, directed by the second author, has led to an intensive collaboration with HARC over the past six years. The survey was designed and analysed in collaboration with HARC, and we will say a little about the findings below. The workshop programme has been evaluated by HARC through grants to HARC from MENCAP and the MENCAP City Foundation, while individual members of HARC staff have contributed to the workshops themselves. The material developed and collected by the PRMH Project is being synthesised in the information resource with HARC's collaboration.

The PRMH Project survey was the most extensive yet undertaken on the lives and needs of families and carers with a son or daughter with profound and multiple disabilities (Hogg and Lambe, 1988). Some of the nearly 2,000 parents who responded answered over 200 detailed questions in the postal questionnaire, a validation study by Sebba (1989) who visited a sub-sample of families confirming the reliability of their responses through direct assessment and observation of their sons and daughters. The survey, which drew in part for its sampling on work undertaken in HARC on Adult Training Centre provision by Whelan and Speake (1985), established possibly the clearest description on a large sample of the adaptive behaviour, developmental achievements and pattern of impairments yet available.

Though the range of abilities defined was wide, parents reported a highly dependent group whose abilities left a considerable input by parents essential. Thus, 69 per cent and 40 per cent of children and adults, respectively, were totally un-toilet trained, with only 1 per cent and 9 per cent respectively being fully toilet trained. For the two samples of children and adults the respective figures were 90 per cent and 77 per cent unable to wash or dry themselves, 69 per cent and 47 per cent had to be completely dressed and, 55 per cent and 34 per cent needing to be fed entirely by someone else. Importantly, however, in all these areas of adaptive behaviour varying proportions of the individuals *had* made progress towards some degree of independent functioning – more so for adults than for children. Vocal and non-vocal communication were found to be expectedly limited, with 32 per cent of children's parents and 21 per cent of those of adults reporting a total absence of communication. In part, the extent and pattern of additional disabilities were seen to contribute to the slow or limited delay in these areas. It was found that 9.5 per cent of children and 5.0 per cent of adults were reported to have impairments to physical development, vision and hearing. Also, 35.5 per cent and 21.7 per cent had impairment to two modalities, most frequently physical functioning and vision. Where a single additional disability was reported (55 per cent of children and 73 per cent of adults) this was almost invariably physical impairment. Thus, 96 per cent of the children and 93 per cent of adults had some degree of physical impairment, generally severe and involving loss of ambulation. Overall, behavioural difficulties were reported by over 70 per cent of parents and varying degrees of sleep problems in over 80 per cent. A variety of medical conditions were noted, particularly epilepsy, in the region of 60 per cent. A wide range of drug prescription involving anticonvulsants and psychotropic medication was reported, including multiple drug prescription. These figures are reported by Hogg (1991a) and are placed in a wider context of drug prescription to people with intellectual disabilities in Hogg (1991b).

The consequences of the extent of disabilities and limitation on adaptive behaviour, together with the medical and behavioural problems reported, had profound consequences for parents. The average time spent in basic caring activities was between seven and eight hours, with some spending sixteen hours. Informally, confirmation has come for the accuracy of these figures from parents who, provoked by our report to examine their own situation, have added up the time spent in care activities and to their own surprise found the figures confirmed. It is not unknown for parents to have to get up in the early hours of the morning to begin preparing their child for school, or even to prepare their child the night before.

Clearly the degree and kind of support merited by families who undertake such an onerous primary caring role is both extensive and diverse. Recommendations targeted on all aspects of services emerge from the report. For the PRMH Project itself, however, a contribution has been made in the light of the needs expressed through their survey responses by parents. Seven major areas of need were identified:

(1) Dental care;
(2) physical management in the home;
(3) communication and feeding;
(4) managing difficult behaviours;
(5) evolving approaches to leisure;
(6) preparation for the future – legal and residential considerations;
(7) understanding benefits and allowances.

The PRMH Project has substantially implemented this programme of workshops which has involved a first phase workshop which HARC has carefully evaluated, followed by a second phase workshop – also evaluated – and the production of the course materials in the form of a Tutor's Workbook and a Participant's Workbook. The former describes how to run a workshop on a given topic, the latter including all relevant material for those taking part. In addition, a third workbook is available advising on the whole process by which parent workshops can be mounted and resourced – covering funding, identifying and negotiating venues, staffing, transport etc. This workshop model is now being disseminated nationally by MENCAP.

The third objective of the PRMH Project, the development of the information resource, is also being conducted as a joint PRMH Project–HARC initiative. This is providing an unique opportunity to bring together the wealth of academic information developed by HARC over the past decades, and the practical experiences of services and families gathered by the Project.

Collaboration between HARC and the voluntary sector, however, has not stopped with the immediate work just described. With the PRMH Project, HARC has participated in a joint venture with the National Federation of Gateway Clubs to evolve an extensive resource pack concerned with leisure and profound and multiple disabilities. Information ranges from the use of microtechnology in leisure to aromatherapy, from adapted cricket to the design of sensory gardens. The pack draws upon HARC's EC leisure study described above, as well as upon the extensive knowledge of behavioural and medical management noted.

It will not have gone unnoticed that the picture of work in this area that we have drawn has expanded in all directions from the relatively tight learning process orientation we began by describing, to broadly-based investigations into what amounts to the wider, ecological aspects of the lives of people with profound and multiple disabilities. While this widening perspective has taken us some way to developing a more comprehensive picture of the lives of such people and their families, continued debate has introduced new issues, and our view of what is required in terms of services, and where research might cast more light on how we can achieve service objectives, has moved forward.

First, challenges to the proposition that 'all children are educable' have forced us to look closely at what we mean by 'educability' and how we might achieve 'educational' goals. Despite the inclusion of children and young people with profound and multiple disabilities in educational provision, slow or non-existent progress in some instances, despite intensive educational input, has led some commentators to question the appropriateness of the educational model for this group. This had led to the suggestion that education for this group be expanded to embrace all relevant therapeutic techniques (Hogg, 1984), a suggestion that has not been regarded by all commentators as sufficiently all embracing. Peter Evans, a past member of HARC, and his co-author Jean Ware have suggested that

> an exclusively instructional or interventionist approach (i.e. *therapeutic*) may well ignore other features of the environment which would normally be regarded as an essential part of education (and human life) in, for instance the area of affective development (Evans and Ware, 1987).

What emerges as the issue of concern when we become so all-inclusive (that is, response to instruction and/or response to therapy, and/or affective value of experience) is not whether 'educability' has been over extended, but rather that a more holistic view of the person and his or her worth is being proposed, with the implicit value judgement that different individual's *capabilities* do not warrant the assumption that human lives have differing degrees of worth. In practical terms with respect to instruction *per se* the consequence of such a view is broadly the same as for Baer (1981), that though it has not been proven that all people can learn, in terms of intervention we will continue to act *as if they can*. With respect to educational *practice*, such a view has led to an increasingly holistic approach to education, with a clearer emphasis on the whole person (Bray *et al.*, 1988). In addition, active consideration of the place of pupils with profound disabilities in the National Curriculum is ensuring that educational segregation by default is avoided, as well as giving an added impulse to innovative curricula work with this group.

The second major emergent theme of the past decade is in reality already intrinsically involved in Evans' and Ware's (1987) discussion. Following on significant developments in the field of child development which have counterbalanced the preoccupation of Western culture with intellectual excellence and its development, *affective* growth and experience have emerged as significant themes in the wider literature on intellectual disability (see Brown *et al.*, 1989 for a full discussion). Consideration of affective experience has also extended to people with profound and multiple disabilities, for example, in the work of Gleason (1988) and of Latchford (1989). The scene is set in this work to provide practical approaches to the assessment and monitoring of affective experience in such people, not only in educational settings, but possibly in leisure contexts where evidence of choice and preference are central to the very concept of leisure. Assessment of affect through observation or even physiological procedures may be seen as a development on a par with the advance in interviewing techniques developed with more able people with intellectual disabilities. Such methods enable us to establish not only 'service users' views' as part of the movement towards consumerism in service provision, but also to extend the means and modalities through which people communicate their experience of their quality of life.

There is evidence in many countries and throughout the UK of a growing sensitivity to the holistic needs of people with profound disabilities. That Peter Mittler encouraged these trends over two decades ago is to his credit, but it is perhaps more significant that he also created the conditions that enabled many of us working in HARC to engage in this humanly significant field and to carry it forward elsewhere. Twenty-one years on, the last of those colleagues who joined him in 1969 has moved on to develop an extensive, and it is intended, holistically-orientated day service for adults with profound and multiple disabilities. This service, the White Top Centre, Dundee, is to be developed with a research input from several departments of the Univeristy of Dundee, ranging from Social Work and Psychology, through to Orthopaedics and Microtechnology. Perhaps in ten years time, for Peter Mittler's seventieth birthday, the authors will have the opportunity of describing the outcome of this development, and again illustrating the long term consequences of his vision and support those many years ago.

References

Baer, D. M. (1981) A hung jury and a Scottish verdict: 'not proven', *Analysis and Intervention in Developmental Disabilities*, 1, 91–7.

Beveridge, S. (1986) Mothers' interactive styles: their relationship to a programme of parent teaching. Ph.D. Thesis, University of Manchester.

Bray, A., MacArthur, J. and Ballard, K. D. (1988) Education for pupils with profound disabilities: issues of policy, curriculum, teaching methods, and evaluation, *European Journal of Special Educational Needs*, 4, 207–24.

Bricker, W. A. (1970) Identifying and modifying behavioral deficits, *American Journal of Mental Deficiency*, 75, 16–21.

Brown, R., Bayer, M. B. and MacFarlane, C. (1989) (eds) *Rehabilitation Programmes: Performance and Quality of Life of Adults with Developmental Handicap Volume 1*, Toronto, Lugus.

Cavet, J. (1990) Occupational and leisure activities for people with profound retardation and multiple impairments: a study of the use of creative activities to facilitate social integration. Supported by the division for Action in Favour of Disabled People, Commission of the European Community. Hester Adrian Research Centre, University of Manchester.

Dunst, C. (1980) *A Clinical and Educational Manual for Use with the Uzgiris and Hunt Scales of Infant Psychological Development*. Austin, Texas, Pro-Ed.

Evans, P. and Ware, J. (1987) *'Special Care' Provision: The Education of Children with Profound and Multiple Learning Difficulties*. Windsor, NFER-Nelson.

Fuller, P. R. (1949) Operant conditioning of a vegetative human organism, *American Journal of Psychology*, 62, 587–90.

Gleason, J. (1988) Intent on play: social-cultural dimensions of the group life of persons with profound developmental disabilities, *European Journal of Special Educational Needs*, 4, 239–51.

Hogg, J. (1983) Sensory and social reinforcement of head-turning in a profoundly retarded multiply handicapped child, *British Journal of Clinical Psychology*, 22, 33–40.

Hogg, J. (1984) Abnormality, learning and development in profoundly intellectually impaired people and the issue of educability. Paper presented to the 'Current perspectives on learning in mentally handicapped people' symposium held at the Annual conference of the British Psychological Society, University of Warwick, April.

Hogg, J. (1991a) The administration of psychotropic and anticonvulsant drugs to children and adults with profound mental handicap and multiple disabilities, *Journal of Mental Deficiency Research* (in press).

Hogg, J. (1991b) The administration of psychotropic and anticonvulsant drugs to children and adults with profound mental retardation and multiple disabilities. London, MENCAP.

Hogg, J., Foxen, T. and McBrien, J. A. (1979) *Training Staff Responsible for Profoundly Retarded Multiply Handicapped Children: An Application of Kiernan and Riddick's Staff Training Programme*, Hester Adrian Research Centre, University of Manchester.

Hogg, J., Foxen, T. H. and McBrien, J. A. (1981) Issues in the training and evaluation of behaviour modification skills for staff working with profoundly retarded multiply handicapped children, *Behavioural Psychotherapy*, 9, 345–57.

Hogg, J. and Lambe, L. (1988) *Sons and Daughters with Profound Retardation and Multiple Handicaps Attending Schools and Social Education Centres: Final Report*. London, MENCAP.

Hogg, J., Remington, R. E. and Foxen T. (1979b) Classical conditioning of profoundly retarded, multiply handicapped children, *Developmental Medicine and Child Neurology*, 21,779–86.

Hogg, J. and Sebba, J. (1986) *Profound Retardation and Multiple Impairment: Volume 1: Development and Learning*. London, Croom Helm.

Kiernan, C. C. and Riddick, B. (1973) *A Draft Programme for Training in Operant Techniques: Practical Units*. London, Thomas Coram Research Unit.

Latchford, G. (1989) Towards an understanding of profound mental handicap. Ph.D Thesis, University of Edinburgh.

McBrien, J. A. and Foxen, T. H. (1987) A pyramid model of staff training in behavioural methods: The EDY Project, In J. Hogg and P. Mittler (eds) *Staff Training in Mental Handicap*, pp. 375–427, London, Croom Helm.

Remington, R. E., Foxen. T. and Hogg, J. (1977) Auditory reinforcement in profoundly retarded, multiply handicapped children, *American Journal of Mental Deficiency*, 82, 299–304.

Sebba, J. (1978) A system for assessment and intervention for pre-school profoundly retarded and multiply handicapped children. M.Ed. Thesis, University of Manchester.

Sebba, J. (1987) *Education of People with Profound and Multiple Handicaps: Resource Materials for Staff Training*. Manchester, Manchester University Press.

Sebba, J. (1989) Validation study, PRMH Project Paper 7, London, MENCAP.

Segal, S. S. (1974) *No Child is Ineducable*, Oxford, Pergamon.

Uzgiris, I. C. and Hunt, J. McV. (1975) *Assessment in Infancy: Ordinal Scales of Psychological Development*, Urbana, IL., University of Illinois.

Whelan, E. and Speake, B. (1985) *A National Survey of Day Provision in England and Wales for Mentally Handicapped Adults with Special Needs: Final Report to the Department of Health and Social Security*. Hester Adrian Research Centre, University of Manchester.

Woodward, M. W. (1979) Piaget's theory and the study of mental retardation in N. R. Ellis (ed.) *Handbook of Mental Deficiency, Psychological Theory and Research*, (2nd Edn), Hillsdale NJ, Lawrence Erlbaum.

Woodward, M. W. (1959) The behaviour of idiots interpreted by Piaget's theory of sensorimotor development, *British Journal of Education Psychology*, 29, 60–71.

CHAPTER 5

Staff Training and Development

Colin Robson and Judy Sebba

Introduction

The training and development of staff working with people with learning difficulties is a broad and complex subject. Inevitably, this chapter will discuss some areas relatively superficially while focusing on others in more detail. An attempt is made to highlight the main general issues, rather than describing developments in training for each of the relevant work forces. The general issues will mainly be illustrated by examples from the training of teachers as this is the area in which the authors have carried out much of their own research, but an attempt will be made to cover other areas.

The chapter will describe the main trends in service provision for people with learning difficulties that are considered to have had an impact upon patterns of staff training and development. Some of the changes in these patterns over the past twenty years will be described briefly. There has been considerable research on the effectiveness of training in terms of subsequent development of the service provision. This research will be selectively summarised with respect to a few specific issues. Finally, a brief glimpse into the crystal ball will be offered in order to speculate about possible future developments.

It should be noted that the other contributors to this volume are people who without exception have been responsible for major developments and research in staff training for people with learning difficulties. It is likely therefore, that in every chapter there will be material relevant to the discussion. In addition, Peter Mittler himself has continued to maintain a major interest in staff development both nationally and internationally with particular commitments to the areas of multi-professional work and work in developing countries.

Major changes in services for people with learning difficulties

Two changes stand out which have primarily affected health and education services respectively.

Community care

By far the most important change in health-related services for people with learning difficulties that has been occurring over the past twenty years has been the community care programme. Research on hospitals and monitoring of practices in them, which for years have been carried out by the National Development Team, led to an increasing commitment to hospital closures. Initially, admissions of children were stopped and most health authorities drew up longer term plans for the total closure of the hospitals. This obviously needed to be accompanied by massive increases in the provision of services in the community, and it was this that has continued to provide the greatest area of controversy. There are clear concerns about whether the quantity of community-based service provision justifies continued resettlement of residents from the hospitals.

One major implication has been that some staff previously working in the hospitals were offered redeployment in the community services, potentially requiring retraining. In addition, large numbers of staff have been required to work in community-based housing and most of these people have no formal qualifications or training. The implications of this for patterns of training are considerable.

Education

Changes in education services have been largely the result of a series of Education Acts and government reports. The Education Act of 1970 brought the education of pupils with severe learning difficulties within the education system for the first time. Teachers who worked in these schools were required to have qualified teacher status and since many had worked within the Junior Training Centres run by the Department of Health for many years, they tended not to have this status. A programme of gradual change was introduced specifying a number of years within which they needed to secure secondment on to a course. In practice, there are still one or two teachers in many schools for pupils with severe learning difficulties in England and Wales who do not have qualified teacher status.

The 1981 Education Act abolished the previous categories of Educationally Subnormal (Severe) and Educationally Subnormal (Moderate), replacing these and other categories with the more generalised label of 'children with special educational needs'. However, in practice, since the schools were redesignated schools for pupils with severe learning difficulties and those for pupils with moderate learning difficulties, the pupils within them became referred to by the same labels. The Act did reflect the views of the Warnock Report that had preceded it, by suggesting that pupils be integrated into mainstream schools wherever possible. Hence, while hospitals were beginning to resettle residents in the community, schools started setting up, or in some cases extending, their links with mainstream schools, enabling more pupils to spend at least part of their week with pupils in these schools. The move towards integration has been greatest for pupils with moderate learning difficulties where some local authorities have closed separate provision, although the suspicion has been voiced that this was primarily on financial grounds and associated with falling rolls in secondary schools arising from demographic changes.

Dramatic changes in the education services appear likely to be brought about by the 1988 Education Reform Act which includes amongst its many clauses, the introduction of the National Curriculum for *all* pupils and Local Management of Schools. To date (late 1990), few special schools have been offered the opportunity to fully manage their own budgets but this is likely to have a direct effect on a substantial number of special schools in the future. Indeed, all special schools are likely to be affected if only because mainstream schools linking with them and holding delegated budgets, may need to review the link arrangements. There are concerns that this process will threaten both new and well established links, but there is little evidence as yet, that this is happening.

The impact of National Curriculum on pupils with severe learning difficulties is too complex an area to cover here. Suffice to suggest that in many schools the review of the curriculum instigated by the Act is leading to consideration of many activities not traditionally offered to those pupils. This has considerable implications for the in-service training needs of teachers, nursery nurses and assistants who might have been previously unaware, that if, for example, they were melting cheese for a sauce (as part of what they might think of as home economics) this could form the basis for an understanding of 'the effect of heat on food' which falls within the science area of the National Curriculum.

Trends in training

From carer to professional

One notable trend is the growth of professionalism for those working with people with learning difficulties. The 1970 Education Act legally required teachers of pupils with severe learning difficulties to have qualified teacher status, in recognition of the need for these pupils to be educated, rather than simply well cared for. Likewise, the nursing profession continued to strive for an increase in the number of qualified nurses to work in hospitals. Adult Training Centres preferred to employ staff with one of a number of professional qualifications seen as appropriate (for example, social work, teaching, etc.).

Expansion of specialist training

For those staff wishing to pursue a career in working with people with learning difficulties, opportunities to gain a specialist qualification expanded. For example, nurses could become a Registered Nurse of the Mentally Handicapped, Social Workers could do a Post Qualifying course in working with people with a mental handicap (although only one such course exists) and teachers could either initially train in mental handicap or undertake an advanced qualification after some experience. More recently, this specialist initial training for teachers has been phased out with a substantial, but not currently sufficient provision of in-service specialist courses and is being reviewed. In addition, a few specialist, advanced qualifications have developed for staff wishing to teach people with learning difficulties in further education.

Coverage of learning difficulties within generic training

The initial training of staff, for whom only part of their job involves working with people with learning difficulties is more likely to include some 'disability awareness' now than occurred in the past. These staff might include GPs, generic social workers, health visitors, further education lecturers and some physiotherapists, speech therapists, occupational therapists and psychologists who do not have a post specialising in learning difficulties. In addition, all teaching qualifications are supposed to include coverage on special educational needs although the evidence suggests this varies in both quantity and quality.

Input on learning difficulties on generic training has been a necessary response to the changes in services described above which has led to the greater likelihood of these professionals coming into contact with people with learning difficulties. In addition, the growing awareness that many people have learning difficulties at some point and within some sphere of their lives, makes the applicability of this type of training more widespread. The recognition of the importance of multi-professional work, discussed elsewhere in this volume may also be a contributory factor.

Development of joint training

The growth in multi-professional work in services for people with learning difficulties has identified the need to develop a shared philosophy. This is hampered by the isolated professionalism encouraged by many initial training courses and the genuinely different theoretical standpoints that have been popular within any particular profession. For example, if psychology training was at its most behavioural when social work training was at its most humanistic or psychodynamic, staff qualifying during that time might need to invest considerable effort in understanding one another prior to working collaboratively.

One way of encouraging staff to work more closely across professional boundaries was provided by the development of opportunities for joint training. This was assisted by the reorganising of funding for training which created specific joint funding money. One of the purposes to which this could be put was the provision of training and staff development which aimed to attract staff from both social services and health. Attempts have been made, successfully on some occasions, to get these courses jointly validated.

By far the most extensive example of joint training at the in-service level, within services for people with learning difficulties was provided by the Staff Development Initiative arising from the All Wales Strategy. This initiative provided a range of courses at different levels, regionally, which were attended by staff from all services concerned with those with learning difficulties and parents. Hundreds of staff were involved in this initiative and the impact of it is still being evaluated. There have been several other attempts at joint in-service training but this still appears to be the exception rather than the norm.

Increasing power of the service provider

A trend particularly noticeable in education but discernible in other services, has been for the service provider to have a stronger voice in the nature and extent of the in-service training provided. Increasingly, the prime aim of the training has been to assist in delivering the service rather than to fulfill the personal needs of the practitioner. This is implemented by grant regulations where effectively the local education authority buys the training it needs. The trend is, of course, not specific to the learning difficulties field, but has had major effects.

There has been a substantial reduction in the number of one year, full-time, in-service courses, through lack of support from secondments. This has had a particularly serious effect on areas such as training for learning difficulties where small teams of tutors can ill afford depletion. Other effects are more beneficial in that, for example, whereas in the past some institutions of higher education essentially provided those courses that they wished to teach, courses are now increasingly tailored to needs as perceived by providers. Local management schemes further devolve funding for in-service training down to school level, which is likely to intensify this trend. Training becomes more school-focused in the sense of being targeted to specific school needs, and in some cases physically based within the school.

More of the training is being provided by local authority personnel such as advisers and other support staff, as well as teachers themselves. This in turn generates a new training need in that many such staff are in this taking on a new role. Potential problems of quality control have been addressed in some areas by collaborative arrangements between local authorities and higher education institutions, for example a modular Special Needs Certificate and Diploma which is largely taught by Humberside Education Authority staff and validated by Hull University (Robson and Wright, 1989).

Development of distance learning

As indicated in the previous section changes in the funding arrangements for many professionals working with people with learning difficulties have limited the opportunities to participate in full-time training courses. Some individuals have never had the opportunity for full-time study for a variety of reasons and in some rural areas the geographical availability of training is too limited. In addition, much of the evidence from studies of the effectiveness of staff training summarised in the next section, suggests that training away from the work place is less effective than that which takes place 'on the job'.

For these reasons, and in order to make training as accessible as possible to the widest range of people, there has been a growth in distance learning opportunities. The Open University initially offered 'The Handicapped Person in the Community', followed by 'Patterns for Living', courses aimed at non-qualified staff, parents and anyone else who wished to pursue them. More recently, an advanced version of the Patterns for Living course has been launched. In addition, a full range of modules addressing learning difficulties is offered within the Open University's programme within education and social sciences.

Another major contribution to a specialist field through distance learning has been the course run from Birmingham University leading to a mandatory advanced, teaching qualification in visual impairment (Chapman, 1982). This course has successfully run for nearly ten years through a distance learning mode, enabling teachers who because of their specific professional interest are likely to be geographically dispersed, with sometimes only two or three in a whole county, to participate. It is a unique course in that it was the first distance learning course to be set up outside the Open University and was initially based on a full-time, university-based version of the same course.

Pyramid training

During the 1970s and 1980s a considerable number of training packages have been published ranging from those aimed at a specific audience on a specific topic (for instance 'Preventive Approaches to Disruption' Chisholm *et al.*, 1986) to those aimed at a variety of professionals and covering a number of topics (e.g. Education of the Developmentally Young Foxen and McBrien, 1981). They have provided training to a wider range of staff through a 'pyramid' model in which the initial sessions train the trainers who subsequently take staff in the services within their own areas through the training.

Advantages of pyramid training include accessibility of the material and ideas to the widest possible audience, training based in the workplace (and therefore, potentially, many staff from one service can be trained together), and the costs are reduced. Disadvantages include the lack of control on the part of the originators of the material over how it is used (and therefore, potential dilution/misrepresentation of the material), lack of control over potential evaluation of it and limited opportunity of cross fertilisation of ideas which can arise when staff from different services meet together. Attempts have been made to use currently available material for training in countries other than the one in which it was devised. This may be problematic because of cultural incompatibilities, and needs careful adaptations particularly for developing countries. A recent initiative involving pyramid training in developing countries (Ainscow, 1991) has attempted to take into account the different cultures within which the 'trainers' are working.

Alongside developments in pyramid training, there has been an increase in modularisation of existing courses and a tendency for new courses to be set up with a modular structure. This increases the flexibility in the pattern of the course, enabling staff to pick and choose the content and weight of the workload at different times. It has also led to more collaborative ventures between institutions of higher education and services (for instance, social services, local education authorities, health services, etc.). Thus, local initiatives that may be worthy of wider dissemination may be scrutinised and then validated towards a qualification. In practice, this is critical since it enables staff who are regular course attenders and sacrifice much of their own time to staff development to at least receive some recognition for doing so.

Research on the effectiveness of staff training

The *raison d'être* of staff training and development is that it will improve practice. However, it is evident from the extensive reviews of staff training (e.g. Fullan, 1982; Hogg and Mittler, 1987; Hopkins, 1989; Showers et al., 1987) that the relationship between training and institutional change is complex and the evidence suggests most training is of limited long term effect. A variety of factors influence this relationship including characteristics of the individuals who participate in training, characteristics of the institutions in which they work and models of training offered. In addition, since most staff training and development is not evaluated, the information on its effects are limited.

Characteristics of staff

In terms of characteristics of the participants, Showers et al. (1987) have concluded from a meta-analysis of 200 research studies on staff development (not specifically addressing learning difficulties) that individual teaching styles and values orientations do not often affect teachers' abilities to learn from staff development. However, a basic level of knowledge or skill in a new approach is helpful. A word of warning to the trainers comes from the finding that initial enthusiasm for training, while reassuring to the providers has relatively little influence on learning.

Characteristics of institutions

The characteristics of institutions which may influence responsiveness to change include support from the manager or headteacher (e.g. Robson *et al.*, 1988), the quality of staff relationships (e.g. Evans and Hopkins, 1988) and whether the institution is currently experiencing 'innovation overload' (Fullan *et al.*, 1990). In addition, Landesman-Dwyer and Knowles (1987) identify a key variable in predicting longer term effects to be the degree to which the job demands are consistent with or complement the goals of the staff training programme. This would appear to relate to a major issue within models of training.

Models of training

For many years the emphasis in explanations of why people with learning difficulties sometimes failed to learn was on the perceived characteristics of the individual, often using the label of a syndrome. More recently, explanations have focused to a greater extent, although importantly not exclusively, on the possible inappropriateness of the teaching approach. Staff training and development has been through a similar process. Initially, the explanation given for why staff failed to change was because they lacked motivation, did not understand the techniques, were too rigid, etc. Currently, staff trainers are much more critical of the approach to training that is adopted.

The gap between research and practice is as wide in this field as anywhere. The research evidence has been accumulating for years about the need to enter staff training with negotiated objectives between trainer and participants (e.g. Robson *et al.*, 1988; Landesman-Dwyer and Knowles, 1987). As Fullan (1982) reminded us, sustained change in curriculum and instruction depends heavily on a shared understanding about the nature of the innovation and what it can accomplish. Hence, staff training and development must seek to establish shared objectives from the outset and yet most initiatives which take place fail to address this fundamental issue.

From the 200 studies which Showers *et al.* (1987) analysed, it appeared that where or when training takes place or who the trainer is, are much less important than the training design. Many researchers and staff developers have been suggesting for years that staff training must be as close to the 'real life' work situation as possible. Showers *et al.* make it clear that the theory–demonstration–practice–feedback combination is vital to ensuring transfer of skills into the work situation. Table 5.1 is adapted from Joyce and Showers (1988) and reflects their research findings on models of training, in which the magnitude of the effect is considerably enhanced when training involves two people observing one another's practice of the skills. Whether the trainer does the 'coaching' or it is done by a peer, leads to the same level of effectiveness. More surprisingly, it has been found that peer coaching involving observation only, without any opportunity for discussion, is just as effective.

Table 5.1 Effect sizes for training outcomes by training components (expressed as a magnitude of change on a scale on which 1.0 indicates change of 1 standard deviation)

Training components and combinations	Training Outcomes		
	Knowledge	Skill	Transfer of training
Information	0.63	0.35	0.00
Theory	0.15	0.50	0.00
Demonstration	1.65	0.26	0.00
Theory, demonstration, practice and feedback	1.31	1.18	0.39
Theory, demonstration, practice, feedback and peer coaching	2.71	1.25	1.68

(*Source*: Adapted from Joyce and Showers, 1988)

Staff training and development involving peer or trainer coaching is seen as creating the conditions under which sufficient levels of knowledge and skill are developed to sustain and support practice until transfer of skills has taken place. At this point it is assumed that the staff have cognitively assimilated the practice sufficiently for it to be re-selected and used at any time, appropriately and integratively. However, surveys of staff development practice reviewed throughout this section, suggest that only a small proportion of programmes offered combine the necessary components to sustain practice to the point of transfer.

The future for training

Crystal ball gazing is a hazardous sport. Writing in 1990 we do not have any great measure of confidence that what we might have written in 1980 would bear much resemblance to contemporary reality. It seems fair to suggest, however, that many of the trends that we have highlighted are set to continue. Developments in community care and the National Curriculum are going to have important long term effects. A more diversified, locally responsive in-service training pattern also appears likely although there is something paradoxical about linking this to a national curriculum.

The political and economic context will clearly influence developments. At the time of writing, education and training bids fair to be a major battle-ground for the first general election of the 1990s, and its outcome may well provide a turning point. Continuation of a right-wing government could see the withering away of initial training courses in ideologically suspect education departments through the development of licenced teacher schemes with on-the-job training.

However, it may be that economic constraints will severely limit potential developments. A sustained recession, possibly deepened by a major increase in oil prices, could throttle the best intentions of providing the necessary training resources. The European dimension will loom larger as 1992 approaches and is passed. Changes in award structures are likely, as is the cross-transfer of staff bringing different perspectives. While, in the past, many countries have looked to the UK for ideas about training, developments in continental Europe, in part funded by EEC money (e.g. Marchesi, 1986), could well influence our own approaches.

There do appear, however, to be trends in training likely to be independent of such factors. The modularisation of education and training is proceeding apace. Credit accumulation and transfer schemes are developing very quickly. These might provide the predominant framework for training in five to ten years time, the accreditation of prior experience and learning as counting toward academic and professional awards will form an important part of such schemes. Training institutions will increasingly 'franchise' their courses so that constituent parts, even the whole course, may be taught by, say a college of further education or the training division of a social services department. More generally, an increasing proportion of training will take place 'in-house' by education, health or social services staff, with the addition of bought-in expertise. Links to local higher education institutions may be retained primarily to take advantage of their ability to grant nationally recognised awards; although this might be achieved in some cases by direct relationships with national bodies such as the Council for National Academic Awards (CNAA) or professional organisations.

Such a system is more flexible, responsive, and in some senses more open than the traditional course model. It will necessitate a major change of role for training staff in universities, polytechnics and colleges. This would emphasise consultancy, the development and evaluation of high quality training materials which could be adapted for flexible use in different contexts, high level courses including those to 'train the trainers', and, we would hope, a substantial amount of professionally relevant research to assist in driving the whole scheme. This is not to gainsay the value of 'teacher as researcher' and reflective practitioner models which have much to offer. They highlight a major development task within a system where the training task is devolved to a large extent down to the individual service, school or unit – the need for it to be able to enquire into and improve its own working, and to determine its own needs, including training needs.

Conclusion

Simply increasing the volume or funding of staff training will not produce change. Peter Mittler presented fourteen propositions about staff training in the book edited by him, ourselves and Geoff Davies (Robson *et al.*, 1988). These would seem to still provide useful pointers to consider when discussing the training and development of staff working with people with learning difficulties. They are presented again here as a tribute to one of the most prolific writers on the subject of staff development.

Peter Mittler's fourteen propositions

The major challenges facing staff working in the field of special needs can be baldly summarised in fourteen propositions:

(1) We are all out of date in relation to the tasks which face us.

(2) Everyone in services for children and adults with special needs should be receiving continuous, on the job updating. To this end, there should be a national and local strategic plan of staff development and appraisal for all, from the most senior to the most junior members.

(3) We know very little about the effectiveness of staff training in meeting the needs of participants, the services which employ them or the clients they serve. Yet we continue to call for more and more staff training.

(4) Those who have been trained have not always been given the opportunities to implement their knowledge and skills in the settings in which they work, nor have they been prepared to do so by their training.

(5) Even when such opportunities have been available, the effects are often short-lived. It follows that our training must help people to become effective change agents in their own work settings.

(6) Because we are not clear about the direction of service developments, and therefore of the knowledge and skills required by staff now and in the future, the curriculum content of most staff training courses requires reappraisal and constant review. There needs to be local discussion and decision-making on the knowledge and skills which are considered essential or desirable in teachers (and other professionals) working with students of all ages with special needs (one such list is provided in Hogg and Mittler, 1987).

(7) The organisation of staff development is insufficiently multi-disciplinary and unnecessarily separated from the training of other professionals. Too much training goes on in 'little boxes'. Furthermore, parents and clients are rarely considered as partners in training.

(8) The training of teachers working in special education has too long been segregated from the training of other teachers. Consequently, other teachers have seen special education as someone else's responsibility.

(9) Most courses in the past have trained staff to work in segregated or institutional settings – special schools, day centres, residential homes, etc. In future, we need, in addition, to train staff to work in community settings – e.g. with parents in their own homes, and with children and young people too young or too old to attend schools, in youth clubs and leisure and recreational settings – indeed, wherever people with special needs are living and working.

(10) The role of specialist staff is increasingly one of providing direct support for people with special needs in ordinary settings, as well as supporting staff in ordinary services where necessary. In future, specialist training should aim to equip staff to pass on their knowledge and skills to their colleagues, to families and volunteers and to clients themselves.

(11) Course providers and trainers in colleges and universities will in future need to negotiate with potential students and their employers concerning course content and mode rather than continue to offer courses according to their own interpretation of what is needed. This may mean that staff of higher education institutions will in future need to find ways of encouraging and supporting on the job training in schools, day and residential centres and other work settings.

(12) In order to combat isolation and parochialism, all staff should have regular and frequent opportunities to visit and work in other services in their locality or further afield and to discuss with colleagues and managers the relevance of what they have seen, heard and read to the practice of their own agency. Such visits should be part of the staff development programme of each school and agency and should also form a major element of all training courses.

(13) Every facility should have a small library of relevant books, periodicals and training materials and should in addition have access to a larger resource centre which also contains videotapes and audiotapes illustrating various approaches to working with clients or families.

(14) We must learn to accept that special needs do not cease at sixteen, nineteen or any other age. The education service must accept responsibility for meeting the continuing special educational needs of adults of all ages and levels of ability and provide assistance, training and support to the adult education service in extending its role to this wider population (Robson *et al.*, 1988: 4–5).

References

Ainscow, M. (1991) Towards effective schools for all: an account of the rationale of the UNESCO teacher education project, 'Special Needs in the Classroom', in G. Upton *Staff Training and Special Educational Needs: Innovatory Strategies and Models of Delivery*, London, David Fulton (in press).

Chapman, E. (1982) A new approach to the training of teachers for children with Special Educational Needs, *Educational Review*, 34, 161–8.

Chisholm, B., Kearney, D., Knight, G., Little, H., Morris, S. and Tweddle, D. (1986) *Preventive Approaches to Disruption*. Basingstoke, Macmillan.

Evans, M. and Hopkins, D. (1988) School climate and the psychological state of the individual teacher as factors affecting the utilisation of educational ideas following an in-service course, *British Educational Research Journal*, 14, 211–30.

Foxen, T. and McBrien, J. (1981) *The EDY Course for Mental Handicap Practitioners*. Manchester, Manchester University Press.

Fullan, M. (1982) *The Meaning of Educational Change*. New York, Teacher's College Press.

Fullan, M., Bennett, B. and Rolheiser-Bennett, C. (1990) Linking classroom and school improvement, *Educational Leadership*, 47, 13–19.

Hogg, J. and Mittler, P. (1987) (Eds) *Staff Training in Mental Handicap*. London, Croom Helm.

Hopkins, D. (1989) *Evaluation for School Development*. Milton Keynes, Open University Press.

Joyce, B. and Showers, B. (1988) *Student Achievement Through Staff Development*. New York, Longman.

Landesman-Dwyer, S. and Knowles, M. (1987) Ecological Analysis of Staff Training in Residential Settings, in J. Hogg and P, Mittler (Eds) *Staff Training in Mental Handicap*. London, Croom Helm.

Marchesi, A. M. (1986) Project for integration of pupils with special needs in Spain, *European Journal of Special Needs Education*, 1, 125–33.

Robson, C., Sebba, J., Mittler, P. and Davies, G. (1988) *In-Service Training and Special Educational Needs: Running Short, School-Focused Courses*. Manchester, Manchester University Press.

Robson, C. and Wright, M. (1989) SEN: Towards a modular pattern for SEN, *Support for Learning*, 4, 83–9.

Showers, B., Joyce, B. and Bennett, B. (1987) Synthesis of research on staff development: a framework for future study and a state-of-the-art analysis, *Educational Leadership*, 45, 77–87.

CHAPTER 6

Families and Professionals: Prospects for Partnership

Helen McConachie

Introduction

Disability affects not only an individual child or adult but also members of the immediate and extended family to varying degrees. Professionals who work with people who have learning difficulties therefore need to understand family experiences and reactions in order to give their intervention appropriate context. Research on families has grown in the past thirty years from landmark studies such as those of Farber (1959, 1960) in Chicago and Tizard and Grad (1961) in London. Those studies painted a picture of hardship and stresses leading in some cases to breakdown, and institutionalisation of the child, particularly as adulthood approached.

Such research has undoubtedly had a beneficial effect in terms of social legislation and increased quantity of services available. However, the emphasis on family pathology has obscured understanding of how families actually function, how that may change over time, how families differ in their ways of doing things, how various family members are affected and in turn influence the wellbeing and progress of the child with learning difficulties. The models guiding service provision have been similarly limited in their appropriateness. 'Families of handicapped children' have been approached as a homogeneous group. For example, there has been little study of family differences in seeking help, of families as consumers rather than as passive recipients of services. Traditional welfare provision also fails to recognise the number and variety of sources of support on which families may draw.

Within the past decade there has been a striking shift in the guiding paradigm for research on families of disabled children. The landmark articles might now be suggested as Crnic et al. (1983) and Byrne and Cunningham (1985). These authors reviewed the conceptual background and rather meagre results of past research, and concluded that future research needs to examine the processes by which families creatively adapt to and cope with the stresses of bringing up a disabled child. Logically, the study of families with 'successful' coping is as important in outlining implications for service provision as studying families who are in difficulties.

In the USA, this shift in conceptual model has already been reflected in legislation – the Education of the Handicapped Act Amendments of 1986 (PL 99–457, Part H – Handicapped Infants and Toddlers). These amendments include as a goal for service providers, 'To enhance the capacity of families to meet the special needs of their infants and toddlers with handicaps' (sec. 671(a)(4)). They go beyond 'parent-involvement' and Individual Education Plans (IEPs) to family-based intervention and Individual Family Services Plans (IFSPs). The IFSP has to include a statement of the family's strengths and needs, and this requirement has generated feverish activity towards refining models of family assessment. The IFSP has also to include a statement of expected outcomes both for the child and for the family. This legislation has given impetus to moves towards overcoming traditional barriers between health, social service, educational and therapeutic personnel. Interagency Coordinating Councils have as part of their fundamental policy family involvement in goal-setting and in selection of services (Healy, 1989).

Part H of PL 99-457 applies only to the under-two's at present; however, its philosophy can be expected to permeate across the age range, so that comprehensive family support is planned with a long-term perspective (Turnbull, 1988). Although services for toddlers may have improved in recent years, a recent British study has underlined the fact that the situation for young adults with disabilities and their family carers remains bleak (Thomas et al., 1989).

The aim of this chapter is to outline a conceptual framework for family research, and for delivery of professional services. The findings of recent research studies which adopt some part of such a framework will be reviewed. They have largely focused on families of young children. In the last part of the chapter, implications for the partnership between families and professionals will be suggested. But first some exploration of models of stress and coping is necessary, and an outline of how key concepts have been measured.

Stress and coping

The concept of *stress* is ill-defined, even though it is a much-used term both in everyday life and in health-related research. It can refer both to events or situations impinging on a person, and also to that individual's feelings and reactions. Essentially the concept of stress has been used to indicate a crisis, an abnormal state, and so having a child with severe learning difficulties has been viewed as uniformly stressful. More recent thinking in the social sciences has emphasised instead the normality and ubiquitousness of stress, with effort then being directed toward explaining differences in individual adaptation.

Mothers and fathers of children with learning difficulties have been found as groups to experience greater stress reactions than the normal population (as reviewed in Byrne and Cunningham, 1985; McConachie, 1986). However, attempts to explain observed variation in reactions have been inconclusive, for example, usually not showing correlations between level of severity of disability and stress, or economic circumstances and stress. The problem lies with the traditional 'pathological' model and univariate research strategies looking for simple links between stressor and stress reaction. It is important for research now to define stressors more carefully and to utilise multivariate analyses incorporating a range of background and mediating variables in order to predict adaptation.

One type of factor which has received little attention in the literature on families of children with learning difficulties is life events. Yet there is ample evidence in the mental health literature that the number and type of recent life events experienced may have a strong relationship with a person's physical and mental wellbeing (Pearlin et al., 1981). Parents of a child with learning difficulties are just as likely as anyone to be made redundant or to experience the death of a close family member, and so on. Potentially stressful points in the family life-cycle, such as the child entering or leaving school, need to be considered in research design. Thus a full definition of 'stressors' would include both chronic and short-term.

Interspersed throughout the early literature on stress were clues that parents' perceptions of their situation have a strong mediating influence on their level of adaptation in bringing up their child with severe learning difficulties. For example, Bradshaw and Lawton (1978) found that levels of stress were predicted not by actual housing conditions but rather by whether the mother interviewed considered the family's housing unsuitable; and not by the number of times the mother went out socially, but by whether she felt restricted. Other aspects of parents' perceptions which have been studied include religious beliefs (reviewed by Minnes, 1988a), perceived control over events (e.g. McKinney and Peterson, 1987), and problem–solving ability (e.g. Frey et al., 1989a).

Such beliefs, attitudes and skills are aspects of a person's style of *coping* and are an important part of the equation linking stressors to adaptation. 'Coping' has been defined as 'the cognitive and behavioral efforts made to master, tolerate or reduce external and internal demands and conflicts' (Folkman and Lazarus, 1980: 223). These authors categorise coping responses broadly as problem-focused or emotion-focused. An individual's coping responses are expected to evolve continuously depending on changing perceptions of stressful events, and also to vary according to the type of situation. For example, problem-focused strategies such as 'making a plan of action' are likely to predominate in work-related problems, and emotion-focused strategies such as 'accepting sympathy and understanding from someone' in health-related problems. Many difficulties of definition remain with the concept of 'coping', not least the need to analyse the relative effectiveness of different ways of coping (Roskies and Lazarus, 1980). One can, in addition, imagine in a family with a handicapped child possible problems where the parents adopt conflicting coping strategies. Schwartz (1970) offered an early typology of coping strategies of mothers of handicapped children in their encounters with the medical care system: passive acceptance, active questing, and withdrawal from services. Defining parents' strategies as 'coping' is a challenge to service providers who may be more used to labelling the latter two sets of parents as 'difficult' and 'drop-outs'.

Another approach to definitions of coping is to focus on coping resources, both internal and external. For example, McCubbin and Patterson (1981) have developed a classification of five major coping strategies: internal – 'passive appraisal' (i.e. denial or wishful thinking) and 'reframing' (i.e., redefining a problem so that it appears less stressful); external – using social support, using spiritual support, using professional help. Such a classification can generate implications for intervention, such as negotiating with a family how they would best like to receive outside help and from what source, and offering 'coping skills' training. These will be discussed further in the final section of the chapter.

The social support or *external resources* available to parents of a child with severe learning difficulties also require some definition. Bronfenbrenner (1977) has defined the social ecology of a child as the relationship with four levels of 'nested, concentric structures', that is, settings and events which directly or indirectly involve the child. The family – its membership and pattern of interactions – is the closest structure or system impinging upon the child and parents. The family system is then embedded in networks of everyday relationships with extended family, friends, school contacts and so on. These relationships exist within a more remote network of social structures, such as services potentially offered to parents of a disabled child, ordinary community structures, availability of public transport and so on. Finally, there is also an encompassing level of culture, or rather subcultures, which influence indirectly the interactions and opportunities available to a child and parents. The changing climate of opinion in society regarding disability will help to determine how easily parents can expect to have a wide range of options for their child now and in the future, or whether they feel constantly in struggle against uncaring attitudes. The current literature on families of children with severe learning difficulties generally lacks a unifying social theoretical background, simply defining 'social support' as a list of types of people or agencies, rated on their helpfulness. There are two types of confusion here. One is that individual differences in definitions of 'the family' are not considered beyond whether there are two parents or one in the home. Extended families who live together will give support in very different ways from extended families who live hundreds of miles apart, even though both may be regarded as helpful. The second problem is the term social 'support' – it begs the question of whether contacts are in fact

Table 6.1 Variables commonly included in studies of family stress and coping (and most popular measures)

Stressors - chronic	Resources	Coping style	Outcome

level of severity of disability
child sex
child age
health
behaviour problems
caregiving tasks – time spent
      – perceived difficulty
parent's perceptions of handicap
(e.g. Child Competence factor of QRS-F)
	social support – sources
	      – satisfaction
	      – types
	(e.g. FSS, QSS)
	social network size and density
	spousal relationship (e.g. MAS, DAS)
	family interactions (e.g. FES, FAM)
	contacts with services
		beliefs about control
		religious beliefs
		cognitive coping (WCR)
		e.g. problem-focused,
		seek emotional
		support, wishful
		thinking
			parental adaptation
			(e.g. MI, BDI, PSI,
			Parental Adjustment
			factor of QRS-F)
			
			future anxiety (QRS-F factor)
			
			family adaptation
			(e.g. Family Stress factor of QRS-F)

Stressors – short-term
life events – number
      – perceived strain
	utilitarian resources
	    – parental education
	    – socio-economic
	      indicators
	      including housing,
	      transport, etc.
	    – number of children
	    – single parent
		internal and external
		strategies
		e.g. ability to acquire
		social support,
		reframing, seeking
		information,
		(F-COPES, CHIP)
			child outcomes
			e.g. self-esteem,
			    school achievement
			    social contacts
			    sibling adjustment

Plus: Marlowe Crowne Social Desirability Scale (Crowne and Marlowe, 1964)

QRS-F:	Questionnaire on Resources and Stress, Short Form (Friedrich *et al.*, 1983; Beilke and Friedrich, 1988)
FSS:	Family Support Scale (Dunst *et al.*, 1984)
QSS:	Quantity and Satisfaction with Support Networks (part of Inventory of Parents' Experiences, Crnic and Greenberg, 1983)
MAS:	Marital Adjustment Scale (Locke and Wallace, 1959)
DAS:	Dyadic Adjustment Scale (Spanier, 1976)
FES:	Family Environment Scale (Moos and Moos, 1981)
FAM:	Family Assessment Measure (Skinner *et al.*, 1983)
WCR:	Ways of Coping Questionnaire – Revised (Folkman and Lazarus, 1985)
F-COPES:	Family Coping Strategies Scale (McCubbin *et al.*, 1982)
CHIP:	Coping Health Inventory for Parents, (McCubbin *et al.*, 1983)
MI:	Malaise Inventory (Rutter *et al.*, 1970)
BDI:	Beck Depression Inventory (Beck and Beamesdorker, 1974)
PSI:	Parenting Stress Index (Abidin, 1983)

supportive. There is considerable evidence that contacts with extended family can increase stress (e.g. Kazak and Marvin, 1984) as can contacts with professionals (e.g. Harris and McHale, 1989).

One approach to resolving such problems of generalisation has been to draw up a social network list with an individual so as to look at the size of the network, and also its density (that is, the extent to which those individuals know each other independently). Families of disabled children have generally been found to have smaller, denser networks than comparison families. This tends to mean heavy reliance on close kin for various kinds of support, suggesting considerable pressure on family relationships (Kazak, 1986).

Several studies have included under the heading of resources closer study of family interaction and values, for example, the extent of free expression of feelings, and how achievement-oriented the family is. Qualities of the family system, such as cohesion and adaptability have been shown to relate to levels of conflict and stress (Minnes, 1988a). Satisfaction with the marital relationship is frequently cited as an important factor in parental coping (e.g. Friedrich *et al.*, 1985) and child outcomes (e.g. Sloper *et al.*, 1990). It is, however, important when considering intervention with a family to recognise the cultural limitations of studies in the literature. Different values about appropriate roles for the various family members, communication styles within the family, and patterns of child-rearing will affect considerably the type of support expected and received. In addition, differing cultural views about disability, the possibility of progress, and the shame or otherwise of accepting external help will greatly affect the relationship with professionals offering services (Hanson *et al.*, 1990).

The following section of the chapter will review some findings of recent broad-based studies of families who have a child with severe learning difficulties. Most use multiple regression analysis to predict aspects of parental, family or child adaptation. The *outcome* measures chosen depend on the questions asked by the study; however, the design of any study also depends upon individual emphasis. The family is a source of stress for many people; it also can be a resource for coping with stress and maintaining some balance in life; and the level of family harmony and adaptation could also be seen as an outcome. As an aid to conceptualising the following discussion, variables are grouped in a table under the headings of stressors, resources, coping styles and outcome, but this should be seen as a summary and not a prescription for family research design.

Key factors in adjustment

A number of issues highlighted in broad-based studies of adaptation in families of children with severe learning difficulties will be outlined. However, the emphasis will be on parents; outcomes for the children themselves, siblings, and others are beyond the scope of this brief review.

The relationship between *child characteristics* and parental stress has received continuing attention. Recent studies have taken care to analyse the factor of severity of handicap into the actual demands made on parents. Overall, severity may not be consistently related to parental stress, but children's behaviour problems, unusual caretaking demands and communication skill level are repeatedly found to be (Beckman, 1983; Friedrich et al., 1985; McKinney and Peterson, 1987; Minnes, 1988b; Sloper et al., 1988; Erickson and Upshur, 1989; Frey et al., 1989b). However, conflicting findings are still in evidence. Two studies which have attempted the most comprehensive testing of the coping research model differ on determinants of stress in fathers. Sloper et al. (1988) found that child characteristics did not contribute to the prediction of stress in fathers. However, Frey et al. (1989b) found that communication skill was a major predictor of psychological distress, more so than for mothers. Certainly it seems likely that key factors in adaptation differ between fathers and mothers given contrasting roles and pressures. In the latter study, child communication skill was a key factor in 'parenting stress' for mothers; one way in which this may be influenced was suggested by McConachie (1989), who found that fathers were less involved in sharing child care where the child had no expressive language. Thus fathers may be freer to opt out of day to day interaction, and yet still feel the frustration of not being able to communicate effectively with their disabled child. Note that, in addition to careful differentiation of a factor such as 'severity', it seems also important to differentiate various aspects of parental 'adaptation'.

Where family life style has been used as an outcome measure, child sex and diagnosis have been found significant. The major study by Mink and colleagues using cluster analysis (e.g. Mink et al., 1983) found cohesive, harmonious families to have an overrepresentation of Down's syndrome children and control-oriented families to have an overrepresentation of boys. In this case, increasing behaviour problems with age are likely to be the key factor, rather than maleness as such.

Sloper et al. (1988) appear to be unusual in including *short-term stressors* in their predictor variables. They found perceived strain of recent life events and financial problems negatively related to fathers' satisfaction with life, apparently reflecting fathers' outward-looking role in the family.

The findings on *social support* require careful interpretation. Studies generally find that satisfaction with social support is of more consequence than the number of sources of support (e.g. Dunst et al., 1986; Sloper et al., 1988; Stoneman and Crapps, 1988; Frey et al., 1989a). There are also outcomes for the children. Dunst et al. (1986) found that parents with more supportive social networks reported being less protective of their children, perhaps because they have found they can let others take a role in the child's care.

However, social networks can produce stress even at the same time as providing support. Waisbren (1980) found that, where paternal grandparents were felt supportive, fathers were more involved with their developmentally disabled children and had more positive feelings about the child. But both they and the mothers reported greater stress. One mechanism investigated has been the extent to which members of a family's social network express criticism. This has been found a key factor for fathers (Frey *et al.*, 1989b). Mothers tend to value the amount of assistance provided by the social network more, and are less affected by criticism, particularly where their resistance is bolstered by a positive belief system.

Close friends and family are frequently found important sources of support, but professional sources are of less importance to outcome (e.g. Waisbren, 1980; Minnes *et al.*, 1989). There may be particular effects, however, in these studies, i.e. age (Waisbren – infants) and setting (Minnes – rural families). Parents of institutionalised children will have had more reason to rely on professional contacts, and have been found more positive about professionals' role in their supportive network (Kazak, 1988). Even more so than with family contacts, professionals can generate stress while giving support (Harris and McHale, 1989). For example, they may expect 'parent-involvement' at a time when those parents would like to hand over teaching responsibilities for their child to a trained person (Winton and Turnbull, 1981). The way that services are organised and operate (for instance, lack of coordination, intimidating case conferences) may clearly add to stress even if individual professionals are found supportive (Cunningham and Davis, 1985).

Many studies have emphasised the importance of the *marital relationship* in parental adjustment (e.g. Bristol, 1984; Abbott and Meredith, 1986; McKinney and Peterson, 1987; Bristol *et al.*, 1988; Wallander *et al.*, 1989). Marital satisfaction was not found highly predictive of parental stress by Sloper *et al.* (1988), but was predictive of parents' perceived satisfaction with life, especially for fathers. It was not reported separately in the Frey *et al.* papers, but was found highly predictive of adjustment for both mothers and fathers, in particular showing a negative association for fathers between marital satisfaction and the use of 'avoidance' as a coping strategy (Frey, 1990).

Where studies have included measures of cognitive *coping* style, it has been found highly predictive of parental wellbeing and satisfaction with life. In particular, positive comparative appraisals (such as 'We're blessed that she's physically healthy') and practical coping (such as 'I try to make myself feel better by exercising or something') are positively related, and passive acceptance (such as 'I accept it, since nothing can be done') negatively related (Sloper *et al.*, 1988; Frey *et al.*, 1989b). There is a clear relationship between these types of measures and studies of cognitive appraisals in depression (e.g. Beck, 1976) which then suggest possibly fruitful routes for intervention.

It may be useful here to summarise the risk factors for poor quality of life and stress in families found in one study, that of Sloper *et al.* (1988).

● high behaviour problems in the child
● high excitability in the child
● low child functioning
● high levels of strain from current life events
● marital dissatisfaction

- lack of family cohesion
- lack of active-recreational involvement in the family
- lack of strong moral-religious emphasis in the family
- socio-economic factors of unemployment, lack of a car, inadequate housing
- parental coping strategies – low use of practical coping/high use of passive acceptance in dealing with child-related problems.

Few studies have included in their design the possibility of looking at *change* over time. However, the Sloper and Frey studies do enable us to look at some major influences over a two year interval. In both, measures of parental adjustment to the child have importance. Sloper *et al.* (1988) found that behaviour problems were more likely to decrease when mothers had shown positive adjustment to the child (with the initial level of behaviour problems controlled in the analysis). Frey *et al.* (1989a) also measured fathers' adjustment to the child, and found this factor predictive of greater gains in children's social competence. Fathers' adjustment to the child at year one was also found a significant predictor of mothers' adjustment to the child at year three. These findings reinforce the importance of including fathers in overall intervention strategy. They also emphasise the necessity of further longitudinal studies in order to map the cyclical chain of influence from children's behaviour to parental response to children's adaptation, and so on (McKinney and Peterson, 1987).

A handful of studies have focused on 'successfully coping' families in order to try to learn what strategies might be suggested. For example, Trute and Hauch (1988a, b) interviewed a sample of families selected by clinicians from a much larger population served by a child development centre. The children were of a wide range of severity of disability, and the families of a wide range of incomes. However, only one out of forty was a single-parent family. These families had extended family systems which gave high levels of support in terms of child care, physical assistance, advice and information, and emotional support. The mothers tended in addition to have a network of friendships, that is, a range of women friends who did not necessarily know each other but who provided a social outlet (c.f. Kazak, 1988). Other parents of handicapped children have also been cited as important in the support network of successfully coping families (Bristol, 1984).

Implications

The model of stress and coping presented in this chapter has received considerable research support. Significant risk factors for stress in parents of young disabled children have been identified under all the headings suggested. The clear implication for service providers is that they need to adopt a similarly broad-based framework in conceptualising their role in supporting families. However, this does not simply mean having multiple goals for intervention; the strategy has to take account of the family as an interdependent system, recognising that change in one set of interactions will have effects on all others.

Early identification of behaviour problems, and appropriate and systematic advice to parents on behaviour management is indicated by the research. Sloper *et al.* (1988) point out that several resource factors mediated the perceived stress of behaviour problems, including whether mothers went out to work. Thus, it would be essential for the intervention strategy not to demand intensive involvement of mothers' time in such a way that finding or maintaining employment is made more difficult. Indeed, it may be of considerable indirect benefit to the key problem of behaviour to increase the family's respite care resources through finding an experienced child-minder, through offering behaviour management advice to extended family members or neighbours, or through involving a volunteer in taking the child out at weekends.

The recognition of the importance of major life events in adding to strain implies flexibility in how services are offered to a family. For example, support with child care may need to be more often after a father is made redundant, not less often because he is now at home. What may be less well appreciated by professionals is the parental strain experienced at times of transition for the disabled child. For example, at school-entry many services (such as home-teachers and peripatetic advisers) withdraw their support, and school staff may not easily substitute for their counselling role. School-leaving is generally more traumatic. Parents and other family members need to learn the skills required for future planning, making transitions, and establishing new support networks.

The findings on parents' social networks suggest several implications for intervention. Where parents are relying heavily on a small family network for all kinds of support, it may help to extend the possible sources, for example, by introducing them to a 'link' family who could assist with child care, and potentially with information and emotional support. In addition, parents may benefit from help in developing problem-solving skills with their social network. Since family members are the most likely to offer criticism as well as support, parents may need to learn skills of assertiveness in dealing with inappropriate comments as well as in asking for help. It may be easier to work out strategies and to practise responses in a group with other parents of disabled children (Schilling *et al.*, 1984). Grandparents who seem insensitive to parents or troubled by the child's disability may benefit from direct information from professionals, or from reading literature (e.g. Crutcher, 1988).

The importance of the mother–father relationship to family cohesion and child wellbeing was emphasised in many studies. It is therefore essential for intervention teams not to unbalance the relationship through piling commitments concerning the disabled child on to the mother. The role of fathers in their child's positive development is an important one. Where fathers are prevented from enjoying interaction through problems in understanding their child, support can be given directly to show fathers how to observe their child more closely (perhaps using videotape of interaction) and reinforcing their success in following the child's focus of interest (McConachie, 1986). It is important not simply to see fathers as 'surrogate mothers'; they have potentially a unique role with their disabled child, and this needs individual negotiation with the professional team (Gallagher et al., 1983).

The research findings have emphasised the role of informal support networks, which professionals do not necessarily recognise. Urey and Viar (1990) gave paediatricians and parents questionnaires about mental health support. The two groups gave rather different answers when ranking the most important providers; parents gave the highest overall ranking to other parents of a disabled child, while paediatricians nominated a psychologist or social worker, giving other parents a low ranking. It seems vitally important for professionals to see their role as supporting the family's informal network, and offering additional expertise where it is wanted, not taking over from the family's preferred sources.

Professional services must realise the potential stresses they impose on families. It is not uncommon for a family to have as many as ten 'helping' professionals involved (e.g. physiotherapist, speech therapist, health visitor, neurologist, psychologist, social worker, peripatetic adviser for the visually impaired, etc.) all taking up family time and giving well-intentioned advice about what more the parents (or rather, mother) can do to further the child's development. The need for a key worker or link person, as envisaged in the Warnock Report (DES, 1978), has not diminished. The current findings in research suggest that the role should be more than simply coordinating services; it could encompass a responsibility for negotiating with a family the range of supports they would like and from what source. The literature also reflects a general consensus on the need for training so that every professional becomes a 'family-counsellor', able to respond to the individual problems and strengths of families and understanding the family as a system.

The final area of findings to address is the importance of cognitive coping skills. Once a family's usual coping skills have been identified, professionals can support these, and introduce others. For example, parents may be helped to find benefits that come from an otherwise stressful event or compare themselves to others who are less fortunate (Summers, 1989). Coping self-statements can be modelled by the professional counsellor to counteract negative and self-derogatory thoughts (Roskies and Lazarus, 1980; Schilling et al., 1984). This is not to deny the real problems that parents face, but to recognise the role that perceptions of events can have in mediating stress reactions. One example of this approach being applied to a service for disabled children and their families is described in Kushlick et al. (1984). Professionals need also to organise their services in such a way as to ensure that family members experience being competent and solving problems (not having them solved), feeling in control of events, exercising choice, expressing anger, and so on.

The first requirement for future relationships based on partnership may be that professionals learn to ask family members the right questions. This is perhaps the greatest usefulness of the current research model and preliminary findings. In the wake of PL 99-457, a variety of additional measures are being developed of family strengths (e.g. Trivette et al., 1990) and family needs (e.g. Seligman and Darling, 1989). There remains a problem about too great a reliance on self-report measures. For example, is a parent who expresses no needs in regard to helping their disabled child really better off than a parent who expresses some needs (Sheehan and Sites, 1989)? There is also little guidance at present on how to take into account cultural differences in allowing individuals from outside the family to help (e.g. Smith and Ryan, 1987).

The findings on key factors in parental stress and family functioning form a basis for service planning and priorities. That is not to say that families which are coping successfully, have a supportive social network and a positive outlook should have no services. Rather, they may choose to have relatively little direct involvement at present with the services offered. However, the knowledge of potential risk factors is at least a more rational basis for planning than what currently happens – administrative convenience, and uneven access depending on social status and parental determination (Black, 1980; Baxter, 1989).

Conclusion

Current research literature reflects optimism about the future prospects for partnership between families and professionals. In the USA, the optimism seems to have been generated by the changes in law and the creativity required for their implementation. There are model services described which embody the important facets of family support (e.g. Bailey *et al.*, 1986; Seligman and Darling, 1989). In Britain too, legislation will play a role. The 1989 Government White Paper 'Caring for People' has proposed that case managers will hold a budget for a disabled person to choose services, as consumer rather than recipient, which suggests an opportunity to assess strengths and needs in a broad and interactive framework. The 1986 Disabled Persons Act allowed for assessment of need of disabled individuals and of carers, particularly at the time of transition from school (sections 5/6, implemented in 1990). The aim of whole family support could be built into such assessments, particularly if it is complementary to good practice in the earlier services for children with severe learning difficulties.

The chapter has presented a conceptual model of family stress and coping; the challenge now is for families and professionals to translate its implications into working support strategies.

References

Abbott, D. A. and Meredith, W. H. (1986) Strengths of parents with retarded children, *Family Relations*, 35, 371–5.

Abidin, R. R. (1983) *Parenting Stress Index Manual* Charlottesville, VA, Pediatric Psychology Press.

Bailey, D. B., Simeonsson, R. J., Winton, P. J., Huntington, G. S., Comfort, M., Isbell, P., O'Donnell, K.J. and Helm, J.M. (1986) Family-focused intervention: a functional model for planning, implementing and evaluating individual family services in early intervention, *Journal of the Division for Early Childhood*, 10(2), 156–71.

Baxter, C. (1989) Parental access to assistance from services: social status and age-related differences, *Australia and New Zealand Journal of Developmental Disabilities*, 15(1), 15–25.

Beck, A. T. (1976) *Cognitive Therapy and Emotional Disorders*, New York, International Universities Press.

Beck, A. T. and Beamesdorfer, A. (1974) Assessment of depression: the depression inventory, in P. Pichot (ed.) *Psychological Measurements in Psychopharmacology* 7, 151–69. Basel, Karger.

Beckman, P. J. (1983) Influence of selected child characteristics on stress in families of handicapped infants, *American Journal of Mental Deficiency*, 88, 150–6.

Beilke, R. L. and Friedrich, W. N. (1988) Factor analysis of the QRS-F, unpublished manuscript, University of Washington, Seattle.

Black, D. (1980) 'Inequalities in health'. Report of a research working group, Department of Health and Social Security, London.

Bradshaw, J. and Lawton, D. (1978) Tracing the causes of stress in families with handicapped children, *British Journal of Social Work*, 8(2), 181–92.

Bristol, M. M. (1984) Family resources and successful adaptation to autistic children, in E. Schopler and G. B. Mesibov (eds) *The Effects of Autism on the Family*, pp. 289–310. New York, Plenum Press.

Bristol, M.M., Gallagher, J. J. and Schopler, E. (1988) Mothers and fathers of young developmentally disabled and nondisabled boys: adaptation and spousal support, *Developmental Psychology*, 24(3), 441–51.

Bronfenbrenner, U. (1977) Towards an experimental ecology of human development, *American Psychologist*, 32, 513–31.

Byrne, E. A. and Cunningham, C. C. (1985) The effects of mentally handicapped children on families – a conceptual review, *Journal of Child Psychology and Psychiatry*, 26(6), 847–64.

Crnic, K. A., Friedrich, W. N. and Greenberg, M. T. (1983) Adaptation of families with mentally retarded children: a model of stress, coping and family ecology, *American Journal of Mental Deficiency*, 88(2), 125–38.

Crnic, K. A. and Greenberg, M. T. (1983) *Inventory of Parent Experiences Manual*. University of Washington, Seattle.

Crowne, D. P. and Marlowe, D. (1964) *The Approval Motive*. New York, Wiley.

Crutcher, D. (1988) Parents and grandparents of children with Down syndrome, in C. Tingey (ed.) *Down Syndrome: A Resource Handbook*, pp. 65–75. Boston, College-Hill Press.

Cunningham, C. C. and Davis, H. (1985) *Working with Parents: Frameworks for Collaboration*. Milton Keynes, Open University Press.

Department of Education and Science (1978) *Special educational needs: report of the committee of enquiry into the education of handicapped children and young people*, The Warnock Report, Cmnd 7212. London, HMSO.

Dunst, C. J., Jenkins, V. and Trivette, C. M. (1984) The Family Support Scale: reliability and validity, *Journal of Individual, Family, and Community Wellness*, 1(4), 45–52.

Dunst, C. J., Trivette, C. M. and Cross, A. H. (1986) Mediating influences of social support: personal, family, and child outcomes, *American Journal of Mental Deficiency*, 90(4), 403–17.

Erickson, M. and Upshur, C. C. (1989) Caretaking burden and social support: comparison of mothers of infants with and without disabilities, *American Journal on Mental Retardation*, 94(3), 250–8.

Farber, B. (1959) Effects of a severely mentally retarded child on family integration, *Monographs of the Society for Research in Child Development*, 24(71).

Farber, B. (1960) Family organization and crisis: maintenance of integration in families with a severely mentally retarded child, *Monographs of the Society for Research in Child Development*, 25(75).

Folkman, S. and Lazarus, R. S. (1980) An analysis of coping in a middle-aged community sample, *Journal of Health and Social Behavior*, 21, 219–39.

Folkman, S. and Lazarus, R. S. (1985) If it changes it must be a process. A study of emotion and coping during three stages of a college examination, *Journal of Personality and Social Psychology*, 48, 150–70.

Frey, K. S. (1990) Personal communication, University of Washington.

Frey, K. S., Fewell, R. R. and Vadasy, P. F. (1989a). Parental adjustment and changes in child outcome among families of young handicapped children, *Topics in Early Childhood Special Education*, 8(4), 38–57.

Frey, K. S., Greenberg, M. T. and Fewell, R. R. (1989b) Stress and coping among parents of handicapped children: a multidimensional approach, *American Journal on Mental Retardation*, 94(3), 240–9.

Friedrich, W. N., Greenberg, M. T. and Crnic, K. (1983) A shortform of the Questionnaire on Resources and Stress, *American Journal of Mental Deficiency*, 88(1), 41–8.

Friedrich, W. N., Wilturner, L. T. and Cohen, D. S. (1985) Coping resources and parenting mentally retarded children, *American Journal of Mental Deficiency*, 90(2), 130–9.

Gallagher, J. J., Beckman, P. J. and Cross, A. H. (1983) Families of handicapped children: sources of stress and its amelioration, *Exceptional Children*, 50(1), 10–19.

Hanson, M. J., Lynch, E. W. and Wayman, K. I. (1990) Honoring the cultural diversity of families when gathering data, *Topics in Early Childhood Special Education*, 10(1), 112–31.

Harris, V. S. and McHale, S. M. (1989) Family life problems, daily caregiving activities, and the psychological well-being of mothers of mentally retarded children, *American Journal on Mental Retardation*, 94(3), 231–9.

Healy, A. (1989) The individual, the family and the community – cooperation is the future, *Developmental Medicine and Child Neurology*, 31(5), 567–8.

Kazak, A. E. (1986) Families with physically handicapped children: social ecology and family systems, *Family Process*, 25, 265–81.

Kazak, A. E. (1988) Stress and social networks in families with older institutionalized retarded children, *Journal of Social and Clinical Psychology*, 6(3/4), 448–61.

Kazak, A. E. and Marvin, R. S. (1984) Differences, difficulties and adaptations. Stress and social networks in families with a handicapped child, *Family Relations*, 33, 67–77.

Kushlick, A., Smith, J. and Gold, A. (1985) An intervention package to teach parents of severely retarded and severely noncompliant children and adults at home to teach their child new relevant skills, in B. Daly, S. Kerfoot, A. Sigston and J. Addington (eds) *Portage: The Importance of Parents*, pp. 119–37. Windsor, NFER-Nelson.

Locke, H. and Wallace, K. (1959) Short marital adjustment and prediction tests: their reliability and validity, *Marriage and Family Living*, 21, 251–5.

McConachie, H. (1986) *Parents and Young Mentally Handicapped Children: A Review of Research Issues*. London, Croom Helm.

McConachie, H. (1989) Mothers' and fathers' interaction with their young mentally handicapped children, *International Journal of Behavioral Development*, 12(2), 239–55.

McCubbin, H. I., Larsen, A. S. and Olson, P.H. (1982) F-COPES: Family coping strategies, in D. H. Olson, H. I. McCubbin, H. Barnes, A. Larsen, M. Muxen and M. Wilson (eds) *Family Inventories*, pp. 101–19. St Paul, MN, University of Minnesota.

McCubbin, H. I., McCubbin, M. A., Patterson, J. M., Cauble, A. E., Wilson, L. R. and Warwick, W. (1983) CHIP – Coping Health Inventory for Parents: an assessment of parental coping patterns in the care of the chronically ill child, *Journal of Marriage and the Family*, 45, 359–70.

McCubbin, H. I. and Patterson, J. M. (1981) *Systematic Assessment of Family Stress, Resources, and Coping*. St Paul, MN, Family Stress and Coping Project, University of Minnesota.

McKinney, B. and Peterson, R. A. (1987) Predictors of stress in parents of developmentally disabled children, *Journal of Pediatric Psychology*, 12(1), 133–50.

Mink, I. T., Nihira, K. and Meyers, C. E. (1983) Taxonomy of family life styles: 1. Homes with TMR children, *American Journal of Mental Deficiency*, 87(5), 484–97.

Minnes, P. M. (1988a) Family stress associated with a developmentally handicapped child, *International Review of Research in Mental Retardation*, 15, 195–226.

Minnes, P. M. (1988b) Family resources and stress associated with having a mentally retarded child, *American Journal on Mental Retardation*, 93(2), 184–92.

Minnes, P. M., McShane, J., Forkes, S., Green, S., Clement, B. and Card, L. (1989) Coping resources of parents of developmentally handicapped children living in rural communities, *Australia and New Zealand Journal of Developmental Disabilities*, 15(2), 109–18.

Moos, R. H. and Moos, B. C. (1981) *Family Environment Scale Manual*. Palo Alto, California, Consulting Psychologists Press.

Pearlin, L. I., Lieberman, M. A., Menaghan, E. G. and Mullan, J. T. (1981) The stress process, *Journal of Health and Social Behavior*, 22, 337–56.

Roskies, E. and Lazarus, R.S. (1980) Coping theory and the teaching of coping skills, in P.O. Davidson and S.M. Davidson (eds) *Behavioral Medicine: Changing Health Lifestyles*, pp. 38–69. New York, Brunner/Mazel.

Rutter, M., Tizard, J. and Whitmore, K. (1970) *Education, Health and Behaviour*. London, Longman.

Schilling, R.F., Gilchrist, L.D. and Schinke, S.P. (1984) Coping and social support in families of developmentally disabled children, *Family Relations*, 33, 47–54.

Schwartz, C.G. (1970) Strategies and tactics of parents of mentally handicapped children, in N.R. Bernstein (ed.) *Diminished People*, pp. 73–105. Boston, Little, Brown and Co.

Seligman, M. and Darling, R.B. (1989) *Ordinary Families, Special Children*. New York, Guilford Press.

Sheehan, R. and Sites, J. (1989) Implications of PL 99-457 for assessment, *Topics in Early Childhood Special Education*, 8(4), 103–15.

Skinner, H.A., Steinhauer, P.D. and Santa-Barbara, J. (1983) The Family Assessment Measure, *Canadian Journal of Community Mental Health*, 2(2), 91–105.

Sloper, P., Cunningham, C.C., Knussen, C. and Turner, S. (1988) A study of the process of adaptation in a cohort of children with Down's syndrome and their families. Final report to the Department of Health and Social Security, Manchester University, Hester Adrian Research Centre.

Sloper, P., Turner, S., Knussen, C. and Cunningham, C. (1990) Social life of school children with Down's syndrome, *Child: care, health and development*, 16(4), 211–18.

Smith, M.J. and Ryan, A.S. (1987) Chinese-American families of children with developmental disabilities: an explanatory study of reactions to service providers, *Mental Retardation*, 25, 345–50.

Spanier, G. (1976) Measuring dyadic adjustment: scale for assessing the quality of marriage and other dyads, *Journal of Marriage and the Family*, 38, 15–28.

Stoneman, Z. and Crapps, J.M. (1988) Correlates of stress, perceived competence and depression among family care providers, *American Journal on Mental Retardation*, 93(2), 166–73.

Summers, J.A. (1989) Personal communication, Beach Center, University of Kansas.

Thomas, A.P., Bax, M.C.O. and Smyth, D.P.L. (1989) *The Health and Social Needs of Young Adults with Physical Disabilities*. Clinics in Developmental Medicine, No. 106. London, Mac Keith Press.

Tizard, J. and Grad, J.G. (1961) *The Mentally Handicapped and their Families*, Maudsley Monographs, 7. London, Oxford University Press.

Trivette, C., Dunst, C.J., Deal, A.G., Hamer, A.W. and Propst, S. (1990) Assessing family strengths and family functioning style, *Topics in Early Childhood Special Education*, 10(1), 16–35.

Trute, B. and Hauch, C. (1988a) Social network attributes of families with positive adaptation to the birth of a developmentally disabled child, *Canadian Journal of Community Mental Health*, 7(1), 5–16.

Trute, B. and Hauch, C. (1988b) Building on family strength: a study of families with positive adjustment to the birth of a developmentally disabled child, *Journal of Marital and Family Therapy*, 14(2), 185–93.

Turnbull, A.P. (1988) The challenge of providing comprehensive support to families, *Education and Training in Mental Retardation*, 23, 261–72.

Urey, J. R. and Viar, V. (1990) Use of mental health and support services among families of children with disabilities: discrepant views of parents and paediatricians, *Mental Handicap Research*, 3(1), 81–8.

Waisbren, S. E. (1980) Parents' reaction after the birth of a developmentally disabled child, *American Journal of Mental Deficiency*, 84(4), 345–51.

Wallander, J. L., Varni, J. W., Babani, L., DeHaan, C. B., Wilcox, K. T. and Bannis, H. T. (1989) The social environment and the adaptation of mothers of physically handicapped children, *Journal of Pediatric Psychology*, 14(3), 371–88.

Winton, P. J. and Turnbull, A. P. (1981) Parent involvement as viewed by parents of preschool handicapped children, *Topics in Early Childhood Special Education*, 1(3), 11–19.

CHAPTER 7

What Future for Voluntary Organisations?

Philippa Russell

What is the voluntary sector?

[The Voluntary Sector] should cooperate closely with the State Services, perhaps even carrying out specialised work under agency arrangements . . . but whatever the decision made, it must be taken in the full knowledge of the needs to be met and bearing in mind that it is always the historic role of the charity to pioneer and take risks . . . [it] has greater flexibility, ability to set new standards or to undertake new work without seeking fresh statutory powers . . . to make additional or special provision for people suffering from certain types of disadvantage or disabilities . . . to work *outwards* from the individual in need to help the services he needs rather than the reverse process of discovering an individual and providing a service. (The Nathan Committee, 1950).

Although written forty years ago, the Nathan Report accurately anticipates the new contract culture of the 1990s, with voluntary agencies increasingly moving to service provision within the context of the Children Act 1989 and the new community care arrangements. But the notion of a voluntary organisation solely as another contractor in an increasingly pluralist society – almost as the respectable end of the growing private sector – would be unnecessarily limited.

The Nathan Report was the first major review of voluntary organisations to acknowledge the major changes which were sweeping through them in mid-twentieth century. Historically many of the great voluntary organisations were built upon Victorian philanthropism, usually providing for children or people with disabilities in larger institutional settings. Patrons contributed financially but rarely became directly involved with the people they were trying to help. Money was raised by active fund-raising, which in turn depended upon often negative images of the disadvantaged and 'needy' people requiring help. Thomas Coram found that one of the most effective ways of raising money for his Bloomsbury Foundation was to invite the wealthy ladies of London to tour the buildings and watch the children at their Sunday lunch! The large long-stay mental handicap hospitals like Redhill and St. Lawrences were also charitable bodies in their day – eventually handed over to the new NHS in the late 1940s. Picnics and guided tours were also common, with no particular thought to the feelings of the residents beyond the fact that their cleanliness and general care were sufficiently good to attract contributions.

But, as the Nathan Report anticipated, from the 1950s the role and image of the voluntary sector began to change. Whilst the emphasis remained on innovative work and 'good practice', the payment of fees by local and health authorities for direct care for their clients, together with greater professionalism, meant that the voluntary sector was in effect becoming a major service provider. Increasingly it was also working on jointly planned and often joint financed initiatives in local communities.

The Oxford English Dictionary describes a voluntary organisation as 'maintained or supported solely or largely by free will offerings and free from state interference and control'. However, this has become increasingly untrue in the special needs fields, where many voluntary agencies have major injections of funding from local and central government – and where indeed the client group (for example children in special schools run by voluntary bodies) may actually be wholly funded by their local authorities. Indeed, as the joint report from the National Council of Social Services and Personal Social Services Council (Unell, 1979) clearly shows, Victorian-style philanthropism has been in continuing decline as a source of finance for voluntary activity, and fees for professional services form the major part of annual income. Even the new free sources of money (such as funds raised through Telethon and Children in Need) tend to be spent on voluntary agency activities which are already at least part funded through statutory sources – and often with service users directly funded through their local authorities. The growth of fees and funding from local or health authorities has inevitably coloured some of the developments of the voluntary sector – and will continue to influence them over the next decade. For a start, fees imply some mutual and *shared* accountability which could affect the ability of the organisation to be innovative and take risks. Second the acceptance of fees presumes a reliable and regular service – which to function adequately must be fully utilised. Many voluntary organisations are also into the unhappy business of marketing their services and to some extent being market-driven in the care they offer.

But voluntary organisations are not all large. Many are small and informal self-help and mutual support groups. As the Wolfenden Committee, looking at the voluntary sector in the late 1970s noted, the diversity was so great that one could identify a veritable Noah's ark of voluntary organisations 'ranging from the Killer Whale to the Termite Ant, from the Benares Tiger to the humble Doremouse' (Wolfenden Committee, 1978).

In general families with children of disability or special needs have used four different systems of care:

(1)   Informal *social* caring, the 'gift relationship' described by Titmuss in which families, friends and the wider community provide informal networks of support. The notion of informal care and support is written into the government's White Paper 'Caring for People'. But neighbours, volunteers and extended family and friends may need extra additional support to cope with disability – or indeed to fully understand the needs of families as carers. Some parents and carers also fear the vulnerability of children to volunteers who may recieve little preparation or training and are often short-term.

(2)   The *commercial system*, by which clients purchase direct services. The community care arrangements presuppose that more families will be charged for services – despite evidence in the OPCS Reports (1989) that families with a disabled member are adversely financially affected by caring at home. In the USA the private care system is well established – and there is a corresponding growth of *private* health, social care and education systems in the UK.

(3)   The *statutory* sector, which traditionally provided a universal service but which is increasingly adopting a 'purchaser, provider role' with the new arrangements for case management and community care. Local management of schools seems likely to similarly reduce the overall strategic influence and direct resourcing of the LEA and to see much more local accountability for the actual use of services.

(4)   The *voluntary* sector, which in fact complements, supplements and influences the other systems. Historically all our services in the UK, educational, social and health provision, have emerged from voluntary initiatives and campaigns for better provision. Many voluntary organisations still provide both an analytical and a campaigning role in pursuing better services for vulnerable people. But the potential conflict between direct service provision and pressure group activities (which may offend the purchasing authorities) should not be minimised during the coming decade. Similarly many voluntary organisations are very small local groups which provide a highly individual support network to a group of local people. Many small groups are affiliated to large organisations (for example Contact a Family and MENCAP) and it is increasingly common to find parents – and people with disabilities – belonging to a number of different voluntary organisations for different needs

Family support: working with parents of children with special needs

The 1970s and 1980s saw the emergence of a strong professional commitment to working in families – and an acknowledgement of the emotional as well as practical needs of families with a child with a disability or special needs. The 'self help' movement began with the development and expansion of the local groups of national organisations like MENCAP, the National Deaf Children's Society and the Spastics Society and has since proliferated in diverse settings, with some smaller voluntary organisations and self-help groups working closely with professional services and attaching themselves to child development centres, schools or playgroups. The concept of 'self-help' and mutual support is a seductive one for service providers and planners. The White Paper on Community Care, 'Caring for People' advocated greater investment by local authorities in voluntary organisations which could provide presentation, counselling and personal support networks, acknowledging that such services do not work without financial and professional support.

But there is growing evidence that 'self-help' and the voluntary sector cannot provide a total service for many families. Enabling parents to become more competent may indeed reduce the need for other services. But the voluntary sector cannot exist in a vacuum and should be seen as part of a network of provision. Spontaneity is important, but so is the enabler – MENCAP groups have always worked through support from regional and national offices. Contact a Family operates from a local basis but has national direction and support – from trained staff if necessary. However, the 1990s seem likely to see a rapid increase in voluntary organisations who work *with* statutory agencies and see themselves as part of a 'mixed economy' of care. The Children Act 1989 formally acknowledges this emerging and complementary role of family support, requiring local authorities not only to publicise the availability of support through voluntary organisations under the Schedule Two duties for 'children in need', but also to consider using such services as part of their new 'purchaser' rather than 'provider' role. Many of the larger voluntary organisations, like Barnardos, already provide specialist and professional services, including family centres, foster-care and respite care schemes and school-leaving programmes. But marrying these new *professional* roles with those of the burgeoning small-scale informal support groups may require some radical new thinking in local authorities (where the role of the voluntary sector in 'minimising the impact of their disability on children' (Children Act) is likely to be significant). Parent groups and voluntary organisations are likely to have the most accurate information on local needs – and in meeting individual needs will require real opportunities to feed this knowledge into the planning system. The proposed independent inspection units under the Community Care arrangements seem likely to include members of the voluntary sector. Involving the voluntary organisations in quality assurance procedures is not new. Community Health Councils have offered this opportunity for nearly a decade. But *inspecting* services and managing complaints procedures will also necessitate the voluntary sector looking at itself and being willing to change and respond to new needs.

One of the challenges for both voluntary and statutory organisations is balancing the new and positive attitudes of parents towards an 'ordinary life' for them as families and their children – and for much greater integration into mainstream services – with the counterbalance that many families encounter real problems which, if unmet, will achieve the opposite to the desired integration and actually lead to pressure for a return to more traditional services.

In looking at the role of the voluntary sector in providing such family support, it is important to ask what sort of lives families with children with special needs are leading in the 1990s.

The background to living with disability: family dynamics and special needs

It has been estimated (Office of Population and Census Surveys, 1989) that there are about 360,000 children with disabilities living in the UK. The vast majority (355,000) live with natural or foster parents in their local community. The same survey tells us that many families are unaware of the sources of help available to them, that 38 per cent of families had never belonged to a voluntary organisation (and did not know they existed). Only 27 per cent of parents knew that respite care existed – and only 4 per cent actually used it. The most common professionals cited by parents as being 'most often seen' were GPs, hospital doctors and consultants, followed by teachers and health visitors. Despite the significance of the new Children Act and the community care arrangements, only 12 per cent of parents of children living at home saw a social worker regularly. One third of those children who were living in 'communal' (i.e residential) establishments were there because parents or foster families found their health or behaviour problems too difficult to cope with – and, presumably, because inadequate support at home was available. The families had generally lower incomes than their equivalents in the community and single parents were likely to rely wholly on state benefits. Although the OPCS figures make gloomy reading, they also indicate the importance of information and of communication with parents. Practical parenting means receiving financial allowances, knowing about voluntary organisations, using respite care – it also means taking power and acting confidently in asking for help. This chapter considers a number of crucial needs for families and how parents may be best encouraged to use available services.

The birth of *any* child can be a traumatic as well as a happy event for the parents concerned. Parenthood brings alarming new responsibilities, as well as pleasures. When a new baby has a disability, the initial diagnosis may be devastating for the parents. Recent research by Cunningham and Davis (1985) and others clearly shows us how important it is to recognise the impact of disability on parental expectations and self-image. But, as Hewett noted in 1970, 'the general tendency to characterise parents of handicapped children as guilt-ridden anxiety-laden... over-protective and rejecting beings is unfair. They are, rather, vulnerable families faced with a major challenge for which they require support as well as counselling, and respect rather than any global assumptions about 'pathological abnormality'. Many disabled children require high levels of *practical* support in their day-to-day lives. A study by Glendinning (1983) found that 50.1 per cent of the 361 severely disabled children in her survey could not be left alone, unsupervised for more than ten minutes at a time in any one day. Wilkin (1979) and Baldwin (1987) have emphasised the burdens placed upon *mothers*, with little support from neighbours or other relatives.

Cooke and Bradshaw (1986) found that disabled children in a study of families using the Family Fund were *more* likely than other children to experience at least one spell in a one-parent family. These spells were longer than for families with non-disabled children and those families with the more severely disabled children were less likely to be reconstituted into new marriages or relationships. It is obvious that physical restrictions of care will limit families' social networks. But the Cooke and Bradshaw research indicates the importance of looking at the *family* networks and structures and individual needs when there is a disabled child, and at the implications for care and support within that family. Wolkind (1981) and others have shown the high incidence of depression and low self-esteem amongst all young parents in disadvantaged inner-city areas. The social context of disability is therefore of crucial importance in determining whether positive approaches to parent support will be effective for both family and child. Supporting disabled children and their families will require a range of services. However, ensuring that services are effective, fully used and sensitive to consumer needs requires constant review and assimilation by professionals, carers and managers. The significance of recent research for the development of good quality community services is often not appreciated or considered in setting priorities for the future. Such priorities for support must include access to services in statutory *and* voluntary agencies: respite day care and financial advice to reduce the additional costs of disability in the family.

In terms of overall family support, the voluntary sector seems likely to extend and augment its role into the 1990s. Organisations like MENCAP, AFASIC, the Spastics Society and the Royal National Institute for the Blind can provide information, advocacy, counselling – and ensure that family needs are fed into local and central government thinking. An evaluation of parent members of Contact a Family (Hatch and Hinton, 1987) found that parent members were more effective users of statutory services, were less isolated and had more positive expectations of their child – and, as one mother commented succinctly,

> we learned to be assertive, not aggressive; hopeful not depres-
> sed ... and we have learned that 'empowerment' means a *group*
> process when people like us gain greater control over those resources
> and people who affect our lives and develop a real partnership by so
> doing. But it takes a voluntary organisation to help us achieve this
> goal!

Special educational needs: partnership with parents and the voluntary sector

The voluntary sector has played a central role in shaping policy and in making provision for children with specific disabilities or special educational needs. The Warnock Committee and the subsequent 1981 Education Act owe much to persistent lobbies from the voluntary sector for equal opportunities in education and for a greater integration of parents into assessment and provision for special needs. Indeed the 1981 Education Act gives a legal role to voluntary organisations as sources of advice and support for parents of children with special needs. Circular 22/89 on Assessment and Statementing reminds LEAs of the unique contribution of the voluntary sector as providers of educational advice and as advocates during assessment. Section 10 of the same Act requires health authorities who identify a child with potential special educational needs not only to inform the LEA but to tell parents of the name of the voluntary organisation if they feel it would be appropriate. However, as Goacher et al. (1988) noted in the report of the DES funded review of the implementation of the 1981 Act, government endorsement of the contribution of the voluntary sector has not been equitably implemented in practice. This research study by the Institute of Education, London University found that only 17 per cent of authorities had regular planning meetings with voluntary organisations about policy and practice for special educational needs. Only 11 per cent involved the voluntary sector in training for special educational needs. And many voluntary organisations were being involved too late in disagreements about assessment decisions, when their negotiating skills and independent status could have secured more balanced discussion at an earlier stage.

But, despite problems in renegotiating the relationships between professionals and parents following the implementation of the 1981 Education Act, there have been some significant developments in working together. As Peter Mittler noted, in 'Guidelines for Partnership' prepared for the International League of Societies for People with Mental Handicap (World Rehabilitation Fund, 1989),

> Growth and learning in children can only be understood in relation to the various environments in which the child is living. These include the family, peers, schools, the local community and wider society. The study of child development calls for an examination of ways in which the child interacts with, affects and learns from these environmental influences. We can neither study nor teach the child in isolation. (Mittler, 1987)

Peter Mittler sees partnership as mutual accountability between parents and professionals – but he also rightly acknowledges the diversity of relationships and the need to avoid a single recipe approach. He envisaged 'an infinite range of particular forms of working relationships depending on the context within which the work is undertaken and how the family lives'. He also identified the key factor in positive partnerships as 'mutual respect of the different qualities and skills which both sides bring to the partnership relationship' (Mittler, 1989).

Perhaps the most positive area for 'partnership' with parents and the voluntary sector to show itself in action – and where such partnership arrangements seem likely to be a major feature in subsequent service development – is in the field of early years education.

Historically there has been no single service for young children under five with or without special needs in the UK. Indeed, as Wolfendale noted,

> Pre-school provision in the United Kingdom has evolved in a quite distinctive way and is currently characterised by a plethora of types of provision with an array of different service providers comprising the statutory services and the voluntary sector. (Wolfendale, 1989)

The pre-school playgroup movement is the largest provider for this age group, with growing numbers of playgroups or opportunity groups accepting children with a range of special needs. Although some LEAs have seen the provision of nursery placements for the majority of their under-fives population as a major priority, others have provided little, with the majority of children using voluntary provision (and a lesser number, day care through social services). With the demographic changes in the population forecast for the 1990s and the expected large-scale demand for all young women to enter the work-place, future trends seem likely to link early education with an extended day or day care (often provided through the voluntary sector) or for combinations of voluntary and private day-care through work-place crèches and community nurseries. The position within these very diverse settings for young children with special needs remains problematic – and one early indicator is that statutory services will have to diversify their own patterns of working and providing an outreach advisory service if they are to fulfill the legal requirements of both the 1981 Education Act and the 1989 Children Act to identify children who are likely to have special needs.

Some early education programmes (particularly in the voluntary sector) have centred upon compensatory education and early stimulation – many modelling themselves upon the USA 'Highscope' or 'Headstart' programmes (also run by voluntary organisations). Literature on early intervention programmes where the child's developmental delay appears to be induced or directly affected by socio-economic factors within the family or local community does not entirely clarify whether the positive outcomes observed are directly related to improving the child's long-term educational performance or to improving the parents' competence and self-confidence. But research by Sylva (1986), Woodhead (1985) and Kegan *et al.* (1987) has clearly shown the significance of realistic goal setting in terms of reinforcing children's competence and sense of self-worth and the parents' positive expectations of their children. As many children with special educational needs come from socially disadvantaged backgrounds (with the 1989 Reports from the Office of Population and Census Surveys clearly indicating the connections between poverty and disability in a family member), the capacity of the *voluntary* sector to work on many levels – including home visiting and family support as well as through direct provision – is likely to be a significant resource during the changing circumstances of the 1990s.

As noted above, the major provider of early education and social experience for children under five is the *playgroup* movement. Indeed many children combine experience in a nursery class or school with a playgroup placement and a number of playgroups now receive additional support and guidance from the LEA. In terms of children with SEN, a growing number of LEAs are now funding placements in playgroups and opportunity groups and giving such groups access to the educational psychological service and other specialist facilities within the LEA. Needless to say a playgroup also has much to share in terms of a child's social and educational development with the nursery provision or reception class to which that child subsequently moves.

At a time when there is growing emphasis from central government upon partnerships between the local and health authorities and the voluntary section, it is worth noting that such partnerships can and do work. A successful example of a specialist resource working with the *wider* community is the Blythe School Integrated Playgroup (Carpenter, 1988). The playgroup is for children with and without SEN and provides an under-fives educational experience for children in an area where there is no alternative nursery provision. The playgroup is based within a school for children with severe learning difficulties and the advantages of such an arrangement have been:

(1)   That children with special needs can receive an integrated mainstream placement.

(2)   That such a placement follows John Fish (1989) in advocating integration as 'planned interaction' and 'a process not a state'. Many parents of children with severe learning difficulties or complex physical difficulties are afraid that integration without coherent planning and resources might be a token exercise and actually deny the child specialist services. The Blythe Playgroup has access to the expertise and resources of a special school and its support services.

(3)   That the children with special needs and their families have a real opportunity to meet and work with children with a range of abilities. The integration therefore not only fulfils individual needs, but provides a wider community awareness about disability.

(4)   That the programmes offered in the playgroup are helpful to planning subsequent entry to primary or special school for all participants. The Blythe School has successfully developed curriculum plans which take account of the National Curriculum for children with severe learning difficulties and some children follow part of this curriculum in neighbouring primary schools with appropriate support.

(5)   That many young children have learning or developmental difficulties, health or behaviour problems that need early and effective intervention. These children have gained from access to the special resources of Blythe School and their parents have also gained from the well developed shared assessment and record keeping which is a characteristic of the 'special' education sector of the present time.

(6) The collaboration between a statutory and a voluntary agency in the same building can work – and is viewed positively by the local community.

Planning partnerships of this nature will be crucial in view of the shortfall of nursery education in mainstream and special schools within many LEAs. In these circumstances partnerships between the voluntary and statutory services create better integrated services and make the best use of scarce resources.

Nationally there is growing evidence of consortia arrangements between the voluntary sector and statutory services in the provision of early educational experience. However, there is also growing evidence that such 'partnership' arrangements are ineffective unless there are mutually agreed referral policies and LEAs are able to allocate teaching, advisory and psychological services to where children with special needs are placed – whether in a local authority or voluntary setting. But despite a growing commitment at professional and management levels towards coordinated services, there appear to be many barriers to improving practice. The House of Commons Select Committee on the Education of the Under Fives (1989) noted that 'there is no evidence on a national scale of the high degree of cooperation necessary to achieve the best use of existing resources . . . or a clear collective view of the shape of the desired comprehensive service for the under-fives'. Evidence to the same committee by the Association of County Councils found that about 33 per cent of their members had some form of central co-ordinating mechanism, a joint arrangement between social services and education, whether it be a subcommittee, advisory, consultative or coordinating group or working party'. The ACC did not refer to either child health or the voluntary sector, a fact underlined by the National Children's Bureau's Report on working together, which found coordination between all stakeholders to be reflected in joint management of under-fives services in only about 15 per cent of cases. The Fish Committee (1985) similarly found a low incidence of joint management of under-fives provision, but noted the success of those services which did reflect a genuine input from all relevant agencies – and from the voluntary sector in particular.

Perhaps the future of the voluntary agencies as joint managers and participants in integrated services for young children is best illustrated by the success of home based early education programmes like Portage. Although Portage is primarily run through the education service (with some 300 schemes drawing upon special monies through the Education Support Grants – which will end in 1991), the voluntary sector has itself run some schemes and developed others in partnership with statutory agencies.

Robert Cameron (1989) reviewing 'teaching parents to teach children', has noted the importance of acknowledging that parents have *three* specific educational roles when a child has a disability or special educational need. First parents need to understand how to teach a child everyday skills. Second they need help in managing difficult or disruptive behaviour which the child may acquire. Third parents can work co-operatively with teachers in reinforcing and developing educational programmes. Since the mid-1970s, the Portage home teaching model has become increasingly popular and it has been estimated (Cameron, 1989) that there are now over 300 schemes in the UK. Portage is characterised by focusing upon helping parents to teach children with special needs within their own homes.

The strength of Portage and other home based learning programmes is that they:

(1) Involve the strengths and knowledge which parents already hold;
(2) Involve a trained home visitor who is able to link back to a wider network of professionals;
(3) Provide an essentially private service, inasmuch as it can take place in a venue chosen by the parents;
(4) Enable parents to select their own priorities not only in terms of cognitive development but in seeking practical solutions for difficult behaviour;
(5) Matches the actual level of parental involvement to individual family dynamics. Home based learning programmes such as Portage can be combined with other forms of pre-school provision such as nursery classes, day care arrangements etc.

Many voluntary organisations already provide early education and intervention programmes, usually part-funded through LEAs. With the ending of the Educational Support Grant special funding for Portage Schemes (which resulted in some 300 being initiated over a three year period), it is interesting (and potentially worrying) to speculate that the voluntary sector may yet again find itself compensating for a service that has disappeared. Although many voluntary organisations like SENSE (through their Ealing and Birmingham Centres for young deaf/blind children) and KIDS (through Portage programmes attached to their family centres) already operate home-based learning programmes, it is unlikely that the voluntary sector as a whole could fund and manage all the current Portage projects – and the developments planned for expansion of services in those already operating.

One of the major successes of a good Portage scheme is that it permits information to travel between parents and professionals and provides a detailed data base on a child which can be utilised by subsequent service providers. Portage additionally provides a 'key worker' approach in offering support to parents through a familiar individual and in facilitating transfer of information between parents and a range of professionals, using an individualised teaching programme which is based upon a realistic assessment of the child's existing skills and providing positive monitoring and recording procedures. Its future expansion and consolidation, however, seems likely to depend either on voluntary agencies taking the lead for the development of future schemes – or in partnership arrangements between LEAs and the voluntary sector which ensure that Portage is seen as an integral part of any package of any early learning service for children who may have special educational needs.

The partnerships which have been emerging in the pre-school sector are now beginning to develop between schools and parents of older children. In the USA, the effectiveness of Public Law 94:142 (the equivalent of the UK's 1981 Education Act) has to a considerable extent been attributed to the contributions of parent and voluntary organisations. The parent coalitions and the parent counsellors (directly funded by federal money) have enabled parents to have a collective as well as an individual voice in the development of special education systems. Equally importantly, parents have been assured of the availability of a 'named person' during assessment – a concept of parent advocacy developed in the DES Warnock Report (1978) and endorsed by the Fish Committee (1985) but seldom implemented in practice. Although there has been a long tradition of health authorities and social services departments using joint finance money (often in partnership with a voluntary organisation) to support parent-led activities, there has been little similar allocation of resources by LEAs. However, the Voluntary Council for Handicapped Children, one year on in a three year DES funded project to look at and promote more effective partnership with parents and special educational provision, has identified some encouraging pointers for the future. More LEAs are now actively working with parents and the voluntary sector in planning 'whole authority' policies and in looking for ways of providing information, counselling and support in assessment. In South Wales, three education departments have collaborated with the Spastics Society, MENCAP in Wales and Wales Council for the Disabled in order to establish SNAP (the Special Needs Advisory Project). This Project has recruited, trained and supported a panel of volunteer advisers who can act as the Warnock 'named person' with parents whose children have been identified as having a special educational need. The evaluation of the project has clearly demonstrated the effectiveness of using trained volunteers as parent advisers and advocates – and the importance of acknowledging the emotional and personal stress surrounding assessment for many families. The ILEA/Elfrida Rathbone Parent Advocacy Project in Camden in north London shows similar increase in parent satisfaction, when the local authority funded an independent parent adviser, based within a local voluntary organisation, to work with parents who have experienced difficulties during assessment.

An evaluation of a parent adviser scheme at the London Hospital (Cunningham and Davis, 1985) has indicated that many of the most vulnerable parents – particularly those from minority ethnic groups or socially disadvantaged backgrounds – benefit from sensitive counselling and listening – even without explicit professional advice. In effect 'empowerment' and 'partnership', however defined, are unlikely to be effective without time, continuity and an awareness of the multi-faceted nature of family life, where special needs may be only one of a cluster of problems affecting parents at any one time. A 'parent to parent' scheme run by KIDS in north London similarly found an overwhelming need for friendship and emotional support before a parent was asked to take an active role in any programme.

Representation and advocacy do not, however, necessarily come cheap.

The commitment to independent representation and advocacy through the voluntary sector in both Circular 22/89 on Assessment and Statements under the 1981 Act and in the White Paper on Community Care, *Caring for People*, is not accompanied by a clear recommendation to statutory agencies to fund such initiatives. Indeed Sections 1–3 of the Disabled Persons Act 1986, which would require local authorities to provide representation and advocacy to disabled people during assessment, have never been implemented because of the resource consequences.

Funding for increasingly complex services in the voluntary sector is likely to become problematic in the 1990s, as the voluntary sector itself not only becomes more service-oriented (with priorities in some organisations therefore primarily directed to their fee-paying 'customers') but also because there is likely to be an escalation of demand not only for local authority money (already adversely affected in some areas by community charge capping) but also by changes in the statutory services themselves. The NHS reviews, particularly where hospitals and units opt for independent trust status, may have a serious adverse affect on voluntary organisations who have often had strong links with child development teams and other community services (and sometimes operated from NHS premises). In the new market-conscious economy of the health service, such support may be hard to find.

Equally the overall strategic role and budget of the LEA will be affected in those authorities where a number of secondary schools have opted out, and by the individual decisions of governing bodies with regard to priorities for local management of schools. It remains to be seen if parents will press in larger numbers for statements (which will hopefully offer financial resources) but will find in practice that many LEAs are reluctant or unable to increase their statementing numbers because of lack of centrally held resources. But the outlook may not be all negative. The voluntary sector has always been flexible and adaptable. Sources of 'new' money which are completely independent – seem to be increasing annually through media events like Telethon and Children in Need. Equally voluntary organisations may themselves be found to be cost-effective in maximising customer use of services, in avoiding appeals and wasteful confrontations, and in becoming part of the planning and monitoring systems for the new arrangements and attract financial support to achieve these goals.

What is clear is that parents and voluntary organisations need training, not only by themselves but with the wider network of agencies within which they will be operating in the future.

A pilot course run by the Voluntary Council for Handicapped Children, the ILEA and Parents in Partnership on 'partnership in assessment' for teachers, parents and administrators in the London boroughs found that training *together* could produce radical changes in attitudes simply by offering the opportunities for all parties in assessment to understand each others perceptions. The teachers and administrators found themselves shocked and surprised by some of the parents' feelings and experiences. Parents found that mutual support produced confidence – and that they themselves made better use of the assessment process through understanding the rational for the procedures relating to assessment – and sharing in some of the resource dilemmas of the administrators. Most importantly joint training offered parents the opportunity to become trainers – not only of other parents but of professionals and their local communities, and to directly influence the organisation and future shape of special educational provision in their localities.

It also seems likely that in terms of special educational needs, we shall see our own versions of the USA 'parent coalitions', which are not disability-specific and take a holistic approach to special needs. Parents in Partnership, Network 81, Contact a Family and KIDS are examples of the new non-denominational approach (which works with the existing major national voluntary bodies but which provide a network of support for all parents with special needs in the school system). At present such groupings tend not to include parents of children with emotional and behavioural difficulties – perhaps that is the challenge for the 1990s in terms of developing community and family support networks.

The voluntary sector in the 1990s

The Chinese symbol for 'danger' also signifies 'opportunity' – an appropriate talisman for the 1990s, when we are likely to see the best of intentions at times contradicted and threatened by problems in resourcing; conflicts in partnership between key agencies and a plethora of new legislation with its attendant reviews and turbulence in all services for people with disability. 1992 will also see the advent of a more clearly defined European identity – and we will have the chance to draw upon the best of practices as well as needing to reject some of the more paternalistic attitudes to special education from some of our EEC neighbours.

It is not inappropriate to think of Europe, because television programmes of children with physical and developmental disabilities in Romania are sharply contrasted to the highly coordinated and effective programmes of the Peto Institute in Budapest. And in both instances, it is the voluntary sector which is taking the major initiative in seeking better lives for children with disabilities.

The next decade will see major changes in the way in which human services are provided in the UK. The National Curriculum, the impact of local management of schools, the Children Act and the new community care arrangements all signify major challenges for children with disabilities and their families. But none of these changes need be negative. High resourcing levels produced the large institutions we are now anxious to close. The concept of 'empowerment' of parents and children and young people is beginning to bite. Empowerment goes further than partnership. It is a group process where people who have lacked equal access to resources gain greater control over those resources which affect their lives and acquire the skills to not only participate in but also to be directive over services and life-styles. The 1981 Act – bureaucratic as some of its procedures have been – has moved us down the road of acknowledging that parents have an expert role to play in the development of their own child. The Children Act (1989) emphasises the need to listen to children – and gives children greater powers in participating in decision-making about their own lives. Children may even seek orders from the Courts to secure services they need – and they may refuse examinations or treatments which they feel is inappropriate. The new community care arrangements fully acknowledge the voluntary sector – and the consumer – as integral components in any successful local service for people with disabilities. The voluntary sector has always lived with change. It has taken risks; it has expected high standards; above all else it has espoused empowerment – and perhaps the major challenge for next century will be to acknowledge the international potential of voluntary organisations not only in working together within a supposedly united Europe but in sharing several centuries of experience, triumphs – and some failures – with a new voluntary movement over the next decade.

References

Baldwin, S. (1987) *The Cost of Caring*. London, Routledge & Kegan Paul.

Brimblecombe, F. and Russell, P. (1987) *Honeylands: Developing a Service for Families with Handicapped Children*. National Children's Bureau.

Cameron, R. (1989) Teaching parents to teach children: the Portage approach to special needs, in N. Jones (ed.) *Special Educational Needs Review*, vol 1, London, Falmer Press.

Carpenter, B. (1988) Integration: The Coleshill experience, *British Journal of Special Education*, 3, September.

Cook, K. and Bradshaw, J. (1986) Child Disablement and Family Disolution and Reconstitution, *Development Medicine and Child Neurology*, 28, 610–16.

Cunningham, C. and Davis, H. (1985) *Working with Parents: Patterns for Collaboration*. Milton Keynes, Open University Press.

DES (1978) *Special Educational Needs* (Report of Warnock Committee), London, HMSO.

DES (1989) Circular 22/89: *Assessments and Statements of Special Educational Needs: Procedures with the Education, Health and Social Services*, DES Publication Unit.

DES/HMI (1990) *Education Observed: Special Needs Issues: A Survey by HMI*, London, HMSO.

DOH (1990) *Caring for People*, London, HMSO.

Fish, J. (Chair) (1985) *Equal Educational Opportunities for All?* Report of the Committee of Enquiry into Special Educational Needs, ILEA.

Goacher, B., Evans, J., Welton, J. and Wedell, K. (1988) *Policy and Provision for Special Educational Needs*, London, Cassell Education.

Glendinning, C. (1983) *Unshared Care: Parents and their Disabled Children*. London, Routledge & Kegan Paul.

Hatch, S. and Hinton, T. (1987) *Self-Help in Practice: A Study of Contact a Family in Wandsworth*, London, Community Care/Social Work Monographs.

Hewett, S. (1970) *Handicapped Children and their Families: A Survey*, Nottingham University.

House of Commons Education, Science and Arts Committee (1987) *Enquiry into the Implementation of the 1981 Act*, London, HMSO.

House of Commons Education, Science and Arts Committee (1989) *Enquiry into Nursery Education*, London, HMSO.

Mittler, P. (1989) Working together: guidelines for partnership between professionals and parents of children and young people with disabilities, in Monograph 39, *Family Supports for Families with a Disabled Member*, Dortothy Kerzner Lipsky (ed.), New York, World Rehabilitation Fund.

Nathan Committee (1950) *Report of the Committee on the Law and Practice Relating to Charitable Trusts*, London, HMSO.

Office of Population and Census Surveys (1989) Report 6, *Disabled Children Services, Transport and Education*, London, HMSO.

Robson, P. (1989) *Special Needs in Ordinary Schools: Pre-School Provision for Children with Special Needs*, London, Cassell Education.

Sylva, K. (1986) *Monitoring the High Scope Training Programme*, University of Oxford, Department of Social and Administrative Studies.

Unwell, J. (1979) *Voluntary Social Services: Financial Resources*, National Council of Social Services/Personal Social Services Council, Bedford Square Press.

Wilkin, D. (1979) *Caring for the Mentally Handicapped Child*. London, Croom Helm.

Wolfendale, S. (1989) Parental involvement and power sharing in special educational needs, in *Parental Involvement: Developing Networks Between School, Home and Community*, S. Wolfendale, (ed.) London, Cassell Education.

Wolfenden Committee (1978) *The Future of Voluntary Organisations*, London, Croom Helm.

Wolkind, S. (1981) Depression in Mothers of Young Children, *Archives of Disease in Childhood*, 56(1), 1–3.

Woodland, M. (1985) Pre-school education has long-term effects: but can they be generalised? *Oxford Review of Education*, 11, (2), 133–5.

CHAPTER 8

Confident Teams and Networks

Bill Fraser and Sally Cheseldine

Retrospect

Peter Mittler, by phrases such as 'people not patients' and 'parents as partners', raised the level of debate on multiprofessional working with mentally handicapped people in the 1970s. The models of working with people with mental handicaps prior to his commanding leadership of the field circa 1972, were still primarily medical and institutional. Theoretically, the process by which different disciplines might become involved in working with a child with severe mental handicaps has changed dramatically since the early 1960s. Then, the bulk of the work would have focused the attentions of professionals from the health services, largely at the instigation of, and under the direction of, the paediatrician who had diagnosed the handicap. The child might well have been described as 'unsuitable for education in schools', with the bulk of the care subsequently landing on the shoulders of the family, with little, if any, support from other agencies. Indeed few other agencies existed specifically to meet the needs of this group.

Twenty years later, we have learned about role blurring and continuous role change (for example, many psychologists and nurses becoming managers), by researching and working together, and by multiprofessional congresses such as IASSMD (International Association for Scientific Study of Mental Deficiency). Peter Mittler set a standard of distinction in the editorship of two proceedings of the congress, and has also led with eminence in the International League of Societies for Persons with Mental Handicap (ILSMH).

Conceptualising seemed simpler in the 1970s. Mental handicap was being logically reformulated as a learning disability, and developmental, educational and clinical psychologists, and social workers, were clearly to take the lead, with health care to be provided by the generic services. This concept remains true, but perhaps has required some qualification because of the complexities of the issues and of the individual 'cases'.

So, what has changed? Is the service more efficient, effective and accessible to all who require it? Or has the development of specialist workers within the differing disciplines led to a situation where there are too many 'cooks'?

Have we in fact come full circle, with the introduction of the concept of 'case managers' who will control the budget, and may see it as their role to decide who is to become involved in any particular case?

Let us illustrate the demands for multidisciplinary working by example:

> Hazel is now eighteen and suffers from Rett's Syndrome. Her history is characteristic. Up to six months of age she showed normal development, and thereafter followed a stagnation period between six and eighteen months. Then virtual continuous hand-wringing appeared, tortuous writhing, flapping in the mid-line, accompanied by tooth-grinding (bruxism), head-banging, and episodic breath-holding which was worse at night. Her abdomen became bloated, and she became insensitive to pain. A miserable screaming mood prevailed. At two and a half years the regression seemed to have ceased. Hazel, now clearly mentally handicapped, appeared to regain some of her original personality. Her moods stabilised and she made some developmental progress, but her night laughing was quite disturbing to her parents. She was growth retarded with tiny cold feet. She had lost intentionality in communications, and with neuromuscular weakness and wasting, now had a wheelchair dependent life. Clinical seizures developed when she was seven years old, which required complicated drug management. She still head-bangs distressingly.

Coordinating care – the child health service, the primary health care team, the psychologist: working together

The emergence in infancy of a neurodevelopmental disorder, the evolution through life of neurological signs of a wide range, coupled with stationary cognitive skills after a stage of regression, disruption of communicative development, and abnormal cerebral endorphin activity as found in subgroups of pervasive developmentally disturbed children such as Hazel, represents the need for close collaboration between the developmental psychologist, the clinical psychologist, developmental paediatrician, the speech therapist, the physiotherapist, the teacher, a physician who is trusted by the family, and a neuropharmacologist who understands this individual's complex medication requirements.

The family doctor

The general practitioner, with the dentist, is the service provider who is contacted most consistently by people with a mental handicap (Gollay, 1981;

Evans *et al.*, 1987, 1988). Most clients with a mental handicap throughout the world enter the Mental Handicap Services via a medical contact (Rowitz, 1981). The general practitioner is the only continuous medical contact (Lowe and de Paiva, 1990), yet general practitioners receive little training in mental handicap (Ineichen and Russell, 1980). People with mental handicaps and their families have difficulty communicating successfully with their doctors (Beange and Bauman, 1990), who in turn have insufficient consultation time for such people (Kinnell, 1987). Murdoch and Anderson (1990) have shown that parents are critical of general practitioners for their low expectations and relative reluctance to organise regular health checks and to refer for further opinions on sensory deficits. The general practitioner also seldom asks about specific areas such as sleep problems, yet some 30 per cent of families experience various sleep difficulties with their handicapped offspring.

The general practitioner is particularly unconfident in dealing with psychiatric and psychological problems, yet these additional health problems, which ought to present interesting challenges to the general practitioner, are crucial in limiting the handicapped person's engagement in quality-life with others. Nowadays general practitioners are keen to learn about mental handicap and to acquire the skills for the new era of community care. For this they also require a clinical specialist nurse, for example, from a Community Mental Handicap Team, to prompt them about the special health care needs of handicapped people and also to bring to their notice the problems that the handicapped person has been unable to communicate about. While this might not be the only role of the nurse, it is a crucial link with the professional who is likely to have most contact.

General practitioners now have considerable access to computers, and it is estimated that by April 1991 77 per cent of practices will have one. They are generally used for patient registration, repeat prescriptions, call and recall, but some 36 per cent of systems can communicate with other systems, and some suites of programmes can provide *aides-mémoire* to process consultations. In any practice only two to five patients have a mental handicap, and 'at a touch' consultation checklists for people with Down's Syndrome would be well worth developing. Add in the data from the physiotherapist's computer, and the speech therapist's, and enter by network to the social work register or a Bulletin Board. This latter can operate not only as a record of up-dated documents (work schedules, duty rosters) but also as a message delivery and exchange system. In coordination with FAX and telephone conferences it can help community workers to feel part of a team.

The psychologist

From the point of view of the clinical psychologist the ideal situation would be involvement from the beginning, perhaps from when the child is seen in the Multidisciplinary Assessment Unit, so that long-term, forward planning could be the norm. Unfortunately this rarely happens. Referral to clinical psychology services typically happens when people have 'tried everything', and the psychologist is seen as the last resort. Perhaps the psychologist is seen as the disciplinarian – the tough guy who will use the strong technology of a behavioural approach to cure all ills.

Whenever referral is made, a model of observation/assessment of need, followed by intervention with evaluation/continued assessment would be used. However, even within this simple model, there have been changes of emphasis over recent years. The concept of 'functional assessment' reflects progress from the days of intellectual assessment, and implies the use of an assessment to inform intervention rather than merely to hang a label on a person.

Where a child is self-injuring, the use of functional analysis to try to ascertain causes and maintaining factors for the behaviour would be a common first step. For many psychologists, however, the simple 'ABC' paradigm (Antecedents, Behaviours, Consequences) is too simplistic, and while it may provide a useful frequency count for baseline records, would not be expected to tell us much about the reasons for the behaviour. Far more sophisticated analogue studies (e.g. Iwata *et al.*, 1982) are used to examine variations in behaviour patterns under differing conditions, with the object of then basing intervention around teaching alternative behaviours with equal, but more appropriate, communicative functions (Bird *et al.*, 1989).

Functional/analogue analysis may well indicate why a behaviour appears at a certain time, although it is often the case that it has different functions on different occasions. Perhaps the important issue is that it is usually adaptive in giving the individual control over his or her environment. In this context, it may be more profitable to expend energy examining the behaviours of others who are around the individual and considering how they do *not* respond to more appropriate cues.

In the matrix of events that might cause challenging behaviours, we have to take into account not only environmentally dependent factors such as aberrant behaviours that have been inadvertently reinforced, and failed communication, but also environmentally independent 'biomedical' factors, such as homeostasis, over- and under-arousal, developmental, organic and functional mental illness (Baumeister, 1989).

Intervention needs to reflect the many facets of behaviour exposed through functional analysis. There are also many instances where it is the behaviour of the caregivers or the nature of the environment that needs to be changed, with a subsequent 'improvement' in the behaviour of the individual. The 'constructional' approach to behaviour focuses on adding to the repertoire of skills rather than on removing behavioural 'excesses', and incorporates all that is good about behavioural technology. It may be naïve though to expect to teach all social skills using the same technology that we would use to teach assembly of a bicycle pump, because that largely ignores the role of the social context (Lovett, 1985) and the rules (or inconsistencies) by which the rest of the society operates.

For learning to take place, it is crucial that the severely and profoundly handicapped person responds to cues from the environment. Responsiveness is a function of arousal and alertness. For the psychologist to be most effective, he or she needs more help from the neurophysiologists in assessing this alertness prior to scheduling the day so that skill training is optimally introduced (Espie and Tweedie, in press). To quote Sternberg and Richards (1989) 'questions will continue to be raised concerning whether individuals with the most debilitating types of handicap benefit from the provision of educational services'.

Elements of punishment are still used in many behaviour change programmes, with the justification that they lead to rapid 'improvement'. While many workers would deny such techniques are used, and only consider the application of specific physical stimuli, such as electric shocks, lemon juice and slaps, to come under this heading, it is often unwittingly tagged on to the more positive aspects of a behavioural programme – 'If John does X reward him with Y, but if he doesn't, take away Z' – punishment by removal (Yule and Carr, 1980). Many opportunities to learn more appropriate skills, such as excursions and 'therapeutic' sessions, are removed as a sanction because of failure to comply with often arbitrary rules in a totally unrelated setting. Yet for people who are *not* labelled 'handicapped' we often allow ourselves these treats precisely because we have had a bad day.

The normalisation, or social role valorisation movement, would argue strongly against the use of punitive devaluating techniques. Similarly the 'gentle approach' (McGee *et al.*, 1987) represents a firm move away from anything that might be construed as punitive, while implementing the positive aspects of a behavioural approach (Jones, 1990).

Baumeister's (1989) classification seems to support two apparently conflicting ideologies; first, that of gentle therapy, and second, that of neuropharmacology. If a handicapped person is suffering from physical pain, then gentle therapy based on the premise of humanisation of all, to teach bonding to those who have distanced themselves (by pain and distress), obeys the basic principle of caring – *primum non nocere*. Also, studies of the opioid antagonists have found that beta-endorphins play a part in brain development and learning, and high levels are found not only in Rett's, but in many other syndromes with self-injurious behaviour, preventing pain and distress reactions, and mandating a search for suitable medical remedies. Recently, dramatic improvements with Naltrexone have been reported in Rett's syndrome symptoms such as hand-wringing and screaming, during the administration of the drug. To combine 'punishment' techniques with a psychopharmalogical regime which involves (justifiable) lowering of the pain threshold, would be quite intolerable. The recent reintroduction of psychobiological concepts, in a balanced way, into the management of handicapped people with behaviour problems is timely.

Working together

How does all this fit into a multidisciplinary approach?

The idea of sharing such things as computer networks, mentioned above, by primary health care teams, is underpinned by the idea that there will be more shared assumptions. We are now in a more sophisticated normalisation epoch which means that in order to make normalisation work, we must have specialists to enable handicapped people to live ordinary lives, and to gain in health sufficiently to acquire skills and to engage in work activities.

All those involved will have different expectations of one another. Where a child is concerned, we might expect to see primarily the parents, but also a health visitor, paediatrician, general practitioner, pre-school teacher, clinical psychologist, community nurse and social worker involved. Each of these, however, might expect to see other professionals invited to participate – speech therapist, educational psychologist, respite carer, psychiatrist with special interest in mental handicap, physiotherapist, home-help organiser and so on. As the child becomes older, yet others may start to take a part – teacher, day centre worker, residential worker, befriender and advocate, community support worker and occupational therapist.

Many will be expected to perform their functions irrespective of whether there are behavioural difficulties – the general practitioner to give access to good health care, the social worker to ensure access to the appropriate benefits and emotional supports. Others will offer their services 'once the behaviour has been modified', while yet others will be expected to come up with 'solutions' to the problems. Whatever the pattern of involvement, it is unlikely that all will be part of a truly multidisciplinary force. Instead most will be tried at some stage with the end result that, in contrast to the Cheshire Cat, the problems rather than the smile will remain.

Many of these people will operate through a Community Mental Handicap Team, but the way, and the success with which these teams function varies considerably from district to district. The general approach adopted often depends on the views of the most forceful person in the group. If the problem behaviour is only experienced in certain settings, for example, the home, referral via the general practitioner may lead to only the involvement of health professionals initially, whereas a referral from the day centre may be more likely directed towards social services. To have full multidisciplinary involvement relies on good communication and a sound knowledge of what each profession can offer. There is also a need for trust and respect for the skills that each profession has.

Gentle education of Hazel may have to be combined with trials of medication. Physical deficits require appreciation of the need for a degree of prosthetic environment, that is, extra flexicare staff, a location accessible to the therapists, and a habitat offering a range of nearby daytime opportunities. Normalisation needs enabling measures.

But who is the specialist in communication? Who will advise on physical activities to replace inappropriate behaviours? Who can be an advocate? Why a psychiatrist rather than a psychologist? Why a community mental handicap nurse rather than social work assistant? Perhaps it has been the very lack of suitably trained staff in the field of mental handicap in general that has now led to the situation where many learn something about it and consequently seem to offer similar skills. No wonder the service's users often seem confused – but do they actually get a better service? When all is going well, there are almost queues on the front door step, yet when there are problems, the experts are called in to give their advice (Kushlick's 'DC ten minutes'), and it is the full-time, less well trained staff, or parents, who are expected to deal with the individual for the rest of the time.

Closing ranks

There is often an assumption that just because professionals use the same jargon, they are talking about the same thing. Nothing could be further from the truth. Speech therapy is very specific about the terms it uses to describe language disorders, yet many professionals claim to work on aspects of communication. Similarly psychologists know exactly what they mean by positive and negative reinforcement, or by time out, yet these terms are often used incorrectly or simplistically by others. The concepts of 'normalisation' and 'gentle teaching' are excellent examples of how terminology is rapidly absorbed into the professional vocabulary with very little standardisation of usage.

Terms become slogans which may with time obscure their original purpose. Normalisation ought to mean managers paying more attention to bettering the lives of people with learning difficulties, and less to emphasising the importance of the 'social address' at which the interventions take place (Zigler *et al.*, 1990). This differing emphasis has been a cause of unconstructive tension between professionals: researchers and clinicians viewing advocates and social reformers as 'anti-evaluation' and 'anti-science' (Schopler, 1989), while the latter have recently indeed said that 'value systems cannot and should not be subjected to empirical testing' (Greenspan and Cerreto, 1989). The disagreements span philosophical principles; normalisation, gentle teaching versus aversive methods, mainstreaming, deinstitutionalisation and the need for special services.

Even the concept of the definitive 'multi-disciplinary team' is open to question. Perhaps it is only in the eye of the beholder. There is undoubtedly multiprofessional work going on in the lives of many people with handicaps, but not necessarily through a delineated team. Yet perhaps these workers have another factor that will push them towards unity. We must 'close ranks' as workers with the learning disabled to face the onslaught in business practice of the profit motive.

It is interesting how effortlessly the traditional NHS and educational systems have slipped into the new business approaches, accepting the over-riding concerns of measuring outcomes of programmes and procedures, and counting the product cost (assuming that basic quality assurance exists). We must also learn together some hard lessons about marketing of skills. People with mental handicaps and their families have been particular victims of professional preciousness, and often it is the professionals' rather than their own demands that are met – psychiatrists doing 'psychotherapy' for the few, rather than running epilepsy clinics for the many; psychologists working with people with mild/moderate handicaps with interesting behaviour problems, rather than with people with profound handicaps or those who are too troublesome; nurses and physiotherapists working in Community

Mental Handicap Teams doing social work, whilst in the future what is likely to be asked of them is their distinctive professional skill, that is, nursing or physiotherapy.

Many people at 'grass roots' level are now arguing that team meetings are a waste of valuable clinical time, and serve no purpose other than the exchange of information which could more effectively be conveyed via a computer bulletin board. This uncertain existence has been eroded further by the government White Papers, which make the future of Community Mental Handicap Teams questionable, and one can envisage the above health care professionals being attached instead to the primary health care teams (if they don't get jobs as case managers).

In the US, the issue of economics has led in the last twenty years to non-physician practitioners such as pharmacists, nurse practitioners and optometrists gaining limited drug prescribing privileges, along with dentists. On Indian reservations, clinical psychologists have been prescribing medication for several years, and there is now a possibility, particularly in the US Department of Defense where doctors are difficult to recruit, of appropriately trained psychologists prescribing psychotropic medications in the diagnosis and treatment of nervous, mental and organic pain disorders under certain conditions. The American Psychological Association has endorsed the development of curricula including pharmacology for psychologists (Rhein, 1990). Notwithstanding understandable misgivings, this ending of the 'closed shop' is likely to be in the interests of handicapped people, and could be balanced by similar appropriate training to allow physicians to undertake neuropsychological tests, presently the preserve of clinical psychologists. The closed shop belongs with the 1970s not the 1990s.

How can we change the adversarial climate so that scientists, clinicians, advocates, managers and social policy changers can be complementary in enabling people with handicaps to live more ordinary lives? Menolascino and Stark (1990) propose that it will be the interaction of learning together that reconciles the disciplines and reverses the polarisation, the functions of training being to translate client needs to researchers, and vice versa, and to disseminate research and innovation to theoreticians and advocates, and vice versa. This involves shared assumptions, shared value systems, shared training in communicating with people with handicaps, shared premises and shared hardware and software. One is still astonished at the misconceptions that each profession has about the others' expertise, techniques and technologies, hierarchies and grades, and attitudes (and salaries!).

Trends in therapies and treatments or approaches come and go, and we should be wary of any team that considers that it has 'got it right'. Research continually adds to our knowledge and shapes our outlook. We must not become complacent. There is perhaps an important role here for those who have carried out postgraduate study to lead the way in developing an awareness of what is new and going on beyond the boundaries of the team.

Schools of learning difficulty

In the argument for maximising the use of generic services, the need for centres of excellence in mental handicap has been played down, on the grounds that centres are elitist and non-normative, yet advances in mental handicap have stemmed not from generic services but from units with *special* mandates to help people with mental handicaps (for instance in this country the Hester Adrian Research Centre which was developed under the stewardship of Peter Mittler). Through gradual starvation of funds, such centres in the US and the UK are looking to training as a way of surviving in an era of radical populism: witness the US University Affiliated Projects, whose purpose is by examples of good practice to teach high quality, multiprofessional, medical, educational and community living projects, (for example the John F. Kennedy Institute at the John Hopkins University, Baltimore, where medical personnel are trained in large part by other disciplines). In Britain, rigid professional training programmes mean that mental handicap is a 'tail end' topic in most disciplines which are accountable for training mental handicap practices. Project 2000 will end the RNMD. We require more diplomas and degrees which represent shared learning and are specific to learning disability, as at the University of Keele, Winchester, and planned for Humberside. Such courses need to offer opportunities for dual qualifications in nursing and social work.

The achievement of access to generic services for people with learning disabilities is still some way off. The training of enabling professionals sophisticated in multiprofessional practice has only just started.

References

Baumeister, A. A. (1989) Causes of severe maladaptive behavior in persons with severe mental retardation: a review of hypotheses. Presentation given to the National Institutes of Health, Bethesda, Maryland.

Beange, H. and Bauman, A. (1990) Health care for the developmentally disabled. Is it necessary? in W. Fraser (ed.) *Key Issues in Mental Retardation* London, Routledge.

Bird, F., Dores, P. A., Moniz, D. and Robinson, J. (1989) Reducing severe aggressive and self-injurious behaviours with functional communication training, *American Journal on Mental Retardation*, 94, 37–48.

Espie, C. and Tweedie, F. M. (1991) Sleep patterns and sleep problems amongst people with mental handicap, *Journal of Mental Deficiency Research*, 35, 25–36.

Evans, G., Beyer, S. and Todd, S. (1987) Evaluation of the All-Wales strategy for people with a mental handicap: a report of the findings of a preliminary survey of people with a mental handicap in the Ceredigion district. Cardiff, Mental Handicap in Wales Applied Research Unit.

Evans, G., Beyer, S. and Todd, S. (1988) Evaluation of the All-Wales strategy for people with a mental handicap: a report of the findings of a preliminary survey of people with a mental handicap in Central Swansea. Cardiff, Mental Handicap in Wales Applied Research Unit.

Gollay, E. (1981) Some conceptual and methodological issues in studying the community adjustment of deinstitutionalised mentally retarded people, in R. H. Bruininks, C. E. Meyers, B. B. Sigford and K. C. Lakin (eds) *Deinstitutionalization and Community Adjustment of Mentally Retarded People.* Washington D.C., American Association on Mental Deficiency.

Greenspan, S. and Cerreto, M. (1989) Normalization, deinstitutionalization and the limits of research: comment on Landesman and Butterfield, *American Psychologist,* 44, 448–9.

Ineichen, B. and Russell, O. (1980) Mental handicap and community care: the viewpoint of the General Practitioner. Department of Mental Health, Research report No. 4. Bristol, University of Bristol.

Iwata, B. A., Dorsey, M. F., Slifer, K. I., Bauman, K. E. and Richman, G. S. (1982) Toward a functional analysis of self-injury, *Analysis and Intervention in Developmental Disabilities,* 2, 3–21.

Jones, R. (1990) Gentle teaching: behaviourism at its best? *Community Living,* 3, 9–10.

Kinnel, H. G. (1987) Community medical care of people with mental handicaps: room for improvement, *Mental Handicap,* 15, 146–51.

Kushlick, A., Felce, D., Palmer, J. and Smith, J. (1976) Evidence to the committee of inquiry into mental handicap nursing and care. Winchester, Health Care Evaluation Research Team.

Lovett, H. (1985) *Cognitive Counselling and Persons with Special Needs: Adapting Behavioral Processes to the Social Context.* New York, Praeger.

Lowe, K. and De Paiva, S. (1990) The evaluation of NIMROD, a community based service for people with mental handicap: client use of services. Cardiff, Mental Handicap in Wales Applied Research Unit, University of Wales College of Medicine.

McGee, J. J., Menolascino, F. J., Hobbs, D. C. and Menousek, P. E. (1987) *Gentle Teaching: A Nonaversive Approach for Helping Persons with Mental Retardation.* New York, Human Sciences Press.

Menolascino, F. J. and Stark, J. A. (1990) Research versus advocacy in the allocation of resources: problems, causes, solutions, *American Journal on Mental Retardation,* 95, 21–5.

Murdoch, J. and Anderson, V. (1990) The management of Down's Syndrome children and their families in general practice, in W. Fraser (ed.) *Key Issues in Mental Retardation.* London, Routledge.

Rhein, R. (1990) Prescribing Psychologists, *British Medical Journal,* 301, 356.

Rowitz, L. (1981) Service paths prior to clinic use by mentally retarded people: a restrospective study, in R. H. Bruininks, C. E. Meyers, B. B. Sigford and K. C. Lakin (eds) *Deinstitutionalization and Community Adjustment of Mentally Retarded People.* Washington D.C., American Association on Mental Deficiency.

Schopler, E. (1989) Excesses of the normalization concept, *American Psychologist,* 44, 447–8.

Sternberg, L. and Richards, G. (1989) Assessing levels of state and arousal in individuals with profound handicaps: a research integration, *Journal of Mental Deficiency Research,* 33 381–7.

Yule, W. and Carr, J. (1980) *Behaviour Modification for the Mentally Handicapped*. London, Croom Helm.

Zigler, E., Hodapp, R. M. and Edison, M. R. (1990) From theory to practice in the care and education of mentally retarded individuals, *American Journal on Mental Retardation*, 95, 1–12.

CHAPTER 9

'We Can Change the Future': Self and Citizen Advocacy

Margaret Flynn and Linda Ward

Introduction

> We all know what handicapped people want are the most ordinary things: to have an ordinary home, some friends, to travel around the community a bit, to have a job and earn some money, to learn. Although these requests seem simple and straightforward, they are still considered radical. Equality is still a radical idea because it means change and change does not come easily. (Day, 1985)

In this chapter we explore two of the most recent and exciting developments in the lives of some people with learning difficulties – the growth of self and citizen advocacy. We draw from a variety of sources to demonstrate that people with learning difficulties, with help from others, can find solutions to the inequities they experience in services dedicated to meet their needs.

Considerations of some key issues surrounding self and citizen advocacy, the setbacks they live with and the opportunities they offer, remind us that these complementary developments cannot be construed as short-term, corrective solutions to the resilience of 'traditional' services. The chapter presents an overview of the multiplicity of essential service initiatives if self and citizen advocacy are to endure and work to create services which are compatible with people's own aspirations and changing needs.

Self advocacy: some key dimensions and early achievements

> Self advocacy is really important in people's lives – until I learned self advocacy skills, I didn't really see myself as a person . . . . With all the

129

labels people put on you – you don't have the confidence. Self advocacy is seeing yourself as a person. ('Nebraska People First', Ward, 1988)

I've done some advocacy courses – I actually taught one at Aycliffe – and I've helped out on a self advocacy course at Prudhoe Hospital. I've tried to involve consumers...and I helped start the Nottingham Advocacy Network...I've done presentations to home helps, I've done presentations to CQSW students at the Polytechnic, and I've done presentations to graduate social workers at Newcastle University. It's helped me to stand up for my rights and it's helped me to be more confident and I'm not frightened of confrontation now. (Binns, 1989)

Since the late 1960s in Sweden and the early 1970s in the USA, Canada, Australia and Britain, self advocacy has grown. Although the triggers initiating self advocacy in these countries were not identical, the international picture suggests that there have been significant and similar gains in respect of people with learning difficulties:

● defining themselves and exploring labels;
● questioning the configurations of power in service settings and the irreproachably well intentioned philosophies of the same;
● exchanging thoughts about their lives, experiences and aspirations through 'participation events';
● initiating self help groups;
● beginning to contribute to the monitoring and evaluation of services;
● confronting the outlawed topics of preparation for independence, real wages and interesting work, personal freedom and intimate relationships and the power advantage of parents and of staff in service settings;
● and seeking to learn the skills required in order to be heard (Nirje, 1972; Shearer, 1973; Williams, 1974; Schaaf et al., 1977; Foss et al., 1978; Browning et al., 1980; Williams and Schoultz, 1982; Crawley, 1983; McKenna, 1986; NDT, 1989).

What is loosely referred to as 'the self advocacy movement' is an international and changing network of individuals and groups who have acquired voices through the negotiations of their daily lives and their introduction of non-disabled people to a picture of the world in which they want to live. It is a world in which different relationships between people with learning difficulties, their families and service personnel are implied; where people are given information, training and experience in making decisions and working with peers to make decisions; a world in which people's decisions are acted upon; and one in which their adult status is recognised.

On an individual, group and collective basis, self advocacy addresses the asymmetry of power between people with learning difficulties and their families and service providers. Self advocacy – people offering their views whether these are solicited or not; being attuned to personal rights and responsibilities; being alert to a growing sense of competence and identity; and learning different ways of conveying views and ideas in order to create change – compel service users, their families and service personnel to ask, 'Whose choices and wishes should be given priority?' (Crawley *et al.*, 1988).

Irrespective of the knowledge that self advocacy brings decision making closer to service users and that it potentially signals an end to the priority of the wishes of families and services over those of service users, the self advocacy movement is fragile. This is largely attributable to the remarkable powerlessness of people with learning difficulties.

The management of power

I am a member of Liverpool Self Advocacy Group. We met on Monday . . . to discuss the document concerning the new day services. This is some of what we thought. We all felt there should be more courses set up in teaching independent living skills to people who will be moving to a group house or flat . . . . Everyone agreed that at the moment some centre staff can be overprotective. (Liverpool Self Advocacy Group, 1989)

The hierarchies in services for people with learning difficulties are steeped in the power relations of the world outside services (Brown and Smith, 1989). The power of managers and service personnel is based on the rarely questioned assumption that their priorities and those of the systems in which they operate should prevail. Without doubt, people with learning difficulties are in an extremely weak position in relation to services. They cannot for example, exert any significant influence by either withholding payment or by opting to withdraw from services. Further, the absence of timetabled opportunities to speak out, their inexperience in doing so and absence of training in this sphere, serve to consolidate their lowly position.

Powerful families and professionals have adopted some very effective procedures which exemplify the power differential under consideration, they:

- propose that self advocates who have acquired confidence and articulacy are 'not really mentally handicapped';
- suggest that self advocates have been manipulated by self-seeking others;
- assert that people with learning difficulties do not understand the good being done on their behalf;
- question the representativeness of self advocates; and
- negate the views and judgements of self advocates on the basis of their label.

Wertheimer (1988) spotlights the conflicts which crowd in on parents whose daughters and sons are involved in self advocacy. The absence of support to parents in, first, renegotiating their relationships with their adult daughters and sons and, second, in redefining their own futures, necessarily inhibits the autonomy of their offspring. The rewarding and positive aspects of relationships with daughters and sons are all too often construed in unhelpful terms rather than nurtured as positive parental advocacy.

Further perils facing self advocates include:

- professionals 'facilitating' self advocacy groups and committees by controlling the agendas, the flow of discussion and information and the subsequent representation of people's views independently of service users;
- professionals working to their own definitions of 'participation' and 'consultation' which are aligned to services' assumptions about what is right and proper for service users;
- professionals believing that the aspirations of self advocates can be met by including one self advocate in a meeting or conference which is top heavy with other professionals;
- professionals overriding the decision of self advocates by reminding them of their previous and sometimes conflicting decisions or by suggesting the 'right' ones for them;
- professionals believing that they are creating the conditions necessary for self advocacy by limiting people's choices to the spheres of food, drink, clothes and leisure pursuits (McKenna, 1986); and
- professionals conceding some lesser changes and improvements in the lives of people with learning difficulties, for example, ways in which they are labelled, but leaving untouched any ideas which challenge the basis of their control (Brown and Smith, 1989).

These are disingenuous and defensive practices which betray the fact that self advocacy is an arena of political struggle. Importantly, the force of efforts is diminished by the steady growth of the self advocacy movement and evidence of its achievements and gains.

Barker and Peck (1987) outline the parameters within which service personnel may enhance, rather than inhibit people's exercise of choice in service settings. We should:

Recognise the problems of imbalance of power.
Seek users and colleagues with a similar perspective and develop local networks.
Create a forum for the introduction of ideas of user involvement.
Be patient.
Recognise the validity of a range of strategies.
Change styles of operating to allow for user involvement.
Watch for styles of meetings, language, setting and agendas.
Help to provide resources for users' initiatives . . .
Be prepared to be ignored.
LET GO! but continue to offer an advice network on users' terms.
Allow users the space to develop their own initiatives.
Network colleagues nationally to spread ideas and initiatives. (Barker and Peck, 1987:28)

Crawley et al. (1988) in 'Getting Going' outline the qualities self advocates should seek in their selection of advisers or 'support people' to assist their groups or committees. As Amans and Darbyshire (1989), Crawley et al.

highlight the tensions inherant in selecting staff members who, by virtue of their employment, cannot be wholly unaligned.

When we share our experiences and thoughts we learn from each other and this process helps us to reformulate our understanding of the world. The opportunity to meet and talk with others is critical to our confidence in speaking from secure positions. In respect of many people with learning difficulties, this position is one of deprivation. It is essential to acknowledge that there are worlds where the experiences of people with learning difficulties do not begin to match those of people who do not have this label. It is also essential that both groups should speak and listen if self advocacy is not to be conditional on service users accepting titbits of autonomy.

Acquiring a collective voice

Trainees committee

This started as a result of a request by me at one of my reviews. As staff had meetings, I thought we should too. I got all the trainees together and asked them who should be on their committees, and we voted for them. We have Dave, a member of staff to record our meetings and help clarify some issues that come up. I chair the meetings. We decide how to spend the money that is made from our Christmas play. We use it to buy everyday things such as a new stackable stereo and some LPs that are in the 'pop' charts. We also discuss things that affect our everyday life at the centre, such as getting the broken locks on the toilet doors repaired. We have found that things we ask about get done. We need to make staff aware of things. (Versey, 1990)

The above quotation was dictated by a woman attending an ATC (Adult Training Centre). It appears in an anthology of writings, poetry and artwork of people with learning difficulties entitled *Know me as I am* (Atkinson and Williams, 1990). The text is remarkable for the quality of its witness, reflecting the breadth but isolation of people's experiences in which the theme of thwarted autonomy recurs.

McKenna (1986) investigated the opportunities for self advocacy in the lives of fifteen adults with learning difficulties who use services. She found that people were typically presented with four types of choices.

(1)   *Fait accompli* or the presentation of a choice made by a helper, e.g., 'I think it's time you went to bed now, don't you?'
(2)   Two or more choices in which the staff member offers the options, e.g., 'You can go out tonight or tomorrow night. Which would you prefer?'
(3)   Prompted free choice in which the staff member initiates the decision making, e.g., 'What shall we do today?'
(4)   Self generated choice, e.g., a staff member will ask 'What did you decide to do today?'

McKenna pointed out that service personnel must exercise considerable skill in order that people whose experience of decision making may be limited, are not encumbered with the responsibility of being expected to make self generated choices within a short period of time. She warned,

> In enabling people to exercise choice for themselves, we should not forget that many services at present do not encourage such independence. To propose abolishing service determined decisions in favour of service user free choice, without assuming a 'service assisted' phase, denies any value a service might have. (McKenna, 1986: 276)

Crawley *et al.* (1988) also recognised that there are tried and tested, structured methods to assist people in acquiring a voice through: getting a group or committee together; learning how to communicate with others, take turns, be assertive, solve problems and make decisions; learning how to run meetings, nominate advisers and find a location for meetings; recruiting people; establishing a newsletter; making the most of people's skills; electing representatives; sustaining interest in the activities of the group; networking with other groups; public speaking and organising conferences.

A recent workshop of American self advocates outlined the ways in which groups and committees of self advocates can assist new people who join them:

> People feel included when: agendas are clear, people are notified by phone and newsletters (or tape for people with trouble reading); meet in accessible community places; transport is available to people who need it; the meeting has clear rules so people feel safe (no fighting or put downs), people feel decisions are made fairly and people who don't understand have a chance to ask questions and get explanations. (O'Brien, 1990)

The same self advocates recognised that the expectation of people making choices with the help they needed to carry them out, has to begin early. Opportunities to make choices and decisions have to be a part of people's lives from the outset.

Political dimensions

Some statements resulting from a two day conference on day services:

- A fair day's wage for a fair day's work;
- Big homes should be closed;
- ATCs should help us to get work but they are not places of work;
- Every ATC and residential setting should have a committee;
- Attenders should be involved in interviewing for staff;
- Training is needed for staff to change their attitudes and the way they 'work';
- There should be opportunity for exchange of information and ideas between centres locally and nationally;
- If staff don't like more independent views of attenders . . . they can get on their bikes;

● Attenders and staff should not be segregated;
● People should choose their key workers and change them if they are no good. (People First, 1989)

Self advocates have demonstrated an increasing willingness to tackle issues within and beyond the systems in which their own lives are embedded. Some recent examples of lobbying at national and local levels for change include:

● self advocates questioning the absence of representation of black people with learning difficulties and the absence of representation of people who have been excluded from services at conferences for researchers and service personnel respectively;
● self advocates in Calderdale contributing to a campaign opposing the opening of a private home for forty people on an industrial site; and
● Barbe Goode, a Canadian self advocate making a presentation to the Supreme Court about a woman with learning difficulties who was to be sterilised. The Supreme Court acknowledged that there should be no non-therapeutic sterilisation of people with learning difficulties.

Clearly the roles and responsibilities assumed by self advocates vary widely. Because membership of some groups is dispersed, conferences and participation events are significant landmarks at which priorities are debated. Although groups and committees do not address identical issues, without doubt, their questions and discussions resonate with the deeper levels of oppression which impact on their lives.

Women and self advocacy

Barbe Goode, a self advocate, in this country on a speaking tour with others involved in the Canadian Association for Community Living – a radical coalition of parents, professionals and people with learning difficulties pressing for a change in Canada's services – offered a useful policy hint that won't cost a penny. She said that the Association would never meet ministers or policy makers without the involvement of someone with learning difficulties, adding perceptively: 'To do otherwise would be like holding a women's meeting which was only attended by men. (Offload, 1990)

It is not surprising that the well known self advocates in this country are men. If we look at self advocacy through a feminist lens, what comes into sharp focus is the unconcious reproduction of power relations in which men adopt leadership roles. Inevitably, their concerns and agendas cannot correspond with the actuality of women's experiences. In efforts to address the ubiquitous sexism in services, a small number of women's groups have surfaced with the help of women service providers. These deal largely with the primacy of female experiences. A video entitled *Between Ourselves* produced by Twentieth Century Vixen shows one such group exploring the problems of public attitudes, rape and child abuse. The existence of women's groups acknowledges the fact that there are worlds where the experiences of women do not match those of men. This is true in some day service contexts in which women are directed towards undervalued domestic tasks and are allocated roles of bleakly unrewarding domesticity (Noonan-Walsh, 1988; Murray and Flynn, 1990).

Citizen advocacy

In the last few years people with mental handicaps have been increasingly advocating for themselves. This has been a new and effective method of social change. Nevertheless, people with handicaps cannot do it all themselves. Some people cannot fight for their rights. For these individuals, friends and family will have to advocate on their behalf. Without their help, the rights of these individuals will only be on paper and, in effect, meaningless. (Day, 1985)

In 1966, the United Cerebral Palsy Association held a national conference in the US. Its purpose was to address the fundamental question concerning so many parents of children with handicaps: 'What will happen to my child when I'm gone?'

The emergence of the citizen advocacy movement in the US was a direct response to that question. Citizen advocacy would provide one means for 'optimising the likelihood that an impaired person would be protected if and when there was no family that could or would do it' (Wolfensberger, 1983). In the absence of family members, an unpaid citizen – or citizen advocate – would defend that person's interests as if they were his or her own.

Twenty five years later there are more than 200 citizen advocacy offices in the US and Canada (Butler *et al.*, 1988) with others in Sweden and Australia (Ward and Page-Hanify, 1986). In the UK there are at least a dozen schemes up and running, with new offices being planned and established all the time (Butler and Forrest, 1990). Citizen advocacy is having a major impact on the lives of individual people with learning difficulties and the agencies set up to serve them. It is helping to challenge conventional wisdom and practice about the lives and rights of people with learning difficulties, by bringing about change for individuals and the communities in which they live.

What is citizen advocacy?

Citizen advocacy is an independent partnership between two people: a volunteer advocate and a person who needs help to represent their interests and to overcome social rejection. (Avon Citizen Advocacy Office, n.d.)

Or, in the words of John O'Brien, one of the leading figures in the citizen advocacy movement in the US:

a valued citizen who is unpaid and independent of human services creates a relationship with a person who is at risk of social exclusion and chooses one or several of many ways to understand, respond to and represent that person's interests as if they were the advocate's own, thus bringing their partner's gifts and concerns into the circles of ordinary community life. (O'Brien, 1987)

Citizen advocacy in the UK

The role of advocacy in securing a better deal for people with learning difficulties was recognised by the Jay Committee in its Report of 1979. Their statement of principles on which a new model of care should be based concluded:

> if we are to establish and maintain high quality services for a group of people who cannot easily articulate and press their just claims, we need someone to intercede on behalf of mentally handicapped people in obtaining services. (*Report of the Committee of Enquiry into Mental Handicap Nursing and Care*, 1979, Para. 93)

Eight years earlier, the UN *Declaration on the Rights of Mentally Retarded Persons* had specifically outlined rights to personal advocacy, protection from exploitation, abuse and degrading treatment and proper legal safeguards where rights were to be restricted or denied (UN, 1971). Although the UK was a signatory to this declaration, official recognition of the need for advocacy on behalf of people with learning difficulties had to wait nearly a decade until the DHSS review of services *Mental Handicap: Progress, Problems and Priorities*. This argued that:

> the most important factor in safeguarding the position of vulnerable patients and ensuring that their rights are upheld is personal contact between the patient and someone whose job it is to explain the position from the patient's point of view. (DHSS, 1980)

However, legislative endorsement for advocacy was not achieved until the Disabled Persons' (Services, Consultation and Representation) Act 1986. The Act, when fully implemented, would give disabled people over the age of sixteen the right to appoint an 'authorised representative' to act on their behalf. Local authorities could also appoint representatives for disabled people who appeared to them to be unable to do so for themselves by reason of physical or mental incapacity. Under the Act, the local authority would be required to permit an authorised representative to act as such in connection with the provision by the authority of any social services, and also to accompany the disabled person to any meeting or interview held by, or on behalf of, the authority in connection with the provision of such services. Authorised representatives would have a right of access to disabled people at all reasonable times when they were living in a wide range of hospital or residential accommodation, including private residential homes and nursing homes (The Act Now Committee, 1990).

Unfortunately, the sections of the Disabled Person's Act relating to authorised representatives (or advocates) have yet to be implemented. Thus initiatives around citizen advocacy in this country still lack statutory backing in practice – in contrast to the US, where the Developmentally Disabled Assistance and Bill of Rights Act requires each American state to establish an independent agency to pursue the individual rights of disabled people.

Citizen advocacy in practice

Advocacy Alliance

Shortly after the DHSS affirmed the need for advocacy (DHSS, 1980) the first advocacy scheme was established in the UK. Advocacy Alliance was launched in June 1981 by five national voluntary organisations – MENCAP, One-to-One, MIND, the Spastics Society and the Leonard Cheshire Foundation, funded by the DHSS, with additional resources from the King's Fund and Mental Health Foundation. Its focus – the needs and interests of residents of three long-stay hospitals to the south west of London – St Ebba's Hospital, Epsom; Normansfield, Teddington and St Lawrence's Hospital, Caterham (Advocacy Alliance, n.d.).

Initial experiences of the Advocacy Alliance are described by Bob Sang, its first coordinator (Sang and O'Brien, 1984). The early impact of three advocacy relationships on the quality of life of the individuals were graphically illustrated in a BBC TV *Open Space* programme featuring the work of the Alliance in 1984 (Advocacy Alliance, 1984).

Sheffield Citizen Advocacy

A second advocacy initiative got underway in the UK in 1984, this time in Sheffield, again funded through a grant from the DHSS. The Sheffield Advocacy Project, while sharing the same fundamental goal as Advocacy Alliance (the matching of vulnerable individuals with volunteer advocates) did not focus exclusively on hospital residents. Those who were isolated or at risk in the community were of equal concern. As Sheffield's experience grew, moreover, so its methods changed. At first it followed the course pursued by Advocacy Alliance. A pool of potential advocates was recruited, long training courses were run, culminating in the linking of advocates to individuals. These individuals (or 'partners' as they are often called by citizen advocacy offices) were often referred to the scheme by professionals and service providers. After a while, the Sheffield scheme decided that locating those individuals most in need of advocacy might be more appropriately done by advocacy office staff. They spent time in institutions and ATCs getting to know people and seeking out those who seemed excluded or generally in need of support.

Recruitment of advocates became much more neighbourhood based using local contacts, like the clergy, to help identify potential volunteers. (Advocacy Alliance had tried, ineffectively, to recruit volunteers through existing voluntary organisations, and via blanket means like TV appeals and newspaper items. Experience in the US, and in later UK projects, suggests recruitment through personal contacts and networks in local communities, aimed at finding an advocate for a particular individual is a more effective recruitment strategy.)

Instead of a lengthy training course, the preparation of advocates became lower key, at most perhaps two or three evening sessions, with more emphasis on learning about the principles of Citizen Advocacy and the situations of specific 'partners'. By its second year Sheffield Advocacy had realised the impossibility of city-wide coverage (given that it employed only one coordinator) and switched to a more localised approach, focusing on particular neighbourhoods at a given time (Forrest, 1986).

Advocacy Alliance and Sheffield Citizen Advocacy have been followed by advocacy offices in Avon, Hereford and Worcester, Camberwell and other parts of the UK. What do we know from their experiences, and experience in the US, about how citizen advocacy should – and does – operate in practice, and what it has achieved?

Key elements in successful citizen advocacy

Harris (1987) and Carle (1984) have both identified key elements in successful citizen advocacy.

- There should be *no conflict of interest*. The advocates loyalty to the person represented is central. The advocate must be free to pursue their partner's rights without concern for job, career or the needs of any organisation. This will be more likely if the advocate is independent of service providers; the advocacy office is independent from service providers (e.g. in location or funding); the advocate, advocacy office and others have a clear understanding of each other's needs.
- Advocacy relationships should be *one-to-one*, so that time and energy can be spent by the advocate in achieving change for one individual. One-to-one relationships also provide a strong counter-balance to the general tendency of services to treat people with learning difficulties in a blanket rather than individualised way (Butler and Forrest, 1990).
- The advocate volunteer should be *unpaid*. (For many people with learning difficulties, the only non-disabled people in their lives are paid to be there. Citizen advocates choose to spend time with their partner of their own free choice).
- The relationships should be *long-term* – since many people with learning difficulties have few long-term relationships in their lives.

A good citizen advocacy office will follow these principles through the activities of its paid staff, its management or core group (local people with a variety of backgrounds, skills and connections) and the advocacy relationships it helps to develop and support. (For more details on the tasks to be undertaken by a successful citizen advocacy programme, see O'Brien (1987).)

Forrest (1986) identifies four steps in the development of individual advocacy relationships: identifying people needing advocates; recruiting advocates; training them and matching them with partners. Beyond this, the advocacy office will need to provide ongoing support and back up to advocates (if they want it); develop the expertise of both staff and management committee; continue to seek out people who may become advocates, supporters or members of the management group and build closer links with the local community (Butler and Forrest, 1990).

What do citizen advocates do?

The roles and tasks undertaken by citizen advocates are as different and varied as the individuals with whom they are involved. What they do will vary over the course of their relationship according to the particular needs, circumstances and wishes of their partner at any one time. How they operate will be influenced by their own personal skills, confidence and personality.

The literature generally categorises the citizen advocacy relationship along two dimensions – instrumental and expressive. The instrumental role is essentially task centred and problem solving – helping a partner to gain access to benefits, services and health care, to move to a new home or get a job, speaking up on their behalf at individual plan meetings, getting medication reviewed, speaking out about ill-treatment and possible abuse.

In the expressive role, the advocate will try to meet (some of) his or her partner's needs for friendship, affection, a sense of belonging. This will involve sharing leisure and perhaps family time together, celebrating birthdays, going out for meals, offering support at times of distress. The advocate will introduce their partner to other individuals in their life, who may themselves form separate relationships with him or her, in turn perhaps fulfilling an expressive role – becoming friends themselves. In this way the partner may gradually become included in the life and social networks of their local community.

In practice, some citizen advocates will fulfil one role, some another – with others performing both, with the emphasis switching over time and circumstances.

What has citizen advocacy achieved?

The literature on citizen advocacy in the US, Australia and the UK, carries many vivid stories of the efficacy of citizen advocacy and its impact on people's lives. (See, for example, Bogdan, 1987; Butler *et al.*, 1988; Morris, 1987; Ward and Page-Hanify, 1986.) These stories – of a couple finally getting married, despite the opposition of local service providers; of a medically fragile, multiply handicapped child in institutional care becoming part of an advocate's own family; of adults being enabled, despite all the obstacles, to move into paid employment or homes of their own; of people getting access to the welfare benefits, health care, social support or educational provision that should be theirs by right – provide powerful testimony to the effectiveness of non-professionals joining forces with vulnerable individuals, to promote and defend their interests as if they were their own.

There is as yet little published research on citizen advocacy in the UK to provide any yardstick against which such powerful individual stories can be appraised. A study currently being undertaken by Ken Simons at the Norah Fry Research Centre, University of Bristol, on the impact of both self and citizen advocacy should go some way towards filling this gap. (Simons, 1990).

The work of citizen advocacy offices can also be evaluated using *CAPE: Standards for Citizen Advocacy Program Evaluation* (O'Brien and Wolfensberger, 1979) and *Learning From Citizen Advocacy Programs* (O'Brien, 1987). These tools were designed to see how well advocacy offices were operating in accordance with the fundamental principles of citizen advocacy. There have, however, been few evaluations of citizen advocacy offices in the UK to date. The report of a recent evaluation of Sheffield Citizen Advocacy (1991) provides useful information on the achievements and experiences of one of the first citizen advocacy offices in the UK.

Issues for the present – and the future

Citizen advocacy offices have now existed in the US for twenty years, and in the UK for ten. So what can be learnt from their accumulation of experience? What are the key issues to be addressed if citizen advocacy is to survive and flourish in the future?

Secure (and independent) funding

In order to avoid potential conflicts of interest, citizen advocacy offices should not (ideally) be funded by statutory agencies (like health authorities or social services departments) which themselves provide the services on which people with learning difficulties may rely. In practice, some citizen advocacy offices are, necessarily, funded from such sources, though every effort is made by them to ensure that the potential for conflicts of interest is minimised. In some cases, local citizen advocacy offices have had to reject funding from statutory agencies with unacceptable 'strings' attached – for example, that the funding provided would be used exclusively to secure advocates for people leaving long-stay hospitals, and not for people equally, or more, isolated and at risk but already living in the community.

In the current economic and political climate, however, local funding of this kind is in any event under threat. It is certainly unlikely to be increasingly available. As Ward and Page-Hanify point out:

> In cost-benefit terms an efficient Citizen Advocacy Program is extremely effective but this preventive concept, like other-low cost options of rehabilitation, is difficult to sell to agencies faced with decisions of short-term expediency. (Ward and Page-Hanify, 1986)

Their argument, that unless some form of legislatively committed funding becomes available, there is the possibility that Citizen Advocacy Programs will remain few in number, may be equally applicable to the UK (though the implementation of the relevant sections of the Disabled Person's Act 1986 would obviously provide a boost to citizen advocacy in this country). In the meantime,

> If individualised services and quality control are really to be the hallmarks of community care in the future, then it is imperative that some mechanism for ensuring the more widespread establishment and maintenance of citizen advocacy offices is found. (Ward, 1990)

What kind of advocacy – and for whom?

Most citizen advocacy offices have tended to emphasise long-term informal advocacy with modest demands. According to Butler and Forrest (1990), this, while perfectly legitimate, has narrowed the range of advocacy roles. They argue that a wider variety of advocacy options should be pursued. Wolfensberger (1983) makes a similar point, with his concern that there has been an emphasis (at least in the US) on instrumental-expressive relationships, with few purely instrumental ones. A correspondingly low emphasis, he maintains, has been placed on the recruitment of formal advocates such as adoptive parents and legal guardians. He also observes that, at least in the early days, citizen advocacy offices in the US appeared to have addressed themselves primarily to individuals with milder 'impairments'. In the UK, there have been criticisms recently that citizen advocacy has become a new form of 'befriending'; it has lost its original energy and anger, and upsets no-one (Brandon, 1990). Such views are hotly disputed by those active in the citizen advocacy movement in the UK, though they are well aware of the dangers of compromise that day-to-day pressures and funding constraints may present (*Community Living*, 1990).

A more recent concern, given our multi-racial society, is the evidence that citizen advocacy is currently primarily about the establishment of relationships with, and on behalf of, white people with learning difficulties. In some places, this issue is now being addressed. Leeds Advocacy, for example, have prioritised the need to recruit advocates for black and ethnic minority people with learning difficulties. They now have black and ethnic minority people on their management committee and have appointed a black coordinator who works primarily, but not specifically, with Asian people with learning difficulties and assists colleagues to understand more clearly black and ethnic minority issues in advocacy (Baxter *et al.*, 1990). In the UK of the 1990s, other citizen advocacy offices will clearly need to do the same.

Small potatoes – big change

For any individual citizen advocate, the issues confronted within the advocacy relationship will be of a different order. What should one do if one's partner reiterates a desire that one should not speak out or make a fuss about abuse or denial of rights for fear of 'causing trouble'? On what basis does one choose which battles to fight, and which to pass over – when to fight on all fronts simultaneously is clearly not a practical possibility? How does one live with the knowledge that the changes secured seem minor in comparison with the scale of change which the claims of social justice demand? Here, feedback and support from others (including citizen advocacy staff) may be of paramount importance in underlining the need to proceed 'one step at a time'. Small steps, as the experience of citizen advocacy generally demonstrates, can lead to powerful changes in individual lives. Mandy Forrest, former coordinator of Sheffield Citizen Advocacy, points out in her account of citizen advocacy in the US:

> Citizen Advocacy is a brave movement. In a nation where profit, status, being expert, consumerism is so important, to make a stand to attempt to get people with disabilities included means having a belief, a dream and optimism. Citizen Advocacy... believes that community members want to get to know others, want to care and want to work towards a more humane society. Citizen Advocacy acknowledges that this can only be done one step at a time, a person at a time. Citizen Advocacy is 'small potatoes'. (Forrest, 1986)

'Small potatoes' maybe – but in the lives of thousands of people with learning difficulties, such 'small potatoes' could mean a great deal.

Self and citizen advocacy in a wider context

> I got a lot off my mind and am sure of myself. I realise other people sometimes have bigger problems than ourselves.... We are hoping to get a meeting together for people from centres and hospitals where we can talk about ourselves and the places we work. I hope that someone will listen to us because I feel they don't at the moment. Families sometimes don't want to know your problems and social services don't always listen either. (Hughes, 1988)

If self and citizen advocacy are to continue to build on their significant gains, we have to be pried away from our allegiances to service responses which congregate people and serve them on a group basis. As users themselves witness, these have a tendency to become static and less alert to people's individual needs over time (Winifred *et al.*, 1990).

Qureshi (1990) outlines the difficulties and conflicts encountered by services working with users in planning and evaluating their own services, running services and planning services across a locality, i.e. user 'satisfaction' surveys are hardly pertinent to unwilling service users; techniques for gathering information from some people are costly and time intensive; some people are not represented in established participatory structures; some service users may wish to distance themselves from other groups of service users; and some users may be so over used that they are more aligned with service systems and less in touch with their original constituencies. Clearly, we have a great deal to learn.

Figure 9.1 Pursuing quality systematically

Internal to enabling authority	Internal to provider agencies	Involving users and community	Established independently
AUTHORITY-WIDE			
• Positive and equitable policies for people with learning disabilities		• Forums for policy dialogue with users, relatives and community representatives	National inspectorates
• Culture of commitment to quality, openness and learning how to do better	• Commitment of generic providers to including people with learning disabilities	• Development of voluntary associations engaged in collective advocacy for and with user interests	External review
• Member scrutiny of performance			
• Planning, management and review processes supporting policy objectives	• As with enabling authorities	• Service review processes involving users and relatives	Regulatory arrangements and 'arms length' local inspection
• Investment in skilled service design and development	– positive policies and appropriate imagery		Voluntary accreditation
• Contracting of services based on standards and performance monitoring	– quality culture – supportive management		
• Complementary investment in staff training, information systems and evaluation	– skilled development – staff training		Evaluation research
LOCAL			
• Emphasis on locality as the focus for comprehensive provision	• Operational policies specifying goals, working arrangements and relationships with other providers	• Users and relatives participation in management committees, advisory groups and review teams for particular services	• As above • Independent advice and advocacy agencies
• Decentralised problem-solving			
• Information and accessible entry to opportunities and services	• Clear job descriptions and staff procedures		
• Active case finding	• Positive monitoring of performance		
	• Quality assurance programmes		
INDIVIDUAL			
• Individual service planning	• Supports to community integration	• Self and citizen advocacy	• Independent case management and brokerage arrangements
• Case management	• Systematic efforts to improve functional abilities	• Circles of support	
• Monitoring of individual provision		• Complaints procedures	

(*Source*: David Towell, 1990)

Reference to Figure 9.1 locates self and citizen advocacy within a wider service context. This figure was conceived by David Towell (1990) to indicate how quality within services can be pursued systematically. The figure addresses the powerful inhibitors to shifting from 'traditional' to user referenced services. It illustrates the multiplicity of service initiatives required and the commitment to a consultative mode at all levels if we are to witness further advances in self and citizen advocacy. Importantly, the figure indicates how marginal self and citizen advocacy are without commitment and coalitions within and across all levels.

The insights of people with learning difficulties into their own experiences and circumstances necessarily surpass those of their listeners, readers and viewers of their videos and art. They are 'expert witnesses' who speak from the secure position of knowledge of their lives and circumstances. What happens to people within and beyond services is deserving of attention.

Many self advocates have eloquently spoken of the harmfulness of the services they have experienced (e.g. Barron, 1989). What is at stake is not the success or failure of self and citizen advocacy, but recognition of the necessity of listening to, understanding and acting on people's preferences and wishes. This requires great changes of the kind outlined in Figure 9.1. Only when the mechanisms for securing and maintaining these changes are established can we anticipate that self and citizen advocacy will touch the lives of many more people with learning difficulties.

References

Act Now Committee (1990) *The Disabled Persons (Services, Consultation and Representation) Act received the Royal Assent on 8th July, 1986 . . . Where is it now?* London, Act Now Committee.

Advocacy Alliance (n.d.) *Guidelines for One-to-one Advocacy in Mental Handicap Hospitals.* London, Advocacy Alliance.

Advocacy Alliance (1984) *It's My Life Anyway.* London, BBC TV/Open Space.

Amans, D. and Darbyshire, C. (1989) A voice of our own, in A. Brechin and J. Walmsley (eds) *Making Connections: Reflecting on the Lives and Experiences of People with Learning Difficulties – A Reader.* Open University, Hodder & Stoughton.

Atkinson, D. and Williams, F. (1990) *'Know me as I am' An Anthology of Prose, Poetry and Art by People with Learning Difficulties.* Open University, Hodder & Stoughton.

Avon Citizen Advocacy (n.d.) *Protecting the Rights of People Who Need Help to Speak Out for Themselves.* Bristol, Avon Citizen Advocacy.

Barker, I . and Peck. E. (1987) *Power in Strange Places – User Empowerment in Mental Health Services.* London, Good Practices in Mental Health.

Barron, D. (1989) Locked away: life in an institution, in A. Brechin and J. Walmsley (eds) *Making Connections: Reflecting on the Lives and Experiences of People with Learning Difficulties – A Reader,* Open University, Hodder & Stoughton.

Baxter, C., Poonia, K., Ward, L. and Nadirshaw, Z. (1990) *Double Discrimination: Issues and Services for People with Learning Difficulties from Black and Ethnic Minority Communities.* London, Kings' Fund Centre/CRE.

146

Binns, A. (1990) Anita's Story (Part 2) in D. Atkinson and F. Williams *'Know me as I am': An Anthology of Prose, Poetry and Art by People with Learning Difficulties.* Open University, Hodder & Stoughton.

Bogdan, R. (1987) *'We Care for our Own'. Citizen Advocacy in Savannah and Macon.* Syracuse University, Centre on Human Policy.

Brandon, D. (1990) 'Is citizen advocacy losing its radical edge?' *Community Living*, April, 1.

Brown, H. and Smith, H. (1989) Whose 'ordinary life' is it anyway? *Disability, Handicap and Society* 4, 2, 105–19.

Browning, P., Rhoades, C. and Crosson, A. (1980) *Advancing Your Citizenship*, Rehabilitation, Research and Training Centre, University of Oregon.

Butler, K., Carr, S. and Sullivan, F. (1988) *Citizen Advocacy: A Powerful Partnership.* London, National Citizen Advocacy.

Butler, K. and Forrest, A. (1990) Citizen Advocacy for people with disabilities in L. Winn, (ed.) *Power to the People: The Key to Responsive Services in Health and Social Care.* London, King's Fund Centre.

Carle, N. (1984) *Key Concepts in Community-based Services.* London, CMH.

Community Living (1990) 'Letters', July, 4–5.

Crawley, B. (1983) *Self Advocacy Manual.* Paper No. 49, Habilitation Technology Project, HARC, University of Manchester.

Crawley, B., Mills, J., Wertheimer, A., Whittaker, A., Williams, P. and Billis, J. (1988) Booklets 1–5: What is self advocacy?; Getting going; Running a group; What next?; Basic skills that help. Learning about self advocacy (LASA), Wembley, Adept Press, CMH.

Day, S. (1985) Rights and advocacy, *Canadian Journal of Mental Retardation*, 35, 1, 3–10.

DHSS (1980) *Mental Handicap: Progress, Problems and Priorities.* London, DHSS.

Forrest, M. (1986) *Citizen Advocacy: Including the Excluded.* Sheffield, Sheffield Citizen Advocacy.

Foss, G., Bostwick, D. and Harris, J. (1978) *Problems of Mentally Retarded Young Adults and Obstacles to their Rehabilitation: A Study of Consumers and Service Providers.* Centre paper No. 12: Rehabilitation Research and Training Centre, University of Oregon, Eugene.

Harris, J. (1987) Citizen Advocacy: four lessons from the North American experience, *Social Work Today*, April 6th, 12–13.

Hughes, P. (1988) Quality of Life, in *The Wigan Weekender* 2, April 22.

Liverpool Self Advocacy Group (1989) Compilation of papers presented to MIND for their 1989 Liverpool Conference, Liverpool, MIND.

McKenna, C. (1986) Self advocacy in the lives of people with mental handicap. Unpublished M.Phil., University of Manchester.

Morris, P. (1987) Making the right match, *Community Living*, Sept/Oct, 8–9.

Murray, J. and Flynn, M. C. (1991) Women with learning disabilities – their training in day services. Working paper in preparation.

National Development Team (1989) Getting it together – the next step. Report on services for people with learning difficulties in Rochdale. London, NDT.

Nirje, B. (1972) The right to self determination, in W. Wolfensberger (ed.) *The Principle of Normalisation in Human Services*. Toronto, National Institute on Mental Retardation.

Noonan-Walsh, P. (1988) Handicapped and female: Two disabilities? in R. McConkey and P. McGinley (eds) *Concepts and Controversies in Services for People with Mental Handicap*. Brothers of Charity Services Galway and St Michael's House, Dublin.

O'Brien, J. (1987) *Learning from Citizen Advocacy Programs*. Atlanta, Georgia Advocacy Office.

O'Brien, J. (1990) *Helping People with Disabilities Speak Effectively for Themselves*. Workshop sponsored by the Research and Training Centre on Community Living at the AAMR Conference, Atlanta, Georgia.

O'Brien, J. and Wolfensberger, W. (1979) *CAPE: Standards for Citizen Advocacy Program Evaluation*. Toronto, National Institute on Mental Retardation.

Offload (1990) Look who's talking, *Community Care*, June 14.

People First (1989) Day Services: a users' account, in A. Brechin and J. Walmsley (eds) *Making Connections: Reflecting on the Lives and Experiences of People with Learning Difficulties - A Reader*. Open University, Hodder & Stoughton.

Qureshi, H. (1990) *Services for People with Disabilities*. Paper presented at 'The needs and resources of people with disabilities' seminar at the Policy Studies Institute, 3-4/12/90.

Report of the Committee of Enquiry into Mental Handicap Nursing and Care (1979) (The Jay Report). London, HMSO.

Sang, B. and O'Brien, J. (1984) *Advocacy: The UK and American Experiences*. London, King's Fund Centre.

Schaaf, V., Hooten, T., Shwartz, T., Young, C., Kerron, J. and Heath, D. (1977) People First: a self help organisation of the retarded, in J. Wortis (ed.) *Mental Retardation and Developmental Disabilities* Vol. IX, New York, Brunner/Mazel.

Shearer, A. (1973) *Listen*. London, CMH.

Sheffield Citizen Advocacy: *Report of the CAPE evaluation of Sheffield Citizen Advocacy*, Sheffield Citizen Advocacy and National Development Team.

Simons, K. (1990) *The Bristol Advocacy Project*. University of Bristol, Norah Fry Research Centre.

Towell, D. (1990) Keynote speech at Institute for Health Policy Studies, 'Measuring and Monitoring Quality in Services for People with Mental Handicap'. 8-9 Nov 1990, University of Southampton.

Twentieth Century Vixen (1990) *Between Ourselves*, Brighton.

United Nations (1981) *Declaration on the Rights of Mentally Retarded Persons*, UN.

Versey, A. (1990) Trainees' Committee, in D. Atkinson and F. Williams (eds) *'Know me as I am': An Anthology of Prose, Poetry and Art by People with Learning Difficulties - A Reader*. Open University, Hodder & Stoughton.

Ward, J. and Page-Hanify, B. (1986) Citizen advocacy in Australia, *Australian Disability Review*, 1, 19–28.

Ward, L. (1990) A programme for change: current issues in services for people with learning difficulties, in T. Booth (ed.) *Better Lives, Changing Services for People with Learning Difficulties*. Sheffield, Joint Unit for Social Services Research/*Community Care*.

Ward, N. (1988) Plenary session of People First conference, outlined by D. Amans and C. Darbyshire, in A. Brechin and J. Walmsley (eds) *Making Connections*.

Wertheimer, A. (1988) *Self Advocacy and Parents – the Impact of Self Advocacy on the Parents of People with Disabilities*. Further Education Unit: Working Together: A series of studies carried out for the UK contribution to the OECD/CERI Disabled Action Programme.

Williams, P. (1974) *A Workshop on Participation*. London, Campaign for the Mentally Handicapped.

Williams, P. and Shoultz, B. (1982) *We Can Speak for Ourselves*. London, Souvenir Press.

Winifred, Paul, Mary, Albert and Edward (1990) *Moving Out from Hospital to our own Homes*. Preston, Carnegie Publishing Ltd.

Wolfensberger, W. (1983) *Reflections on the Status of Citizen Advocacy*. Ontario, National Institute on Mental Retardation.

CHAPTER 10

Obstacles to Community Care

Norma V. Raynes

Background

Community care has been the catch phrase of the 1980s. Not just with regard to services for people with learning difficulties but for all those defined as priority care groups, another catch phrase. Sometimes the services these people received were called the Cinderella services. We learned in the 1970s and 1980s to relabel those people who had a mental handicap as people with learning difficulties. We learnt to statement children and to mainstream them. We learnt to talk about SECs instead of ATCs.

The 1980s were not just the decade of catch phrases and new terminology however. Much actually happened to move children out of institutions and into their parents' or other homes. Much happened to change the shape of the distribution of residential services for adults, both in terms of the location of these services and the source of the provision. As far as day care services, employment and training are concerned little, if we are honest, changed on the ground. Much happened too in the way of government pronouncements. White papers and legislation encouraged new practices. To some degree shifts in funding policy also help to implement 'the policy of community care which enables such people to achieve their full potential' (DHSS, 1989). The people referred to are those affected by problems of ageing, mental illness, mental handicap or physical or sensory disability, all of whom the government has stated need 'to be able to live as independently as possible in their own homes or in "homely" settings in the community'. Community care, so the White Paper states, means 'providing the services and support which people who are affected' by such problems need to achieve such independence in such settings (DHSS, 1989).

149

Residential care

The 1980s saw the government state explicitly that everyone would be better off in their own home and that children should not be admitted to hospital as a place for long term care (DHSS, 1981). The shape and design of these homes was left fairly vague. They were to be homely and in the community, just like, it seemed, the homes of you and me. It was assumed first that this was what everyone wanted; and second, that being physically in the community meant you were integrated in it, that is, you were part of the community. Of course most people with learning difficulties in the community live in their own homes, as they always have done, usually with a family member. However currently some 64,000 people live in staffed accommodation. In the past decade there has been a radical shift in the nature of the residential services provided and the balance of provision has moved from larger to smaller facilities and towards a more mixed economy of care. Places in large NHS hospitals have fallen by 12,000 and we have seen the total closure of some hospitals for people with learning difficulties.

Darenth Park, for example (Wing 1989; Glennester and Korman, 1985). Even the White Paper stated that

> it has become increasingly recognised that the needs of the most handicapped people, even those whose handicap is severe, are largely for social care rather than health care. Increasingly therefore, services are taking the form of packages of social care for people living independently, or supported in small group homes or residential communities. (DHSS, 1989: 12)

There has been a more than corresponding increase in the number of places in small NHS residential facilities and in places provided by local authorities and the private and voluntary sector.

Table 10.1 Changing nature of residential provision for people with learning disabilities

| | Number of residents | | |
	1978	1986	Percentage change
NHS hospital	48,000	36,300	25
NHS community units	–	3,200	–
Local authority (staffed)	10,000	15,800	60
Private sector	1,400	3,900	180
Voluntary sector	2,200	4,700	115
Total	61,600	63,900	4

Many government policy documents have in the 1980s reiterated the importance of aspects of environmental quality (DHSS, 1981, 1988). There is a recurring emphasis on small scale homely environments. The providers of these homes are enjoined to make them places which reflect individual need, providing opportunities for growth and development and a basis from which the fostering of links with the local community can be made. The same government documents encourage the use of community resources available to people in the community in addition to specialist resources which might be needed by some people with learning disabilities. The reality of the shape of available provision if these criteria are used as yard sticks against which we can assess the achievements of the 1980s have been highlighted in a recent study by Raynes *et al.* (1990). They studied a random sample of residential facilities provided by all four sectors, namely local authorities, health authorities and private and voluntary agencies. The sample was stratified by size and covers England with the exception of Greater London. The type of provision they found available is shown in Table 10.2.

Table 10.2 Type of building in which the facilities are located

Type of building	Management agency				
Housing stock	LA	HA	Pte	Vol.	Total
Small (1–4 places)	10	17	0	6	33
Medium (5–8 places)	2	10	7	8	27
Large (9 + places)	4	3	16	10	33
Adjoining houses	6	3	1	1	11
Functioning property					
Small units	2	0	0	1	3
Large units	35	3	0	0	38
Campus-style	0	5	0	0	5
Total number	59	41	24	26	150

Just under 60 per cent of local authority provision is in large scale purpose built hostels and the private sector has the bulk of its provision in houses for nine or more people.

The location of these facilities also revealed variations in their closeness to services for people with other disabilities. Of the homes provided by the local authorities 40 per cent were markedly close to such provision, as was 26 per cent of those provided by health authorities, 11 per cent by the private and 31 per cent by the voluntary sector.

This same study explored the homeliness of the residences and the extent to which the care provided was individualised. Some of the findings reflect improvements in life for people with learning difficulties. For example 98 per cent of the clients had sole and continuous use of personal clothing and their own toiletries. This is very different from the picture painted by King *et al.* (1971), studying provision in the late 1960s. Very few of the children in that study and also the adults in the study in the Tyne (1977) had their own personal clothing or toiletries.

Shops and pubs are close to most houses, within twenty minutes walk in all of the sectors providing homes. However the study by Raynes *et al.* also revealed that the use of community amenities was uniformly low in all sectors. Confirming the work of Flynn (1989) and others, the study found a degree of isolation which was striking in terms of the low level of contact with friends in the community. The majority of people living in the homes in these studies were isolated and lonely. Opportunities to make choices about what to eat or wear and decisions about day-to-day aspects of life was fairly common. Over 80 per cent of the clients in the study by Raynes et al. had key workers who might be presumed to be concerned about their individual needs and futures.

If we think about the alternatives currently available we can now see a range of amenities about which we can reflect. In the 1970s we could not do this. The choice before us seemed to be hospitals, some campus communities, parental homes and a few community units provided by health authorities and hostels provided by local authorities. Now, we have a sur-prisingly large range of provision. Such a situation makes it possible to think about the importance of choice and individual needs.

One of the driving forces behind the ideological shifts of the 1980s, which (if you want to be charitable) may have had, along with some of the research of the 1960s and 1970s, some impact on the policies of the 1980s, was the rejection of the institution as a home. Notions of asylum and sanctity, protection and the community of souls were rejected in favour or normalis-ation, integration and individualised care. Opportunities for growth and development were posited as an antithesis to the institution. Ironically whilst the research of the 1950s and 1960s in mental illness and mental handicap and into institutions for other people argued strongly for the closure of institutions, for which read hospitals in the UK, the research of the 1970s and early 1980s in the USA sounded warning bells about de-institutionalisation. These warning bells were not heard in England. My own view about the basis for policy shifts is that research little informs it. It is more a product of politics and ideology. Ideology is a catalyst but it is also unyielding and dismissive of the researcher and the individual with his or her own needs.

Daytime activities

With regard to day care services the 1980s were mainly the decade of re-labelling. Most adults are still in a day care centre of some kind usually an SEC/ATC. Study after study has shown this, (Raynes et al., 1988; Raynes et al., 1990). The centres have silted up. There is nowhere else to go. However there are signs of more creative thinking about what people with learning difficulties can do during the day. For example there are sheltered work schemes, collectives and new courses in Colleges of Further Education.

For all people with a learning difficulty education is available until they are nineteen. ERA (Educational Reform Act, 1988) requires that everyone follows a core curriculum and this will include those with learning difficulties unless the head of the school determines that they be exempted. The effect of this in practice has yet to be seen since the ERA was only passed in 1988 and the development of the core and foundation subjects is still in process. It could present a wonderful opportunity to extend the practice of educating children of all kinds together and sharing the technology that will make learning possible. All children have to be assessed at key stages to provide a formative assessment for teachers to build upon. This could again provide a basis for growth and development. However the act puts amazing powers in the hands of head teachers with regards to the access of children with learning difficulties to this new set of foundation and core subjects. We have indeed come a long way from the 1950s when so called ineducable children were excluded from learning opportunities. The 1990s are likely to be more exciting.

What are the blocks to community care?

This question assumes that community care is a 'good thing'. Perhaps the first block is this assumption. So let us explore it and see if it is a good thing.

To write such a sentence is to risk the wrath of many, for it is to question an ideological assumption which for ten years has had the quality of a sacred object. The sacred object has been protected and been spread around the country by a *cognoscenti* and one might say a priesthood. Heretics, those who question the new god have been pilloried, not just as unbelievers but as reactionaries and self interested people, caring little for the needs of the 'handicapped'. Who are the unbelievers and what do they want?

Some of the unbelievers it seems to me are the very people for whom the sacred object, community care, is to be provided. There are some people with learning difficulties who do not want to leave their institutions. But they don't know what the real options are, I have heard said, in response to this point of view. If they had lived in the community in small houses they would know it was better than where they are now. They would be happier. I do not know that we know this. We do know that isolation and loneliness lead to depression and at a minimum make life not very happy. I do know that for some of the people with learning difficulties isolation and loneliness and poverty are dominant aspects of their lives. Flynn (1989) tells us that nevertheless none of the people in her study who identified these attributes as part of their lives would want to go back to the hostels and institutions from which they had come. I do not know what people in village communities think about living in the 'outside world' as an option, as opposed to their self-help or other form of community. I do know from research that if the alternative to community care is an institution, in the form of a traditional hospital, I have no doubt that community care is the better option. But I do know that institutions have one important quality with which the options of living in the community are not yet imbued. This is certainty.

One of the other groups who have questioned community care and its quintessential goodness is parents. Indeed so strong is their feeling that they have organised together to establish RESCARE. They actively campaign for the retention of community villages, (and hospitals?). Parents have expressed the desire, following the closure of hospitals, that their children now adults will die before they do. This is real anxiety and real concern for the individual. If we are to hear it we must recognise it and not revile it as protective and infantilising. Institutions look solid, they were solid, they endured and lasted. Will community care do that?

That brings me naturally to another block to community care. It is of course money. The 1980s saw a shift in funding for community based provision. Amongst other things local authorities and health authorities negotiated doweries that returning people could take with them as they moved out of institutions into the community. Funding shifts were agreed. However the crucial White Paper and community care legislation rejected the idea of ring fencing money for services for people with learning difficulties living in the community. This went hand in hand with the shifting of responsibility for providing such services to local authorities. Although there has been a delay in the implementation of this policy, that delay solves no problems, it perpetuates uncertainty and generates anxiety for providers and receivers. The basic source of funding for local authority provision, namely the community charge, is being revised. Those with learning difficulties compete with the elderly, the mentally ill and education for a slice of the local authorities' resources cake. Uncertainty has bred creative schemes and alliances such as those developed by *Housing associations* and MENCAP. It has also generated collaborative cost sharing by statutory and the private and voluntary sectors. The new legislation encourages the purchase of packages of care suggesting flexibility and responsiveness to individual needs. It will not assuage the anxiety of parents however, who want to be sure that their family member with learning difficulty, has a home until death. Preferably it is to be a happy home bereft of poverty and the misery that isolation brings. We should not also disregard studies in the 1980s which showed us that people living with their own families were also isolated in the community and lacking in the support services the White Paper indicates families need.

Out there in the community some other problems confront the pioneering recipients of community care and those who work with them. The most obvious is the community itself. For decades people living in the community have neither seen nor heard of people with learning difficulties, for they have had indeed been put away, especially as they became adults. Parents struggled at home with children but children can blend into the landscape of the community in a way that adults seem less able to do. Visible hostility to the new residents in the community has been repeatedly shown. Residential associations and neighbourhood groups have sprung up to resist the purchase or use of a house in their neighbourhood to become a home for some people with learning difficulties. The Ombudsman has been appealed to. Bitter wrangling has occurred within what was presumed to be a supportive and welcoming neighbourhood. Staff, once working in institutions have had to deal with not just distressed parents but with hostile pedestrians and people in cafes who are quite clear and vocal in their un-welcoming stance to their new neighbours.

These staff in turn are often unsupported by middle managers who have no knowledge of learning difficulties or who understand little of the isolation of the staff and clients in the community. It is not just clients who feel lonely. Staff can feel isolated too. Those staff who were accustomed to work in large institutions had ready made suport networks on tap within the institution. They met colleagues informally at lunch or coffee or on the corridors as well as in formally organised meetings. These encounters gave people an opportunity to share their problems and obtain support from each other. In the community, in the dispersed housing settings, all this has gone and yet staff have to deal with the same problems as before *and* the new ones, some of which are referred to above.

The future

What do we need to move forward so that we can provide services which are sensitive to the needs of people with learning difficulties and their concerned families?

I think first we need to go back to Jack Tizard's concept of continuum of care (Tizard, 1964). We do need a range of residential services, educational, vocational and support services. The White Paper says

> community care means providing the right level of intervention and support to enable people to achieve maximum independence and control over their own lives. For this aim to become a reality the development of a wide range of services provided a variety of settings is essential (DHSS, 1989: 9).

We *do not need* institutional care in the sense of large scale non-individualised facilities. If we have village communities we must ensure that they, like any other provision, provide small group care, reflecting individual needs. In addition we must address the following issues:

(1) The assumption that the community will necessarily meet everyones' needs.
(2) The ring fencing of the fiscal resources for community services for people with learning difficulties. We must insist on this and get it written into legislation.
(3) We must provide training for staff who work in the community to deal with their new neighbours.
(4) We must provide education for the new neighbours to break down their fears and prejudices.
(5) We must find creative ways of opening up learning and job opportunities for adults and children with learning difficulties.
(6) We must ensure that the power of heads of schools to except and exclude children with learning difficulties are carefully monitored so that their education and the education of ordinary children about those who are different from themselves can continue.
(7) We must not underfund those services which are needed by some people with learning difficulties.
(8) We must ensure the further training of professionals, teachers,

doctors, social workers, and home helps so that they understand better the range of the needs of people with learning difficulties.

(9) We must find creative ways of supporting staff in the community.

(10) We must educate middle managers to the needs of their front line staff who are charged with the responsibility of providing homely and integrated community based services.

(11) We must listen to people with learning difficulties.

(12) We must imbue our service providers with the desire to continue to provide high quality sensitive services for individuals.

(13) We must see that those who purchase these services monitor them to ensure that quality continues to be part of the provision.

(14) We must stop worshipping sacred objects and accept the diversity of human need.

(15) We must build on the research and practices of the 1970s and 1980s to make the 1990s and beyond years that truly recognise individuals and their needs.

References

DHSS (1981) *Getting Children out of Hospital*. London, HMSO.

DHSS (1989) *Caring for People: Community Care in the Next Decade*. London, HMSO.

Flynn, M. (1989) Independent living arrangements for adults who are mentally handicapped, in N. Malin (ed.) *Reassessing Community Care*, pp. 302–21. London, Croom Helm.

Glennester, H. and Korman, N. (1985) Closing a hospital: the Darenth Park Project. Occasional paper in social administration. London, Bedford Square Press.

King, R. D., Raynes, N. V. and Tizard, J. (1971) *Patterns of Residential Care*. London, Routledge & Kegan Paul.

Raynes, N. V., Sumpton, R. and Flynn, M. (1988) *Homes for the Mentally Handicapped*. London, Croom Helm.

Raynes, N. V., Wright, K., Shiell, A. and Pettipher, C. M. (1990) An evaluation of the cost and quality of residential services for adults with a mental handicap. Report to the DOH, York University, Centre for Health Economics.

Tizard, J. (1964) *Community Services for the Mentally Handicapped*. Oxford, Oxford University Press.

Tyne, A. (1977) Residential provision for adults who are mentally handicapped. London Campaign for People who are Mentally Handicapped.

Wing, L. (1989) *Hospital Closure and the Resettlement of Residents: The Case of Darenth Park*. Aldershot, Gower.

CHAPTER 11

Changing the Public's Perceptions of Mental Handicap

Roy McConkey

Educating the Community

Educating the community about mental handicap has never been more necessary. An ordinary life in the community for people with severe learning difficulties can only become a reality if we –

- challenge the irrational arguments of the antagonistic,
- counter the indifference of the apathetic and,
- channel the energies of the sympathetic.

The antagonistic

An increasing number of people with learning difficulties now expect to live and work in ordinary settings; no longer are they content to be shut away in far-off 'institutions' or 'colonies'. But the chances of antagonistic responses from the general public have increased, especially as a similar re-settlement policy is underway for other disadvantaged groups such as children in care or people with mental illness. The public's fears are invariably unfounded but until they are challenged effectively, emotions win the day and opportunities are lost for people to live, work and play in the community.

The apathetic

Radical changes in health, education and social services funding will mean increased competition for monies. Advocating the case for mental handicap means winning over apathetic officials, councillors and ultimately the voters.

The sympathetic

The diverse needs of people with severe learning difficulties could never be met through a fully professional workforce – even if society could afford it. A better strategy is to enlist the help of sympathetic people from the community who for a limited time and in specific ways share their talents in helping. In so doing, they will also further the social integration of people with a disability into their local communities.

In short, the ultimate success of care in the community is dependent on the attitudes and reactions of people who have had little or no contact with people who have learning difficulties. Yet despite the thousands of millions of pounds spent each year on services for these people, hardly any is devoted to changing public attitudes.

Families, professionals and self-advocates have done much to improve the quality of services on offer, yet too often they work in isolation from their essential partners – the local community. Educating the public has been made everyone's responsibility and yet it is nobody's.

In this chapter, we shall first explore the dearth of contact which the public have with people with learning difficulties, even when they live in the same neighbourhood. Second, the public's common fears and misperceptions are described and ways of correcting them are outlined. Finally, we examine ways of translating people's goodwill into good actions. Although we can bemoan the past lack of community involvement, much has been learnt about how integration can become a reality in the coming decades.

Who are you?

One fact above all others must be borne in mind as you read this chapter. People's attitudes are not based on first-hand experience. Survey after survey throws up the same result – around three-quarters of the population have never met a person with severe learning difficulties (e.g. MORI, 1982). In part this is due to the past policy of putting people into institutions, coupled with the relatively low frequency of occurrence of this disability – around 1 in 250 people are markedly affected.

But another explanation could be given, namely that the public have actively avoided meeting people with disabilities largely because they feel they would not know what to say or do in their company. We put this notion to the test by concentrating our attitudinal research on people who had more opportunities than most to meet people with a mental handicap, namely the neighbours of community facilities.

For example, we surveyed a statistical sample of 270 neighhbours living in the immediate vicinity of a large day centre for over 70 adults with severe and multiple handicaps who were bussed from their homes in north Dublin each day. The centre opened five days a week for 50 weeks of the year and at the time of our survey had been operating for over two years. Yet only half the people in the district knew of the centre's existence and fewer still – less than one quarter – knew that it was a centre for people with severe learning difficulties. In all, only one in twenty people in that neighbourhood had ever talked to a service-user. Hence it is possible for a centre to be in the community and for neighbours to have nothing to do with it (McConkey, 1987).

Equally surprising were the findings of an Irish national study in which we explored neighbours' reactions to a group home for teenagers or adults with mental handicaps that was located in one of the houses in their estate (McConkey, 1990). Nine group homes were included in the study from various parts of Ireland, North and South. This time we interviewed one person from the 50 immediately adjacent houses to each group home; 426 people in all. We discovered to our surprise that on average, one in ten of the neighbours did not know of the homes' existence and nearly a quarter could not name the handicap of the residents. Although two in five of the neighbours reported talking to a resident of the group home, fewer than one in ten knew the name of even one person from the group home. Neighbours have even less contact with the staff who worked in the houses. Similar disspiriting results have been obtained in various British surveys (e.g. Locker *et al.* 1981; Atkinson and Ward, 1987).

The moral is clear, merely locating day centres or residences in the community is no guarantee that the locals will get to meet people with learning difficulties. Indeed staff in these specialist services may have little perception of their isolation, preoccupied as they are with their work and the fact that many of them live in other parts of the city or town.

Enhancing community contacts

If local people are to meet and get to know people with disabilities, much more planning and organisation is needed. It cannot be left to chance encounters on the street as they obviously do not work.

First, people with learning difficulties should regularly use local community facilities such as shops, cafes, swimming pools etc. It goes without saying that they must cope successfully in these settings. Any bizarre or inappropriate behaviours will put people off and heighten their anxieties. Likewise people are threatened if they encounter a large group of disabled people. They are more likely to chat if they meet one or two handicapped people at a time. Equally neighbours need opportunities of being introduced to people personally (Firth and Rapley, 1990).

Second, community involvement is more likely to come about where there is a settled population and the area provides a range of resources where local people can meet. These criteria should be kept in mind when new locations are chosen for services.

For example, in the national study of group homes, we employed a discriminant analysis procedure to identify the characteristics of people who reported talking to a person from the group home compared to those who had never met such a person. In order of importance, the variables which best discriminated the people who had had contact were:

(1) an involvement in three or more activities within the locality – pubs, schools, churches, sports, resident associations etc.
(2) they lived in small towns rather than cities
(3) the neighhbours had lived in the area for more than five years
(4) they had experience of voluntary work with people who had a severe learning difficulty
(5) females rather than males
(6) people who reported being in frequent contact with their neighbours
(7) people under sixty years of age.

These are suggestive rather than definite guidelines but perhaps it is best to avoid locating services in city neighbourhoods which are replete with senior citizens who have recently retired to the area and who have little or no contact with their neighbours or involvement in community activities!

Third, integration with the local community is much more likely if the clients in the service are drawn from that locality; if the staff who work in the service are from that neighbourhood and live in it, and if local people have some involvement in the running or management of the service (de Lacey, 1988). The sad thing is that these three conditions have rarely been met in the past. Hence service planners must take their share of the blame for perpetuating the public's ignorance of mental handicap.

Misunderstandings

Lack of contact with mental handicap means that myths, stereotypes and confusions linger on. Perhaps the most common is people's confusion of mental handicap with mental illness. For example in a national survey of over 1,400 school pupils aged fifteen and sixteen years, nearly half of them selected 'mental illness' as a suitable alternative to the term 'mental handicap' and one quarter of them went on to select it as the most suitable alternative; ignoring other terms such as 'slow learner', 'retarded' and 'slow developer'. Nor is it a case of childhood ignorance; 20 per cent of employers in a Sheffield survey confused mental handicap with mental illness (Harrison and Tomes, 1990).

The common adjective 'mental' in both conditions is the source of the problem plus the fact that for decades both groups were treated in the same institution, by the same personnel – psychiatrists and nurses. Indeed this still pertains in many parts of the world to this day, despite the call by the International League of Societies for Persons with Mental Handicap for a clear distinction to be made between the services for these two groups.

Much greater effort must be put into explaining mental handicap to the public. Changing the terminology might help, although there is little consensus internationally on an agreed alternative and the risk is that even greater confusion will result. This debate has probably no solution.

Anticipated problems

Public antagonism towards mentally handicapped people has been most marked when it is proposed to open a group home in certain neighbourhoods. This issue is probably the most thoroughly researched aspect of community attitudes.

A USA Gallup Poll (1975) found that 15 per cent of people objected to having 'six mildly or moderately handicapped persons occupying a home in their block'. Comparable figures have been found in surveys in Ireland (Market Research Bureau of Ireland, 1981) and London (Locker *et al.*, 1981). However this figure could be boosted to over 20 per cent when it was suggested to respondents that a vacant house in the neighbourhood – so called 'threat' condition – might be used as a group home (Kastner *et al.*, 1979). Looked on positively this would suggest that four out of five people have no strong objections. But a study by Seltzer and Litchfield (1984) suggests a less rosy picture.

Seltzer and Litchfield found that half of the 43 community residences studied in the Massachusetts area had encountered community opposition and that this was highest during the period immediately before and immediately after the residence opened. Subsequently it diminished considerably. Furthermore opposition was least likely when the community was made aware of the home's existence after the residents had moved in, suggesting that low profile entry strategies might be advantageous.

What are the problems which people anticipate and are they borne out in experience? In Ireland we undertook a major research programme into neighbour's attitudes. In all over 1000 people were interviewed; 426 people were the immediate neighbours of nine staffed group homes and 615 came from fourteen comparable areas with no group home. Subsequently a community service opened in three of these group areas and the reactions of neighbours were monitored before and after the service opened.

Neighbours' perceptions of problems

People's perceptions of problems were investigated in two ways. First they were asked an open question – 'If a house for three or more mentally handicapped people with one or two care staff started up in your neighbourhood do you think that this would give rise to any problems in the neighbourhood?'

In areas with no group homes, 12 per cent of people mentioned one or more concerns – other people objecting, making children anxious, people afraid of them, not enough garden space for the house, children being attacked, lowering house prices; clients wrongly blamed for anything done in the area and that the house could develop into a bigger facility. But only five neighbours (1.7 per cent) of a group home could think of a problem.

Likewise, before a house opened in an area (9 per cent) of people mentioned a potential problem but two years later only one person out of 127 named a problem.

Potential problems

In case people found it difficult to think of problems on the spur of the moment or were reticent to state them outright, we went on to ask all interviewees about nine specific problems that had been mentioned in previous studies (e.g. MORI, 1982). Four of these related to difficulties for the person with the handicap and five for residents in the neighbourhood (see Table 11.1). For each potential problem, respondents were asked to say whether or not it had been or could be a problem, or whether they could not decide.

Table 11.1 Percentage of neighbours perceiving problems

	No group home	Group home	Before	After
			(service opened)	
Problems for the service users				
Teased	46	16	47	2
Victimised	30	7	24	4
Isolated	37	22	31	36
Inadequate professional care	13	5	7	3
Problems for the neighbourhood				
Embarrassment	36	22	39	19
Threat to children	11	1	13	2
Violence	10	2	10	1
House values drop	9	1	8	1
Noise/disturbance	9	1	7	1

As Table 11.1 shows, in nearly every instance people anticipated more problems arising than did occur. Two dominant concerns remained however after the services opened. First, that the service users were isolated and kept to themselves and second, that people were embarrassed in their company – not knowing what to say or how to react to them. Once again, lack of personal contact lies at the root of both.

A survey of employers in Sheffield also found a higher incidence of anticipated problems than was found among those with experience of having a person with learning difficulties on their workforce (Harrison and Tomes, 1990). Forty per cent of employers with no experience thought co-worker acceptance would be a problem, whereas only 4 per cent of 'experienced' employers mentioned this.

Community education

One value of surveys of this kind is to offer reassurance to potential neighbours or employers that their concerns are reasonable and 'normal' but that experience suggests they are unjustified. Information leaflets aimed at potential neighbours can highlight the likelihood that their initial fears and concerns are unfounded. Video-programmes in which neighbours or employees recount their experiences are also a useful educational tool.

Neighbours who happily live beside an existing house might meet with people from another area who are anxious about a house opening in their neighbourhood. Reluctant neighbours or employers are more likely to be reassurred by the experience of people like themselves rather than by the promises of professional service workers.

These results also demonstrate the importance of neighhbours meeting a person with a mental handicap. The usual social interchanges which occur in any neighbourhood can be a significant educational experience in themselves. But integrating people into the life of a community is a very different activity to physically placing them in community settings (Firth and Rapley, 1990). Staff need to make introductions and to provide opportunities for shared activities if the neighbours' feelings of embarrassment – the second most common concern expressed in this study – are to be overcome. Yet staff training, previous work experiences or job descriptions rarely focus on this aspect of working in community settings.

We also need more studies which document and monitor the community integration of residents within neighbourhoods – what works, what doesn't work and the variations across communities and services within neighbour-hoods (Pittock and Potts, 1988). To date research into community residences has been dominated with the functioning and costings of the house.

But the one lesson above all to be drawn from these studies is that the results do not support the stereotype of an uncaring community. The vast majority of people we interviewed were in favour of community care; a high proportion were willing to make contact with the service-users and only a minority foresaw problems. These findings may be particular to these Irish communities but similar research elsewhere suggests that that is not so. Con-sulting with local communities is the best way of determining local reactions and the foundation for building a caring community.

What people want to know

Two topics dominate whenever we have given the public the chance to say what they want to know about mental handicap. First, what do I do if I meet a mentally handicapped person, and second, what causes it?

More attention and money has been spent on the latter, primarily in an attempt to reduce the incidence of handicapped births. However if our data is anything to go by, the messages have become rather confused. For example, in a national survey of secondary school pupils 65 per cent cited 'mothers smoking during pregnancy' as the major cause of mental handicap; quite an over-generalisation! By contrast, other significant causes were known only by a minority of students – lack of oxygen to the brain (43 per cent) and meningitis (39 per cent).

The solution frequently advocated is to have more and bigger publicity drives even extending into television advertising. However the experience of health education campaigns against smoking and alcohol abuse is that information does not necessarily lead to a change in people's behaviour; no matter how well and expensively it is packaged. Rather the emphasis now is on giving people the information when they need it and in a way that makes sense to them.

A common mistake is merely to simplify the medical textbook instead of reworking the information to meet the needs of the target audience. For example with parents who have a young family the emphasis might be on accident prevention; vaccination against childhood illnesses and the risks associated with mothers over thirty-five. With couples contemplating starting a family, details could be given of genetic disorders and their prevention. In both instances, the messages about handicap are best embedded within an overall health promotion context, which leaves people knowing what they can do, rather than inducing unnecessary fears and anxieties which can rebound to the detriment of handicapped people.

How to react with disabled people

The public's wish to know how they should react with their handicapped peers has been ignored. Instead they have been offered trite advice along the lines of 'treat them as you would anyone else'; an impossible task when they appear so patently different from other people.

Educating the public on how to get on with disabled people is not easily done. These people differ greatly in personality, abilities and interests. There is therefore no correct way of interacting with 'them'. Moreover disputes exist among professionals and parents as to what is best for people with disabilities. Some say they need only love and care in the security of familiar surroundings, whereas others maintain that they need to get out and about, doing as much as they can for themselves. All very confusing for the willing helper with no previous experience.

But perhaps the most telling argument against giving the public directives on how they should react towards disabled people, is that it emphasises how different they are and would unwittingly create an even greater barrier. We don't do it for other groups in society – immigrants, old folk, itinerants – so why pick up on people with disabilities?

Yet our experience has been that once people find they can get on with disabled people, they are much more positively disposed towards them. Rokeach (1973) proposed that the attitudes we hold towards other people, are in fact reflections of our own self-concept. If we feel badly about ourselves – for example 'I'm afraid of meeting people with a mental handicap' – then our attitudes towards them will be coloured accordingly. But, he argues, if people's self-concepts can be changed for the better – 'I can get along with mentally handicapped people' – more positive feelings will be expressed to this group. Change has first to occur in the person, before there is a shift in attitudes.

This viewpoint flies in the face of traditional wisdom that attitude change results from giving people lots of information about the disability; hence the call for more television programmes, radio advertising and poster displays! If Rokeach is right, and I suspect he is, then these ventures are a waste of money. They remain attractive to many because they are the easy option.

Reactions to contact

It is commonly asserted that people from the community are not interested in helping. But our research suggests that this is a large over-generalisation. For example when surveying people's attitudes to group homes, we presented them with a list of six ways in which they could be of assistance and asked them to select for each, one of three answers – 'Yes, they would do this', 'maybe' or 'prefer not'. The percentage of people replying 'yes' is shown in Table 11.2.

Table 11.2 Percentage of people willing to have contact

	No group home	Group home	Before	After
			(service opened)	
Talk to them	82	71	89	76
Help in emergency	73	69	78	76
Attend Open Day	69	59	75	69
Have them visit my home	60	49	66	48
I visit them at their place	50	35	58	31
Go on outing	41	32	43	34

In every instance bar helping in emergencies, people living in areas without a group home appeared to be much more willing to help. Sadly it would appear to be a case of words speaking louder than actions. When people knew they could be put to the test, such as in areas where a group home was already established, the percentage of people willing to become involved, dropped dramatically.

Even so, a sizable percentage of people still indicated their willingness to be involved. 'Ah', you say, 'they are only well-intended people who don't know what they are letting themselves in for'. We discovered that was not so. The people most interested in helping are those with past experience of voluntary work and who have been regularly in contact with disabled people. They, more than most neighbours, would know what was in store for them. The sad thing is that many had never been asked to help.

There remains too, the challenge of encouraging the less willing members of the community to become better disposed towards people with mental handicap. In a study of 300 people interviewed at random in three shopping centres around north Dublin, we asked what would encourage them to become more involved in helping people with mental handicaps. 'Support and back-up from professionals' was the most popular incentive – chosen by 40 per cent of people as being the most important, followed by 'if I was helping a person I knew' (30 per cent of people) and if it gave me 'work experience' (a particular favourite with the under twenties). Most people expressed a preference for working with children and with mildly rather than severely handicapped people. When you consider that upwards of one quarter of the people interviewed had experience of doing voluntary work, it may well be possible to persuade more of them to share their time and talents with people who have learning difficulties.

Changing people to change attitudes

One consensus from the welter of international research into changing attitudes towards disabled people is the experience for the able-bodied of actively interacting with peers who are handicapped. They note too that it is the quality of contact rather than the quantity of contact which is important and they warn that certain contacts may actually increase rather than decrease the public's negative impressions.

The features which have produced positive changes can be summarised as follows.

Planned personal contacts

In very many cases people with a mental handicap are their own best ambassadors. They win people over if they meet in an enjoyable, non-threatening way. This is more likely achieved if

- They meet in ordinary places rather than in specialist centres. Hence in the short programme on mental handicap for use with secondary school pupils, which we designed during the CARA project, a group of trainees from the local centre for persons with mental handicap come to visit the pupils in their school.
- The people should share an activity together rather than relying solely on conversation. For example, in our educational module for shop assistants in city centre stores, they take one or two handicapped people on a tour of the store – an educational experience for both partners.
- The people from the community are given opportunities to prepare themselves for the meeting. Our preferred way is to show them a video of people like themselves interacting with mentally handicapped people similar to the ones they are likely to meet.

In our experience it is best if people's first contact is with individuals with whom they can communicate relatively easily. As their confidence increases they can be introduced to people with more severe handicaps.

Contrast these guidelines with most people's introduction to mental handicap – a guided tour of a special centre. Research in the US suggests that such tours rarely change people's attitudes and they may in fact reinforce people's negative beliefs (LeUnes, 1975). Tours do not allow members of the public to meet people with disabilities at a personal level. They don't allow them to share a common activity and little preparation is given to reduce the apprehensions of the tourists other than the assurance that the staff will be on hand to 'protect' you. Afterwards the tourists often enthuse about the facilities and the dedication of the staff and they may perceive them in a more positive way, but invariably they only serve to emphasise the disabilities, not the personalities, of the people observed. They leave with their own inadequacies highlighted, 'I could never do that work' and as Rokeach predicts, thinking less well of the handicapped people.

Why educate the community?

Educating the community is not an end in itself, it is a means to an end. Hence every effort must begin by stating the expected outcomes. Only then can you determine the style and nature of your programme. Methods which can make the public better informed about the causes of mental handicap will not produce volunteers for a summer leisure scheme.

Target groups

The third key to more successful community education is to direct your energies to target groups. These could be key people whom you want to influence – playgroup leaders, clergy, police and local politicians. The great advantage is that your messages about disability can be attuned to these people's own interests and concerns. Moreover, the messages can be got over much more concisely, say in two or three sessions. It is when we talk in generalities that generally nothing gets done and people lose interest.

Multi-media methods

Fourth piece of advice – don't put your faith in one approach. Your educational messages need to be hammered home in different ways – leaflets, talks, discussions, video. Particular use should be made of experiential learning techniques so that people have a chance to discover for themselves the truth of what you tell them. It is this point more than any other, which distinguishes successful attitude change strategies from the well-intentioned failures.

On-going educational programmes

Once-off campaigns are of limited effectiveness. Community education must be on-going, with the occasional peaks perhaps. It is too important a task to be left to a few. Every parent and professional has a role to play and indeed many of the advances we have made are through their efforts, even though they deemed them insignificant ... bringing their handicapped child to church; using the local swimming pool rather than the one in the specialist centre or inviting the local community to use the facilities of their special centre. How much more might be achieved if these were better co-ordinated and supported.

Teamwork

The task cannot be left to one or two dedicated professionals, no matter how experienced and talented they might be. Teamwork is essential for a sustained impact. Among those who should be involved are:

People with mental handicap – they are often their own best advocates. Their involvement in the enterprise should break down the 'them' and 'us' mentality that so pervades present thinking.

Parents or relatives – have the emotional involvement and the direct experience which can silence the sceptic. As most are already 'connected into' local communities through families and friends they can help gain access to many community groups.

Sympathetic people from the community – such as 'volunteer' helpers, employers who have taken people on work experience and next door neighbours to group homes. They are credible witnesses to others in the community; people with whom they can identify. Through their contacts, they too may be able to link you into other groups.

Professional carers and helpers – their role may already involve contact with the community and you would gain from their experiences. They often are aware of the range of needs among people with a disability. Some may have particular expertise to share, e.g. in giving talks, and most could help gain access to certain resources such as video equipment.

'Status' figures in the community – doctor, councillor, clergy. Their advice and ability to open doors may prove valuable even though they will be the first to admit that they know nothing about mental handicap. But it's what they know about the local community that makes them valuable members of the team!

For me, the one person who has actively demonstrated ways of changing people's attitudes and proven their effectiveness is Peter Mittler. So often his 'hunches' have been borne out by subsequent research; the issues he has espoused have become central and his ability to communicate complex ideas simply and practically has not only changed people's thinking but also their practice.

Educating the community is not easy. Service personnel rarely are expected to undertake such work and fewer have been trained for it. It is some comfort to know that we do at least have Peter Mittler's role model to follow as we advance towards the new millenium.

References

Atkinson, D. and Ward, L. (1987) Friends and neighbours: relationships and opportunities in the community for people with mental handicap, in *Reassessing Community Care*, by N. Malin (ed.) 232–48, London, Croom Helm.

de Lacey, E. (1988) Developing community involvement in services, in *Concepts and Controversies in Services for People with Mental Handicap*, by R. McConkey and P. McGinley, (eds), 277–98, Galway, Brothers of Charity.

Firth, H. and Rapley, M. (1990) *From Acquaintance to Friendship: Issues for People with Learning Disabilities*, Kidderminster, BIMH Publications.

Harrison, B. and Tomes, A. (1990) Employers' attitudes to the employment of people with mental handicaps: an empirical study, *Mental Handicap Research*, 3, 196–213.

Kastner, L. S., Rappucci, N. D. and Pezzoli, J. J. (1979) Assessing community attitudes toward mentally retarded persons, *American Journal of Mental Deficiency*, 84, 137–44.

LeUnes, A. (1975) Institutional tour effects on attitudes related to mental retardation, *American Journal of Mental Deficiency*, 79, 732–5.

Locker, D., Rao, B. and Wedell, J. M. (1981) Changing attitudes towards the mentally handicapped: the impact of community care, *Apex: Journal of the British Institute of Mental Handicap*, 9, 92–3, 95, 103.

McConkey, R. (1987) *Who Cares? Community Involvement with Handicapped People*, London, Souvenir Press.

McConkey, R. (1990) Community reactions to group homes: contrasts between people living in areas with and without group homes, in W. I. Fraser (ed.) *Key Issues in Mental Retardation Research*, London, Routledge.

McConkey, R. and McCormack, B. (1983) *Breaking Barriers: Educating People about Disability*, London, Souvenir Press.

Market and Opinion Research International (MORI) (1982) *Public Attitudes Towards the Mentally Handicapped: Research Study Conducted for MENCAP*, London, MENCAP.

Pittock, F. and Potts, M. (1988) Neighbourhood attitudes to people with a mental handicap: a comparative study, *British Journal of Mental Subnormality*, 34, 35–46.

Rokeach, M. (1973) *The Nature of Human Values*, New York, Free Press.

Seltzer, M. M. and Litchfield, L. C. (1984) Community reaction to community residences: a study of factors related to community response, in J. M. Berg, (ed.) *Perspectives and Progress in Mental Retardation: Vol 1*, Baltimore, University Park Press.

CHAPTER 12

Research: Progress and Prospects

Chris Kiernan

Introduction

The invitation of this title could lead in to a catalogue of research 'successes', with possibly a few research 'failures' thrown in to prevent a researcher from being accused of being too arrogant on the part of researchers, followed by a few paragraphs of gloom about the future. There will be elements of this agenda in this chapter, but the opportunity to contribute to this volume has led the author to think about the *raison d'être* for the research process, where it has led us and where we might be going, as well as whether we will ever get there.

In the chapter I will concentrate mainly on research in the education of children and young people with mental handicap. This is, in the main, because this is the area in which Peter Mittler has worked for much of his career, and one in which he is still an active and distinguished contributor, and the area of special education with which I am most familiar. The dedication of this volume to Peter Mittler also gives an excuse for being unashamedly parochial in drawing mainly on work completed or underway in the Hester Adrian Research Centre, which he established and directed for fourteen years.

The answer to the question 'what is research in special education for?' can, at one level, be answered in a very simple way. Research should help the education system teach pupils more effectively. Such research should span the whole spectrum of helping DES policy makers to formulate and evaluate policies for education, helping LEAs to implement national and local policies effectively, helping schools to implement policies, including their own, and helping teachers, within this framework and within the framework of their initial training and in-service training, to teach their pupils.

However, this answer makes a fundamental assumption which needs to be explored. It assumes that the tenets on which special education is based are correct, that the goals of special education, as conceived within the current system, are appropriate.

The reason for starting the discussion at this point is that the idea that science is 'value free', that scientists 'deal only in facts' is now well outmoded. Researchers have their own values which guide their research both in the way in which they conceptualise research problems and, as a consequence, what measures they take and how they then interpret their data. Increasingly research workers are questioning, for a variety of reasons, the concept of the researcher as 'objective technician'. This also leads them to question the fundamental tenets of the systems which they research.

The goals of special education

In 1978 the Warnock Committee framed two long-term goals for education. The first was 'to enlarge a child's knowledge, experience, and imaginative understanding, and thus his awareness of moral values and capacity for enjoyment'. The second was 'to enable him to enter the world after formal education is over as an active participant in society and a responsible contributor to it, capable of achieving as much independence as possible' (HMSO, 1978: 5). The Committee remarked that they were 'fully aware that for some children the first of these goals can be approached only by minute, though for them highly significant, steps, while the second may never be achieved'.

> For some children, enjoyment and understanding may be confined to the hard-won, taught capacity to recognise things and people, and perhaps to name them. For some, independence may in the end amount to no more than the freedom of performance of a task for oneself rather than having someone else do it, even if the task is only getting dressed or feeding oneself (HMSO, 1978: 6)

However, fundamentally, the Committee affirmed that

> education, as we conceive it, is a good, and a specifically human good, to which all human beings are entitled. There exists, therefore a clear obligation to educate the most severely disabled for no other reason than that they are human (HMSO, 1978: 6).

The goals given by the Warnock Committee are consistent with a substantial amount of curriculum development in schools for pupils with severe learning difficulties which has subsequently taken place. Much of this development is consistent with the broadly behaviour approach adopted by Gardner *et al.* (1983) in what they termed a 'Skills Analysis Model'. The approach adopts the basic premise of the behavioural approach to mental handicap. Mental handicap has as its central feature the fact that pupils with severe learning difficulties do not learn skills normally. However, this failure is assumed to be a feature of the learning environment rather than an inherent feature of the 'mentality' of the pupil with severe learning difficulty (Bijou, 1966). If the learning environment can be optimised by the use of behavioural techniques derived from the experimental analysis of behaviour, then the pupil with severe learning difficulties will learn.

The behavioural approach gained substantial currency in the 1970s at least in part because it clearly offered the opportunity for teachers to fulfil their role as professionals who changed pupils' behaviour. In curriculum terms the behavioural approach required educationalists to decide what to teach pupils with severe learning difficulties. The clearest targets were, and still are, the development of everyday living skills. Achievements such as self-feeding, washing, dressing, and caring for toilet needs can be readily broken down into small steps, each of which can be sequenced in line with the basic techniques of behavioural methods. As a consequence such programmes, and programmes concerned with basic pre-academic and academic skills, were well researched and are commonly implemented (Kiernan, 1974, 1985).

These moves are clearly reflected in the form of curriculum by Gardner and her colleagues (1983). The curriculum which has 'clear objectives in terms of specified skills will permit careful assessment of each child's abilities and will enable selection of an appropriate item as the next teaching target for that individual'. Furthermore, such a curriculum

> will provide a structure by means of which the student is enabled to proceed by small steps through a hierarchy of skills, which is not based on normative developmental data but on the breakdown of target skills into constituent elements by a process of skills or task analysis (Gardner *et al.*, 1983: 20).

In other terms whatever can be specified as a skill, and broken down into steps, can be taught. The approach necessarily limits itself to observable behaviour. As Gardner and her colleagues emphasise, the curriculum should be written in the language of behaviour rather than in terms of 'any inferred process'.

The approach was also consistent with an increasingly felt need for accountability in education, an end to which the approach already lent itself in North America. Gardner and her colleagues also see the approach as helping to achieve participation of parents in the pupil's education, a goal stressed by the Warnock Committee (HMSO, 1978, Chapter 9).

Fundamental questions can be raised concerning the conception of the function of education envisaged by Warnock and the way in which curriculum development is pursued in schools for pupils with severe learning difficulties. As already noted, the first goal of education adopted by the Warnock Committee was the enlargement of the pupil's 'knowledge, experience, and imaginative understanding' and therefore the awareness of moral values and 'capacity for enjoyment'. The Committee suggested, however, that enjoyment and understanding may be confined to the 'capacity to recognise things and people, and perhaps to name them'.

These statements stress an essentially technical orientation of education. Knowledge, experience, and imaginative understanding are to be enhanced, although the aim of enlarging imaginative understanding is not further elaborated. The capacity for enjoyment is seen as realised through this process. However, the conception of enjoyment envisaged by the Committee is remarkably limited for some pupils, confined as it is to recognition of things and people and 'perhaps' naming them.

It is arguable that capacity for enjoyment, happiness, or psychological well-being, should be a central goal of education, especially for children and young people with severe learning difficulties. The majority of such pupils will never derive enjoyment from many of the activities normal to their mainstream peers. They will never drive fast cars, excel at sports, construct much admired gardens, or decorate their own houses. Especially for pupils with more severe disabilities their 'enjoyments' may be more at the level of sensory events such as sounds, visual input, or tactile and vestibulary sensations.

The realisation of the goals of education within school curricula appears to give only grudging acknowledgement to the notion that being able to do things which you enjoy is important. Teachers themselves will take obvious personal satisfaction in having taught a pupil to do something which he or she clearly enjoys. Teaching an activity from which a pupil derives a sense of achievement or which clearly enhances the pupils self-esteem will also be satisfying for teachers. However, identifying and teaching such activities is subsumed to other goals. The pupil's enjoyment is, on many occasions, not even seen as a necessary condition of successful education.

Some activities which pupils enjoy may be identified as problem behaviours. This applies in particular to stereotyped or ritualistic behaviour. The pupil whose preferred activity is flicking his fingers in front of his eyes or rocking continuously is seen as having problem behaviour. Clearly these behaviours are problems to teachers if they prevent the pupil from participating in 'educationally' more valid activities. The teacher has to some degree the duty, as a teacher, to intrude on the pupil's preferred activity. However, the question is not one of intrusion but one of what is taught as an alternative to stereotyped behaviour and with what end? All too frequently alternative behaviours are defined as educationally valid for reasons which have little to do with the pupil. So the pupil may be taught to stack rings on a rod, match colours or complete a form board with extrinsic reinforcement in the form of social praise.

The alternative approach would identify what function the behaviour is playing for the child, why it is intrinsically reinforcing. Flicking your fingers in front of your eyes produces varied visual input which is under your control. Given this, a constructive programme might build from within this recognition a series of activities which allow the child to control ever more complex and varied visual inputs. Once a repertoire of activities is established. teaching the child to communicate choices, and to learn complex responses to access activities, will be building on established intrinsic motivation.

Clear statements of this general approach are out of fashion in educational thinking. Stevens (1971) placed great stress on the value of observing children's preferred activities. From such observations, she argued, 'teachers will see how to develop the interests which the children display in free choice sessions and extend them' (1971: 23). She cautions against a narrow interpretation of social education emphasising the importance of considering the child's 'ideas, creations, inventiveness, curiosity, the expression of his own needs and desire, his enjoyment of people who are interested in him' (1971: 14).

The emphasis on developing the pupil's behaviour from within his or her own interests and seeing the extension of these interests as an educationally worthwhile goal runs counter to the basis for much curriculum development. The development of thinking around the National Curriculum in the special needs sector further extends this trend.

In developing this argument I am not suggesting that the attempts to enhance the skills and knowledge of pupils with severe learning difficulties on lines parallel to other children and young people is misguided. However, I am making the suggestion that one important goal of education should be to enable pupils to enjoy their lives. This goal could well lead to radically different approaches to individual programme development than is currently the case.

Two examples might make the point. Research on the leisure pursuits of people with mental handicap show that watching television ranks high (Cheseldine and Jeffree, 1981). Several years ago I saw a leavers' programme in a school for pupils with severe learning difficulties which had taken this seriously. Parts of the programme were built around how pupils could choose their evening's watching by use of newspapers and programme guides. Other parts of the programme involved discussion of preferences, of programme content, and of speculation of what would happen next in favourite series. Through the programme pupils were learning how to make choices, about time, and about control of the TV set. They were also learning how to express, and justify, their preferences. They were learning to share their views with others, to think about future sequences and why one outcome of a set of incidents in a programme was more likely than another. In the age of video recorders they could also have learned how to programme controls, a skill which many of their parents may well have valued given the quality of the typical instruction booklet.

The point of this example is that a whole range of educationally worthwhile aims were being achieved within the framework of an activity which motivated the young people. In addition, the programme taught them something which they could usefully carry forward into their adult lives.

The second example concerns a young man whose only interest was in drawing. His draughtsmanship was shaky but adequate and he drew a range of different subjects, all from memory. However, his teachers saw his interest as an 'obsession'. Rather than building a programme around his preferred activity by, for example, helping him to improve the quality of his drawing, using his drawings to improve his communication and encouraging him to draw from life, he was prevented from drawing in school. The long-term outcome of this decision may have been that his progress in 'legitimate' areas of the curriculum was enhanced. However, in terms of enhancing his happiness and activities he could carry forward to adulthood, the decision seemed to miss important opportunities.

The Warnock Committee's second goal of education is that the child should, after formal education, be 'an active participant in society and a responsible contributor to it, capable of achieving as much independence as possible' (HMSO, 1978: 5). 'Independence' is expanded in terms of 'freedom to perform a task for oneself', even if this is only getting dressed or self-feeding.

The vast majority of children and young people with severe mental handicap will not, as adults, achieve independence in the sense indicated by Warnock. They will be dependent and, to varying degrees, present a 'burden of care'. Furthermore, they will not, in the accepted senses of the terms, be active participants in society or responsible contributors to it.

Without taking too extreme a position, it is possible to argue with the fundamental assumptions underlying these conclusions. In the nature of human society people are not dependent or independent. There are degrees of inter-dependency amongst us all. We each give to other people and other people give to us. We enjoy the company of people we like, are pleased when things go well for them and we are pleased to help when things go wrong for them. Wolfensberger (1983) has argued for a recognition of the common assets which people with mental handicap have. These include 'heart qualities', the ability to 'give life and warmth' and to 'recognise another person and his or her needs', natural spontaneity, responsiveness to kindly human contact, and the ability to relate to other people as people.

Wolfensberger's picture of people with mental handicap is overly simple and, oddly, seems to deny them something of their humanity. Like everyone else, people with mental handicap can be awkward, bad-tempered, anti-social, uncooperative or just plain difficult. Nonetheless the main point is that they are people whom others can love, like and admire. Even children and young people with 'challenging behaviour' can be liked and admired because their behaviour may indicate a 'real spirit' in challenging authority and the world.

Through their inter-relationships with others, people with mental handicap *are* 'active participants' in society. They can and do shape our views of other members of society about them as individuals and about people with mental handicap in general. O'Brien's formulation of Wolfensberger's philosophy sees one of the 'accomplishments' of services for people with mental handicap developing respect for people with mental handicap as valued individuals (O'Brien and Tyne, 1981).

If these considerations were thought through in education they would have wide implications for formal curricula. In practice, again, teachers do pay attention to the social acceptability of the behaviour of children and young people. Aggressive behaviour to peers is commonly identified as a severe management problem which can be socially isolating for the child or young person. Attempts to integrate children and young people into mainstream provision typically emphasise the need to allow both handicapped and mainstream pupils to get to know each other as people and to develop mutually satisfying relationships. However a serious consideration of the importance of development of relationships as part of the curriculum would add substantial dimensions. These would include systematic focus on the relationship between teachers and individual pupils, a focus on the systematic development of peer relationships, such as helping others, and a systematic approach to the development of understanding of the feelings and emotions of other people.

In citing these two areas of education, learning for the promotion of enjoyment or psychological wellbeing and learning to establish and maintain satisfying relationships, I am not suggesting that other educational goals be de-emphasised or abandoned. What I am suggesting is that, both during the school years and in adult life, the ability to gain enjoyment in daily activities, and in personal relationships, is as critical for people with mental handicap as for everyone else. But, as with other aspects of their development, children and young people with severe learning difficulties may need more help and guidance than mainstream pupils. Enjoyment of activities is, arguably, educationally desirable as well as important in terms of adult life. The establishment of mutually enjoyable relationships with other people is similarly educationally desirable, most obviously in the development of communication skills, and critical in 'active participation' in society. Research by Flynn (1989) and others has shown that loneliness is one of the biggest problems experienced by people with mental handicap who live independently. We tend to assume in schools that friendships either happen or do not happen. Arguably, the development of relationships with others should be a central goal of special education.

Models and audiences

The arguments put forward in the previous section were intended to make the point that, as they are currently framed, the goals of education for children and young people with severe learning difficulties are too narrowly drawn. In essence what may be in the 'hidden' curriculum of many schools needs to be given equal formal prominence with already stated goals. It follows that the view of research adopted here is as an aid to educationalists in achieving their stated goals *and* an agent of change. In this latter role researchers may take on the job of changing the perceptions of educationalists about what their goals should be and how they may achieve them.

Within this extended approach researchers may try to influence the development of policy, at the national and at the local level, and also influence practice within schools.

Policy

It is difficult to assess the impact of research on national policy formulation. Policy formulation, by its very nature, is a complex activity involving not only empirical evidence relating to current activity and the likely effect of new policies, but political and economic considerations. Research is then only one of several influences.

Under these circumstances it is not surprising that studies of the impact of research on policy formulation show little effect. However, given that it is likely that some aspects of national policy could be informed by empirical evidence, what is surprising is that the routes available are rather devious.

Thomas (1985), in analysis of the impact of research funded by the Social Science Research Council, formulated three models through which research could affect policy. The first, the 'insider' model involved research which could have an impact on policy because the researcher was either involved directly in policy-making or 'strode the corridors of power'. A variant on this model is the involvement of social scientists and educationalists with the formulation of policies by party politicians (Bulmer, 1982). In both of these instances, but especially in relation to party political involvement, we can assume that researchers are trying to act as change agents. Thomas is able to describe very few examples of the insider approach in education.

Another insider route, less difficult to achieve but still requiring considerable prominence in a field, is through involvement with Committees of Inquiry established by governments. The disadvantage of this approach is that such Committees are rare, the Warnock Committe, on which researchers were represented, and which took evidence from researchers including Peter Mittler, was the most recent.

A second model identified by Thomas is the 'gad-fly'. Here a researcher 'stings' a government through a particularly controversial piece of research which may gain media attention and serve political purposes to an opposition party. The potential for this type of influence has been heightened by the development of a wide range of pressure groups of parents of children and young people with particular conditions or syndromes. Researchers are not infrequently drawn in by these groups to identify the special needs of their sons and daughters. Research then becomes a tool for pressure for development of new resources, especially if causes are taken up by members of Parliament and prominent public figures. The key to this route of influence is that the 'gad-fly' may produce the research but the pressure group operates the sting through its lobby contacts. A current example of this type of interest is work to investigate the Peto Method.

Pressure groups and teacher organisations may also help to operate the third route for influence described by Thomas. This is the slow-drip approach in which researchers, through persistence in presenting research which suggests the need for changes in policy, finally affect policy. This model is described by Weiss (1977) as an 'enlightenment model'. New conceptualisations of an issue trickle and percolate through to policy makers and the general public and create an 'agenda for concern'. As Tizard (1990) points out, this model is attractive to academics but limited in its applicability and difficult to test because of the time-frame assumed necessary before research has its effects. One aspect of its attractiveness to academics may be counter-productive. It excuses the academic from failures to disseminate research through any other than limited means.

Tizard (1990) points out that, in a decentralised system, it may not be clear where policy is made. Certainly, in the last two decades, a great deal of policy making has been devolved to an LEA level. Although this position has been partially reversed in recent years, especially by the introduction of the National Curriculum and other implications of the 1988 Education Act, a great deal of policy-making is still left at the LEA level. One clear example concerns policies relating to the integration of children and young people with severe learning difficulties in mainstream schools, where central government policy is permissive (Education Act, 1981). Following the Warnock Committee Report it would have been quite possible for central government to have funded demonstration integration projects to test the virtues and limitations of integration under optimal conditions. This did not happen but research evidence can still be employed at a local level by researchers wishing to act as advocates or by local educational officers and politicians who wish to formulate policy.

Given the fact that policy-making is complex, may have a short timescale, and is dependent on many factors other than research findings, it is not surprising that there is little evidence of the influence of research on national policy. Additionally, policy-oriented commissioned research may lead the researcher into work which is part of an agenda over which the researcher has no control (Tizard, 1990). Given this fairly gloomy picture it is not surprising that many researchers prefer the 'enlightenment model' or turn to research which is directed at changing practice rather than changing overall policy.

Practice

Research directed at affecting practice may take several forms. Unlike policy-oriented research, where the routes for influence are difficult, practice-oriented research has had well established routes through teacher training and through even more direct methods.

Practice-related research often follows what Weiss (1977) describes as a 'linear model'. In this model, findings from basic research are implemented in action research projects, leading to the development of ideas and methods of operation which can be used by service providers. The final phase of the process should be the evaluation of services developed through research to ensure that results demonstrated in the development phase are maintained in practical settings.

Probably the best examples of the linear model of research in special education derive from work on applied behaviour analysis. Behavioural theory has an explicit technical orientation. It argues that, given that the antecedents and consequences of behaviour can be identified, and the behaviour concerned broken down into its component parts, behaviours can be changed or taught.

Work on the Education of the Developmentally Young (EDY) Project in the Hester Adrian Research Centre represents an excellent example of the linear model. Assisted by a DES grant, Tom Foxen and Judith McBrien developed teaching materials designed to skill teachers in the use of behavioural techniques. The materials were then used, in Manchester, to teach EDY trainers who, on return to their LEAs, taught teachers to use the methods. This pyramid training procedure has continued, based on existing trainers and published materials (Foxen and McBrien, 1981; McBrien and Foxen, 1981). A certain amount of research has been completed to examine the impact of EDY on practice (Farrell, 1989). However, given the large number of teachers and other professionals who have been 'EDYfied' strict control on the use of techniques is simply not feasible.

The strength of the EDY pyramid training approach was that it identified people, usually advisers or educational psychologists, who had the time and authority to take the package directly in to schools.

Other attempts to operate the linear model use an alternative route, through the development of criterion referenced assessment procedures (Kiernan, 1987). The initial stage in the development of these procedures is the identification of behaviours which are believed to be critical in the acquisition of skills. Tests of the ability of the child or young person to perform critical behaviours are then devised. Ideally, these tests are then evaluated for their reliability and validity and the procedures are then, ideally, field tested, to ensure they can be used by the projected audience in the way intended and that training programmes to take the pupil on to the next step can be successfully developed. Finally, they are published.

Several examples of criterion referenced assessment procedures have had some impact on the education of pupils with severe learning difficulties. The Behaviour Assessment Battery (Kiernan and Jones, 1982) tried to reference critical stages in the development of a variety of areas, including aspects of sensory-motor development identified by Piaget. However, with this, and other attempts to develop these procedures, 'critical steps' remain hypotheses which reflect current theory and the imagination of researchers.

Analogue assessment procedures, initially devised in experimental contexts, represent an alternative approach. These procedures are tailored to allow practitioners to test hypotheses concerning the function of high-rate problem behaviours including self-injury or stereotypy. Emerson and his colleagues have recently used videotape and an accompanying manual to make these procedures accessible to practitioners (Emerson et al., 1990).

The great strength of the linear model of research has already been emphasised. The products of research are made immediately accessible to practitioners. However the linear model also has its weaknesses. Inevitably the products of the linear model reflect the theoretical bases which hold when the research begins. As a consequence it is quite possible that, by the time the processes of development are complete, theoretical bases will have changed and the product is outdated. For example research in language and communication has, during the last two decades, shifted attention from the linguistics to the social function of language leaving assessment procedures and intervention packages developed in the 1970s considerably out-dated.

The obvious solution to this problem is that the products of the linear model should be repeatedly up-dated. This up-dating process is rare, partly because the researchers initially concerned may have shifted their interests and partly because the up-dating of published materials will depend on commercial publishing decisions. The high selling EDY materials are currently being up-dated by Peter Farrell, in Peter Mittler's department, partly to take account of substantial changes in thinking on the role of aversive procedures.

A further problem with the linear model is the likelihood of misinterpretation. This problem has been particularly worrying in the case of the use of behavioural techniques. The techniques can be powerful and effective in controlling behaviour. At an extreme, the teacher decides for children and young people 'what will be learned (how and why), whether they like it or not' (Guess and Siegal-Causay, 1985). Guess and his colleagues argue that the approach assumes that pupils are 'not capable of deciding what is best for themselves'. As such, the approach reinforces unequal power relationships between teachers and pupils. No matter what uses the original researchers intended, once they have released their training package they have no control over its use.

Misinterpretation at another level extends these worries. Since the closure of schools in mental handicap hospitals more children and young people with severe problem behaviour are being educated in schools in the community. Kiernan and Kiernan (in preparation) estimate, on the basis of a national postal survey, that there will be an average of five pupils in an average size school for pupils with severe learning difficulties (sixty pupils) with very severe problem behaviours. Research on this level of behaviour problem, by professionals with extended experience of particular problems, suggest that the behaviours may be highly complex and require extensive analysis and carefully monitored intervention. This level of sophistication cannot be developed using EDY style packages. However Kiernan and Kiernan found that EDY was the most commonly quoted source of training in techniques for managing problem behaviour, despite the fact that its developers would agree its limitations.

In affecting practice the enlightenment model can be seen to operate in a more structured way than in relation to policy. Books or papers may be written which have the aim of increasing knowledge, changing attitudes or introducing new skills. However, the impact of research is dependent on books or papers being read and interpreted.

The traditional routes for dissemination of published literature to teachers of pupils with severe learning difficulties have been initial and in-service training. Four year initial teacher training allowed two years of socialisation of students by tutors in special education whose responsibility it was to interpret and distill literature. The replacement of extended initial training with one-year post-experience courses has lessened the strength of training, especially since some students begin courses with already developed ideas derived from their own experience. In addition serious questions can be asked about the effectiveness of local in-service courses and short 'workshops', in particular in affecting attitudes and transmitting skills.

Arguably, the current pattern of initial and in-service training will affect the likelihood of research being disseminated or having an impact. It is generally accepted that teachers rely on such training for their knowledge of new ideas and techniques. Shifts in attitudes, or radical re-orientations in thinking, almost certainly require greater exposure than is provided by short courses.

A contemporary example concerns thinking about problem behaviour. As we have suggested the traditional behavioural model reinforces traditional power relationships and, in the case of problem behaviour, suggests that such behaviour should be approached directly and eliminated. This approach is substantially at variance with a growing body of thinking and research which argues that effective approaches to problem behaviour can only be made through the development of alternative repertoires of behaviour, with a particular emphasis on the development of new skills and ways of expressing needs (Zarkowska and Clements, 1988; Donnellan et al., 1988). This approach is difficult to 'package' within the linear model, not only because it is more complex than the old approach, but because it involves a radical shift of thinking about power relationships. The goal of these approaches is not to control behaviour, but to facilitate the expression of the needs underlying the behaviours in a socially accepted way. In other terms, they represent a move away from purely behavioural analyses to a broadly formulated attempt to infer the 'meaning' of the behaviours for children and young people.

A good deal of research within the enlightenment model has, arguably, contributed to a fairly radical shift in thinking. Research on the involvement of parents in the education of their handicapped children, pioneered in this country by Cliff Cunningham and Dorothy Jeffree, and embedded in the Anson House Pre-School Project (see Hogg, chapter 4, this volume), was widely disseminated). The approach to parents which this work adopted is reflected in the Warnock Committee Report and has been a continuing theme in Peter Mittler's own work. Current educational legislation and practice now embeds parents as crucial in the education of their children.

Other research which can be construed within the enlightenment model has had little apparent impact. Research with its roots in cognitive psychology was produced in substantial volume in the 1960s and 1970s. In the UK, the distinguished work of O'Connor and Hermelin (1963) and O'Connor (1987), in particular, appears to have had no direct impact. A host of other studies on perception and memory seem to have suffered a similar fate (e.g. Herriot et al., 1973).

The non-use of this research may relate to its relative inaccessibility in terms of it being published in technical books or learned journals. Equally it could be argued that the precise practical implications of the work have never been presented in accessible form. A further, more technical argument, is that the research may lack 'ecological validity', in other terms, what happens under the controlled conditions of laboratory experiments does not happen in ordinary learning situations.

All of these factors play a part. However, it is arguable that the problem which this research has suffered is that the conceptual frameworks within which the research has been done are too distinct from those used by practitioners. Behaviourist theory, with its strong emphasis on observable behaviour as the only valid datum, may have played a significant part in making important but difficult work appear irrelevant.

Research prospects

In the first section of this chapter I suggest that researchers had two roles, helping the education system to teach pupils more effectively and bringing about constructive change in education. In particular, the suggestion was made that the goals of education should be extended to encompass pupils' 'enjoyment' or psychological wellbeing and their ability to establish and maintain satisfying relationships.

The highly selective review of the impact of research suggests that, although national and local policies may be influenced, the most obvious route is on practice, in particular through the linear model. The enlightenment model has also had some success, although measuring the impact of this type of research is difficult. It was suggested that the future impact of this type of research will be diminished by changes in the pattern of teacher training. These may also affect research within the linear model.

Prospects for research are always conditioned by available funding and available researchers. On both of these points prospects are not good. Research funding, never particularly generous in this field, is increasingly limited. Funding agencies, especially government departments, are increasingly proactive, severely limiting the possibility that new research agendas will be accepted from researchers themselves. A focus of research on policy can be anticipated, with the likelihood that research will concentrate on the implications of the 1988 Education Act (Kiernan, 1989).

The research community in this country has never been large. It is now increasingly eroded because universities have been forced by the Universities Funding Council to prioritise teaching. Neither universities nor government departments recognise the need to allow researchers to develop career paths. Good young researchers find it difficult to face life on successive two or three year contracts. Funding of research studentships is becoming increasingly sparse. In addition to a brain-drain of able researchers to North America, 1992 may see an increasing brain-drain to Europe. Research in the Hester Adrian Research Centre had, during the last decade, to move to work primarily on adults with mental handicap and, latterly, to other groups of disabled people. The future of the Centre is now under threat.

Within this context researchers in the 1990s and beyond will clearly have a difficult task in maintaining and developing their work. Taking as an example the two areas of development identified by this chapter, both suggest policy changes in terms of the expansion of the National Curriculum, at least as it is interpreted at local level. In addition, they suggest a need to crystalise the attitudes of teachers toward these areas of the curriculum. I suggest in an earlier section that teachers do appear to recognise these areas but in a relatively unsystematic way.

The lessons learned from the linear model suggest that one way forward should be to develop and package basic research in such a way that it is readily interpretable in practical terms. However, the challenge is to develop materials which, in themselves, 'enlighten' and thereby bring about attitude change.

Work on the development of communication skills may clarify this argument. In work with colleagues on communication skills we realised that such skills had two critical features which distinguish them from skills such as self-care or pre-academic skills. The ability to communicate needs, wishes or thoughts is potentially emancipating for the person with learning difficulties. In addition, communication skills help to build the image of the person with mental handicap which shapes his or her social role. Enhancing communication skills provides the foundation on which the individual can build to exert his or her self-advocacy. In other terms, both within schools and in later life, the recognition of the right on the part of the person with mental handicap to express himself or herself, and to be listened to, is essential in the re-shaping of power relationships.

In our own case this thinking led to the linear development of training and assessment materials designed to help teachers and others to encourage communication by children and young people with severe learning difficulties (Kiernan and Reid, 1987; Kiernan et al., 1989). This research, in common with other research on the teaching of communication skills, was behavioural in fundamental theory, but designed to change basic teacher orientation to pupils. Measuring the impact of this research would be a massive task and no claims are made for its effectiveness. I have quoted it only as an example of an approach which might be practicable.

Although the linear model is attractive because it offers a relatively direct route of influence it would be a mistake to suggest that the enlightenment model should be abandoned. Although a great deal is known about mental handicap through research, the search for greater understanding for its own sake, is one crucial source of applicable research.

Research in the education of children and young people with severe mental handicap can be frustrating. Research 'failures' can be deeply disappointing, especially when failures stem from an inability to 'go the last mile' in effective dissemination. Research 'successes' can be tremendously satisfying when the researcher realises that children and young people who he or she has never met, are being helped by teachers who have only read books or articles or been on a course where the work has been discussed. It is the job of researchers to build on hard won experience of effective dissemination, in difficult times, to ensure that they continue to make a contribution.

References

Bijou, S. (1966) A functional analysis of retarded development, in N. R. Ellis (ed.) *International Review of Research in Mental Retardation*. New York, Academic Press.

Bulmer, M. (1982) *The Uses of Social Research*. London, Allen & Unwin.

Cheseldine, S. and Jeffree, D. (1981) Mentally handicapped adolescents: their use of leisure, *Journal of Mental Deficiency Research*, 25, 49–59.

Donellan, A. M., La Vigna, G. W., Negri-Shoultz, N. and Fassbender, L. L. (1988) *Progress Without Punishment*. New York, Teachers College, Columbia University.

Emerson, E., Barrett, S. and Cummings, R. (1990) *Using Analogue Assessment*. Canterbury, Kent, Centre for Applied Psychology of Social Care.

Farrell, P. (ed.) (1989) *EDY: Its Impact on Staff Training in Mental Handicap*. Manchester, Manchester University Press.

Flynn, M. C. (1989) *Independent Living for Adults with Mental Handicap*. London, Cassell Educational Ltd.

Foxen. T. and McBrien, J. (1981) *Training Staff in Behavioural Methods. Trainee Workbook*. Manchester, Manchester University Press.

Gardner, J., Murphy, J. and Crawford, N. (1983) *The Skills Analysis Model*. Kidderminster, BIMH.

Guess, D. and Siegal-Causey, E. (1985) Behavioural control and education of severely handicapped students: who's doing what to whom and why? in D. Bricker and J. Filler (eds) *From Theory to Practice*. Reston, Va, Council for Exceptional Children.

Herriot, P., Green, J. M. and McConkey, R. (1973) *Organisation and Memory*. London, Methuen.

HMSO (1978) *Special Educational Needs*. London, HMSO.

Kiernan, C. C. (1974) Behaviour modification, in A. M. Clarke and A. D. B. Clarke (eds) *Mental Deficiency: The Changing Outlook*. London, Methuen.

Kiernan, C. C. (1985) Behaviour modification, in A. M. Clarke, A. D. B. Clarke and J. M. Berg (eds) *Mental Deficiency: The Changing Outlook*. London, Methuen.

Kiernan, C. C. (1987) Criterion-referenced tests, in J. H. Hogg and N. V. Raynes (eds) *Assessment in Mental Handicap*. London, Croom Helm.

Kiernan, C. C. (1989) Research in the nineties, in R. B. Barnes (ed.) *Mental Handicap, Meeting the Challenge of Change*. Stratford-upon-Avon, NCSE.

Kiernan, C. C. and Jones, M. C. (1982) *The Behaviour Assessment Battery*, (2nd edn) Windsor, NFER-Nelson.

Kiernan, C. C. and Reid, B. D. (1987) *The Pre-Verbal Communication Schedule*. Windsor, NFER-Nelson.

Kiernan, C. C., Reid, B. D. and Goldbart, J. (1987) *Foundations of Communication and Language*. Manchester, Manchester University Press.

McBrien, J. and Foxen, T. (1981) *Training Staff in Behavioural Methods: Instructors Handbook*. Manchester, Manchester University Press.

O'Brien, J. and Tyne, A. (1981) *The Principle of Normalisation: A Foundation for Effective Services*. London, Campaign for Mentally Handicapped People.

O'Connor, N. (1987) Cognitive psychology and mental handicap. *Journal of Mental Deficiency Research*, 31, 329–36.

O'Connor, N. and Hermelin, B. (1963) *Speech and Thought in Severe Subnormality*. London, Pergamon.

Stevens, M. (1971) *The Educational Needs of Severely Subnormal Children*. London, Edward Arnold.

Thomas, P. (1985) *The Aims and Outcomes of Social Policy Research*. London, Croom Helm.

Tizard, B. (1990) Research and policy: is there a link?, *The Psychologist*, 3, 435–40.

Weiss, C. (1977) *Using Social Research in Public Policy-Making*. Lexington, Mass., Lexington Books.

Wolfensberger, W. (1983) Social role valorization: a proposed new term for the principle of normalization, *Mental Retardation*, 21, 234–9.

Zarkowska, E. and Clements, J. (1988) *Problem Behaviour in People with Learning Disabilities*. London, Croom Helm.

Index